ANNALS OF A FORTRESS

ANNALS OF A FORTRESS

Twenty-Two Centuries of Siege Warfare

by

E. VIOLLET-LE-DUC

New Introduction by
Dr Christopher Duffy

Annals of a Fortress
This edition first published 2000 by Wren's Park Publishing, an imprint of
W.J. Williams & Son Ltd.

This edition © Lionel Leventhal Limited, 2000
New Introduction © Dr Christopher Duffy, 2000

All rights reserved. No part of this publication may be reproduced, stored in a retrieval system or transmitted in any form or by any means, electronic, mechanical or otherwise without first seeking the written permission of Greenhill Books.

British Library Cataloguing in Publication Data
A catalogue record for this book is available from the British Library

ISBN 0905-778-59-6

CONTENTS

INTRODUCTION
by Dr Christopher Duffy vii

TRANSLATOR'S NOTE
to the first English-language Edition xvii

CHAPTER I
The First Retreat 1

CHAPTER II
The Oppidum 11

CHAPTER III
The First Siege 26

CHAPTER IV
The Cost of Defenders 65

CHAPTER V
The Second Siege 69

CHAPTER VI
The Permanent Camp – Foundation of a Cité 90

CHAPTER VII
The Fortified Cité 97

CHAPTER VIII
The Third Siege 108

CONTENTS

CHAPTER IX
The Feudal Castle 157

CHAPTER X
The Fourth Siege 178

CHAPTER XI
The First Defences against Fire Artillery 226

CHAPTER XII
The Fifth Siege 239

CHAPTER XIII
The Cité of La Roche-Pont is fortified by Errard de Bar-le-Duc, Engineer to The Most Christian King of France and Navarre 275

CHAPTER XIV
The Sixth Siege..282

CHAPTER XV
The Town of La Roche-Pont is Fortified by M. de Vauban .304

CHAPTER XVI
The Seventh Siege 315

CHAPTER XVII
Conclusion 354

Explanation of some of the Technical Terms used in this book 385

INTRODUCTION

Viollet-le-Duc's *Annals of a Fortress* is best described as an extended historical novel, in which the heroic actor is not an individual, but an imaginary spur of land called 'La Roche-Pont' in Burgundy. The ground is depicted as falling away steeply in three directions, but level on the remaining side, where fortification succeeded fortification in a process which extended for well over 2,000 years. The primitive Gallic *oppidum* underwent siege by the Romans. In the course of time the developing stronghold was captured by the Burgundians, was caught up in medieval feuding, stood out against Louis XI in 1478, protected Richelieu's France against Imperial forces in the Thirty Years War, endured bombardment in 1814, and almost underwent a final siege in the Franco-Prussian War (1870–1). In a kind of appendix Viollet-le-Duc uses the papers of a fictional Captain Jean, a wounded survivor of that last war, to project his own ideas as to how France was to be defended in the future.

The present Greenhill edition represents the fourth time that this book has been put before the public. The French original appeared in 1874 as *Histoire d'une Forteresse*. In the following year Viollet-le-Duc's friend and fellow-architect Benjamin Bucknall produced a lively English translation – published as *Annals of a Fortress* – which forms the main body of the present edition. Arms and Armour Press presented a first reprint in 1983, with an introduction by the eminent scholars Simon Pepper and Quentin Hughes.

On this evidence *Annals of a Fortress* qualifies as a classic, if by that we understand a work which has held its value over the years. We must pause to examine the reasons.

In the first place *Annals of a Fortress* makes very good reading. It is in the best sense an essay in the French form of higher vulgarisation, whereby a respected authority, without condescension, is able to present complex issues to a wider public in an accessible form. The author's 'voice' is distinctive and appealing – eloquent always, but also coloured by that feeling for 'patriotic' landscape that we find in the *Tableau de France* by his countryman Michelet. A comparison with a strongly-flavoured Burgundy wine is not out of place, for *Annals of a Fortress* is best savoured in a period of chosen or enforced idleness – at ease under a tree in a summer garden, perhaps, or when you are laid up with a sports injury.

Annals of a Fortress has also held its place as a remarkably detailed and comprehensive history of fortification. A glance at its immediate predecessors (e.g. H. von Zastrow's *Geschichte der beständigen Befestigung*, 3rd edition, Leipzig, 1854) will show how far Viollet-le-Duc broke away from the fashion of representing ways of fortification as arid 'systems'. Indeed one of the great strengths of Viollet-le-Duc's work is to convey the continuity of topographical continuities in a specific site, and show how these brought about modifications of the geometric norms. The descriptions of the work of Errard de Bar-le-Duc and Vauban at La Roche-Pont are worthy of your particular attention.

Viollet-le-Duc likewise pays due attention to siegecraft (a subject neglected even now), and proceeds to show how the impact of the attack forced defenders to make sometimes radical modifications to their defences in the course of a siege. He succeeds very well in presenting his fortress as a living entity, and not least because as an artist, writer and practitioner, he has integrated text, diagrams and illustrations in a dynamic way.

In an earlier study Viollet-le-Duc had described himself as 'no kind of military engineer, and scarcely entitled to be called an archaeologist' (*Essai sur l'Architecture Militaire du Moyen Age*, 1854, Introduction). That was strictly true, at the time he wrote it, but he was already many other things besides. Eugène Emmanuel Viollet-le-Duc was born on 17 January in the fateful year of 1814, and was the son of an official at the Tuileries Palace. His father was a person of no particular account, but almost by the fact of his birth Eugène Emmanuel was destined to be at the centre of affairs in a city which in his lifetime was to undergo repeated revolutions and one prolonged and terrible siege.

Among the many paradoxes of the career of Viollet-le-Duc was that his acerbic political radicalism was allied with a gift for winning alliances in influential places. As a teenager he helped to build a barricade in the revolution which overthrew Charles X, the last of the Bourbon kings, in 1830. His skills as a largely self-taught artist won him favour at the court of the new Orleans dynasty, and, in 1840, his friend Prosper Mérimée, inspector of the new *Commission des Monuments Historiques*, entrusted him with the restoration of the abbey church of La Madeleine at Vézelay. This was a breakthrough in more than one sense. It was the first work of rescue undertaken in France by a state-funded commission, and more than any other event it launched Viollet-le-Duc on his career as a restorer of medieval architecture. Over the following years we find him supervising works simultaneously at Vézelay, and at the Sainte-Chapelle and the cathedral of Nôtre-Dame in Paris. His bureaucratic power was both ecclesiastical and secular, for he was *Inspecteur-Général des Edifices Diocésains* (from 1848) as well as a governmental architect, and it was as a prominent public figure that he undertook three major enterprises in military reconstruction – the town walls of Carcasonne (probably the best known of all his works) from 1852, and the castle of Pierrefonds and the great tower of Coucy from 1857.

Viollet-le-Duc meanwhile kept himself abreast of all current developments in the arts of the attack and defence of fortresses, and he was caught up with them in the most direct way possible when Paris came under siege from the Prussians on 15 September 1870, after the main French army had been forced to surrender at Sedan, and the Emperor Napoleon III had abdicated the throne. Viollet-le-Duc's most immediate task was to help to defend Fort Noisy, which was one of the detached forts which formed the outworks of the city, but in November he was given a wider remit as lieutenant-colonel in *la Légion Auxiliaire du Génie*. Starving Paris was forced to surrender to the Prussians in January 1871, and in March it was overtaken by a revolution too radical for even Viollet-le-Duc to stomach. He fled the city, but was persuaded to assist the 'Versailles' troops under General MacMahon, who fought their way back into Paris and overcame the Communards among scenes of bloody retribution.

As much a political animal as ever, Viollet-le-Duc wrote a number of articles which excoriated the conservative regime of President Thiers (1871–3), and in 1874 he was elected a town councillor for Montmartre. Seeking at last a little seclusion, he built himself a villa at Lausanne in Switerland, but it was scarcely complete before he died there on 17 September 1879.

The influence of Viollet-le-Duc had still not run its course. In the last section of *Annals of a Fortress* he nailed his colours to the mast as a protagonist of defence in depth, in other words projecting the power of fortification beyond the confines of a town's ramparts. The process had begun in 1747, when Frederick the Great of Prussia had cast a ring of detached forts around Schweidnitz in Silesia. French engineers had been slow to respond. Much controversy had attended the best means of fortifying Paris towards the middle of the nineteenth century, and the outcome was a belt-and-braces compromise, whereby the city acquired both a circlet of detached forts and a continuous enceinte.

Speaking through his 'Captain Jean', Viollet-le-Duc argued that no single fortress was capable of contributing to an active national resistance. The answer must be the creation of fortified zones, in which the fortresses were set out in such a way as to promote dynamic defence on a regional scale. In such a way La Roche-Pont was to serve as the central redoubt of a complex that would embrace Burgundy and part of Franche-Comté, and permit 150,000 French troops to tie down at least twice that number of Germans. In 1878 General Séré de Rivières began the work of refortifying France's frontiers on just such a concept. We cannot establish just how far the new scheme was inspired by Viollet-le-Duc, but it is clear that Eugène Emmanuel was well up with the most advanced military thought of the time.

In terms of civil architecture Viollet-le-Duc did more than any other individual to establish the Gothic Revival in France, and he was undoubtedly aided by the resurgent Catholicism of his period. However his inspiration was not romantic Christianity *à la* Châteaubriand or Pugin, but rather the bleak notion that architecture was the expression of structural needs – an idea later summed up in the phrase that 'style follows function'. Regarding the Gothic forms as the solution of engineering problems, he was less interested in ferreting out clues as to what the original appearance of such-and-such a building actually was, as in remaking it as he thought it ought to have been. He recreated rather than restored, and in the process the original might be obliterated. His best service was, as at Vézelay, to save the basic structure of buildings that would otherwise have ended up as piles of ruins.

While Viollet-le-Duc's manifestly 'new' constructions were lacking in character and individuality, a number of comments in his architectural *Discourses* proved to be very influential indeed. These related to the potentialities of iron-framed buildings that were enclosed within a cladding of non load-bearing masonry. The architects of the budding Chicago School found the suggestions liberating, and, when allied before long with the facility of lifts ('elevators' to Americans) they helped to establish a continuity between the thoughts of that remarkable man, Eugène Emmanuel Viollet-le-Duc, and the appearance of city centres in the third millennium.

In his *Annals of a Fortress* Viollet-le-Duc left open the question as to whether La Roche-Pont had a military future. It would be a worthy enterprise for somebody to write a sequel that took the story of the site from the later 1870s to the present time. We could imagine the familiar locality and the neighbouring eminences being transformed by Séré de Rivières in the 1880s, and then being endowed with armoured cupolas and reinforced concrete as a protection against high-explosive shells from the new generation of siege howitzers. La Roche-Pont and its companion works would have been situated too far to the south to feature even indirectly in the epic defence of Verdun in 1916, but they might have been reinstated in the 1930s as a back-up to the Maginot Line. In this capacity they could well have beaten off an improvised German infantry assault in June 1940, and held out until after the general surrender of France.

La Roche-Pont would then probably have undergone a period of prolonged neglect in the second half of the twentieth century, in which its ramparts were overgrown with trees (the mortal enemies of fortification), its ditches filled with rubbish, and the masonry of its outworks plundered for hardcore. For many years its sole defenders could have been an association of *Amis de la Roche-Pont* under their president M. Lambalot (as much a hero in his own way as Colonel Dubois in 1814), until, in the early 1990s, a reviving appreciation of fortification coincided with local outrage at a proposal to build

Introduction

a burger bar on the remains of the glacis. The notorious riot of 17 October 1994 precipitated a rapid sequence of events. Funds and expertise were made available to clear the ditches, and to clear the vegetation as the first stage in restoring the scarps to their orignal state. Work was already advanced when, in 1997, local enthusiasm together with the demands of tourists led to the decision to open displays in the casemates, and set out signposted walks around the ramparts. Gathering thunder clouds threatened to disperse the crowds during the interminable speeches which attended the opening on 14 July 2000, but M. Lambalot had to shield his eyes against a burst of sunshine when the great gates opened at his command, and he stepped forward to be the first to enter the new-born fortress.

Here, then, is a masterful work and one which is subtle and enchanting in its blending of fact and fiction. But, however entertaining it might be, it is first and foremost a brilliant survey of fortification through the ages and a telling insight into a fundamental aspect of military history.

Dr Christopher Duffy, 2000

The Major Literary Works of Viollet-le-Duc

Essai sur l'Architecture Militaire du Moyen Age, 1854
Dictionnaire Raisonnée de l'Architecture Française, du XIe au XVIe Siècle, 10 vols, 1854–61
Histoire d'une Maison, 1857
Entretiens sur l'Architecture, 1858–72, translated as *Discourses on Architecture*, 1875
Mémoire sur la Défense de Paris, 1871
Histoire d'une Forteresse, 1874, translated as *Annals of a Fortress*, 1875
L'Art russe, 1877
Histoire d'une Hôtel de Ville et d'une Cathédrale, 1878
De la Décoration appliquée aux Édifices, 1879

TRANSLATOR'S NOTE
to
the first English-language edition

THE Fortress whose transmutations during successive ages are so vividly described in the following pages is an ideal one; its supposed situation is on the Cousin, an affluent of the Saône. The practical genius of the author indicates the position which, in view of the new eastern frontier, should be fortified in order to command the Saône.

To his unrivalled talent as an architect, Monsieur Viollet-le-Duc adds the highest qualifications of the military engineer. In this branch of applied science he is a recognised authority; and it may not be out of place to notice here that he was frequently consulted by the late Emperor respecting the permanent defences of the country. It is not too much to assert that if his recommendations had been carried out the investment of Paris would have been rendered impossible, whilst the progress of the German invasion elsewhere would have been attended with greater difficulties. As colonel of engineers, no officer displayed greater energy, skill, or bravery, in the defence of the city; and every operation planned and directed by him during the siege was successful. Within two or three days after the signing of the armistice, the Germans had done their utmost to destroy all evidences of their works of investment. Nothing, however, had escaped the vigilant eye of M. Viollet-le-Duc. In that brief space of time he had surveyed and accurately noted all these works of investment; plans and descriptions of which are given in his interesting memoir of the siege. Upon the outbreak of the Commune, he was solicited by its chiefs to take the military command; and had he not made a timely escape would probably have paid the penalty of his life for refusing that questionable honour. From his retreat at Pierrefonds he was recalled by General MacMahon, to assist the Versailles troops in re-entering Paris. It is deserving of mention that in his absence a devoted band of craftsmen thrice gallantly defended his house from being burnt and pillaged.

In presenting the *Histoire d'une Forteresse* in an English form, the translator has considered it impossible to do justice to the original without adhering to its archaic style and manner; and aware that a translation must lose something either in point of sense or style, his chief aim has been to give a faithful rendering of the sense.

BENJAMIN BUCKNALL,
Architect.

Oystermouth, Swansea,
February 11, 1875.

ANNALS OF A FORTRESS.

"Je sçais bien qu'il faut perdre, qu'il faut gaigner, et n'y a rien d'imprenable ; mais desirez cent mil fois plustost la mort si tous moyens ne vous deffaillent, que dire ce méchant et vilain mot : 'JE LA RENDS.'"—*Comment.* de MONTLUC.

CHAPTER I.

THE FIRST RETREAT.

MANY winters, as we are told by the old men of the district, have passed since human beings first settled in the land of Ohet, a somewhat extensive valley of varying breadth, traversed by a winding stream running southward till it flows into a great river.

The sides of the valley present a series of hills of moderate height, descending by gentle slopes where it widens, and more abruptly where it narrows. On the steeper hill-sides grey crags jut out, and the ground is strewn with fragments of rock. Ascending the stream for some three hours' walk from the point where it joins the great river, we find on the right another stream separating into several small branches in a more elevated valley. In summer, some of these branches dry up, others form pools, whose banks are covered with reeds and water-lilies. The inhabitants of the vale dread this valley, which they believe to be haunted by evil spirits. It is dangerous to wander there, because of the number of bogs covered over with leaves and decaying branches in which the unwary sink. The forest in this valley is so dense, the plants and bushes are so thickly interlaced with the trunks and branches of dead trees, that the rays of the sun hardly penetrate through it, and only illuminate pools of water covered with a mantle of green. A kind of promontory divides the two water-courses at this point (Frontispiece —Fig. 1);—the river running from the north-west, and the smaller stream from the north-north-east. This elevated part of the country is covered with thick woods, and the inhabitants of the valley seldom go there except to hunt the wild ox, the boar, the wolf, and the deer. Beyond, the country seems a wilderness; and strangers who occasionally visit the inhabitants of the vale to exchange amber, copper, gold, salt, and coarse woollen or hempen fabrics for skins of beasts, never come except by the way where flows the great river. The occupants live in families, in the open spaces amid the woods and on the banks of the rivers, inhabiting conical huts, made with stakes set in the ground, joined at the top, and covered with branches, earth, and rushes. The father of the family occupies one of these huts with his wife and children, and as his sons grow up, they build another cabin and take a companion.

The products of the chase and fishing, with the wild roots which they dry and crush between stones, are their only means of subsistence; they do not till the soil, nor have they any flocks or herds. Our informants add that they never had to fight men like themselves, and that if any disputes arise between the families, they call together the oldest chiefs of the other families to arbitrate between them. Those who are unwilling to submit to their judgment are banished from the valley, together with their families; they descend the shores of the great river, and are no more heard of.

When these old men are further asked whether there were other human beings before them settled in the valley, they answer that there were; but that they were small men—dwarfs—who ate earth, and had no bows and arrows to kill the wild beasts, nor hooks to catch fish, nor canoes to cross the river; that at the approach of the present inhabitants, these dwarfs disappeared, and took refuge underground, whence they came out sometimes in the night to do mischief—to cut the fastenings of boats, or sink the boats themselves—to cause children at the breast to die, or to break the bows, or warn the animals of the forest of an intended chase, so that they might get out of the way.

For some time a report has been current—brought by strangers who have found their way along the river into the valley—that an alien race of great stature and strength, with fair hair, and mounted on horses, have already overspread the neighbouring countries, driving away their inhabitants, or killing those who do not fly at their approach; speaking an unknown tongue, and undertaking nothing without first deliberating in great numbers, and consulting the elders and women, sparing none but children, and employing these in labours of all kinds. This news has spread great consternation in the valley; the chiefs of the families meet together, and determine to watch by turns at the mouth of the river; young men posted at regular intervals are to give warning, by loud cries, of the arrival of the fair-haired people, so that all the inhabitants of the valley may be quickly warned, and take refuge with their families in the woods situated on the promontory which divides the river from the smaller stream at their confluence; lastly, each is to furnish himself with provisions such as will be sufficient for a hunting expedition of several days; and then they will consult as to what course shall be adopted.

Meantime, the elders of the people take counsel. They decide that at the first cry of alarm, and while the invaders are entering the valley by one of the banks, all the inhabitants of that side shall cross in the boats to the opposite side shore, in order to unite with those who inhabit that side, and that all together they shall hasten to bring their cargoes to the point where the valley divides, so as to moor the boats below the promontory on the left bank above the mouth of the stream; that the women, children, and old men shall take refuge on the promontory, so that the able-bodied, thus separated from the fair-haired men by the river and the rivulet, will be able to deliberate whether they should use their bows or fly to the forest above. Some days after, just when the sun is beginning to decline, the valley resounds with the cry of alarm, a hundred times repeated, announcing that the fair-haired people are advancing and entering the valley on the western side.

Immediately the whole country—silent but a few minutes before—begins to be filled with a continued hum; most of the inhabitants of the right hasten in their boats to the left bank; but some, either through negligence, or because they have been away from their dwellings, cannot follow the advice of the elders.

In the meantime, the invaders advance with caution: first, a detachment mounted on horses are seen riding round the woods, assembling in the openings, and appearing to deliberate before going further. A body of them have captured some unhappy loiterers among the inhabitants of the valley, who, fastened with cords, are driven onwards by their captors, and closely interrogated, but they do not understand what is said to them.

In a little while, at every visible point in the direction of the river, the valley appears dotted with men on foot and on horseback, and with chariots; and every now and then shouts arise. The sun sinks upon the horizon, but the shouting continues to be heard, and the columns of smoke ascend from all sides; night comes, the valley appears lit up with fires, and silence gradually supervenes.

Assembled at the foot of the promontory, along the banks of the two streams, the men of the land of Ohet have concealed their boats among the bulrushes; they have sent up the women, the children, and the aged to the plateau; they dare not light any fires, lest they should attract the attention of the invaders. The night is spent in fruitless deliberation; some bold young hunters propose to take advantage of the sleep of the fair-haired people to cross the river and fall upon them as they would upon wild beasts, and to kill them all with their stone hatchets; but the chiefs of the families consider that they are too few in number for the execution of any such design; they urge that this body of invaders is perhaps followed by others, that they have horses and can easily escape, that they appear to be tall and strong; and, moreover, that they do not appear to have killed the inhabitants they met with, as the strangers had reported.

At break of day the valley echoes with unusual sounds, such as the inhabitants of the land of Ohet had never heard before. It is not the shouting of men, nor the songs of women, nor the bellowing of wild bulls. These noises spread terror among the fugitives. They all abandon the boats and climb the promontory; there, in the woods, they can see through the trees what is taking place in the valley. They soon perceive a numerous body of men on the opposite side, not far from the river. Some canoes which had been forgotten are being guided up the stream by the invaders. They go through the rushes, unfasten the boats, and draw them up with loud cries on the shore opposite the promontory. These cries are answered from other quarters, and the whole body rush to the shore. But at this juncture the chiefs seem to interfere; they parley for some time, and appear to threaten those who are impatient to get into the boats, often pointing to the plateau above. The main body retire again from the shore, and a dozen men only get into two boats, which make for the opposite bank at the foot of the promontory. With them are two of the inhabitants of the land of Ohet, tied by the neck with leathern thongs. They land together, put the captives before them, and ascend to the plateau. The twelve fair-haired men are armed with sticks, terminated by a long, bright, metal point. Some hold bows in their hands, with the arrows in place. They are dressed in short tunics of ornamented stuffs, their arms bare, and their legs up to the knee bound round with leathern thongs, to which are fastened covered sandals. About their loins is a belt of skin, to which is suspended a bag, also of skin, with the hair of the animal preserved, two knives—one long, the other very short—and a hatchet, the blade of which is of bronze; their necks and wrists are adorned with strings of large glass beads, or with circlets of metal. Many have their hair fastened on the top of their heads, with large pins of bone or bronze; others have their hair divided into long tresses. Their beards have been carefully removed, while their moustaches reach down to their breasts. Their aspect is terrible, for they are tall; their light blue eyes, inclosed by black lines, sparkle like diamonds beneath bushy brows dyed of a brilliant red.

Approaching to within fifty paces of the brow of the promontory, where the ground is somewhat clear, they stop, and one of the captives speaks thus: "The fair-haired people have captured several of us; they have done us no harm; they have not burned our huts, nor killed the women and children. They wish to live in peace with us always, on the same ground. They will not hinder us from hunting or fishing, or from remaining with our wives and children. They say that the land is good, and can support a much greater number of inhabitants than it does now. They bring an abundance of things useful to man. They teach youths to ride, and to use arms against evil men. They say in fine that we have nothing to fear, and that you may return to your dwellings.

"I am told all this by one of their people who speaks as we do, and who once lived in our valley, from which he was banished. They also say that if you will not return to your homes and live in peace with them, they will kill us all like wild beasts, for they are both numerous and strong. They will await your answer here until the sun reaches the middle of its daily course. This is all we have to say."

Several of the elders of the valley then came out of the wood and advanced towards the captives; but the party of fair-haired men made signs to them to come no farther, and fitted their arrows to the strings of their bows. The captive who had already spoken, again addressed them: "Do not come any nearer; deliberate among yourselves, and give an answer quickly. This is all we have to say."

The old men thereupon assembled, and having cut some branches of trees on which they seated themselves, one of them spoke thus: "These fair-haired people with painted faces are more numerous than we; they have murderous weapons, and horses, and are brave; we are not able to drive them out of the valley; if they desire to live with us in peace, as they say they do, why not consider them as friends? Is it to their advantage to kill us? No. They possess many things which we have not, and are provided with what they need. Have you not observed the flocks and herds, the loaded waggons, and the women and children that accompany them? They are not empty-handed robbers. Let us accept the conditions they offer us."

One of the hunters, among the bravest in the valley, then rose and spoke in his turn: "Why do these people with painted faces come into our valley? It is to take possession of it and drive us away. They are strangers to us, and we have never done them any harm. Why do they not remain where they were born? Will there be fish enough in the river and enough wild animals in the forest to feed them and us? They will take all and leave us nothing. Fighting against them is impossible, it is true—but we can fly. There are other valleys and other rivers not far off. Let us take our wives and children with us; I know the woods as far as three days' journey. Let us leave our huts, and our boats, and go and settle far away from these strangers." After the utterance of these contrary opinions a hundred voices were raised; some supporting the advice of the old man, others that of the hunter.

A few young men even wished to fall upon the little troop of strangers and massacre them.

Some of the most venerated of the inhabitants of the Val d'Ohet tried more than once to impose silence and make themselves heard, but the tumult continuing to increase, the assembly was broken up into groups, and the women began to cry out and lament and the children to weep. Meanwhile the little party of fair-haired men had begun to cut some bushes and briars and to make a rampart with them.

Not long afterwards twelve boats crossed the river, and sixty of the strangers came and joined the first twelve. These were bearing twelve oval shields of wicker-work covered with skin. They set up these shields by means of stakes driven in the ground, and placed themselves behind them; only their heads painted red and blue and their sparkling eyes remained visible. They were laughing together loudly.

Midday was at hand, and confusion continued to prevail among the fugitives. Then were heard again those strange sounds which had so much alarmed the unhappy inhabitants of Ohet at dawn; and the shore opposite to the promontory was covered with a multitude of fair-haired men in several detachments, all armed. They began to cross the river, and to seat themselves in a line on the shore beneath the plateau. Then the captive who had already spoken advanced alone toward the forest, and when he was within hearing, said: "My friends, my brethren, you are going to be attacked: and we are to be killed before your eyes. Have pity on yourselves—have pity on us; come down to the fair-haired men; they will do you no sort of harm; they have respected your houses and the women that have fallen into their hands. Do not hope to defend yourselves, for they will kill you with their keen weapons!" At this last appeal the fugitives became silent, and one of the inhabitants of the valley, who had remained since the morning without speaking a word, rose up. He was a short, robust man, of dark complexion and crisp hair; he was well known as a skilful carpenter, and the best boats were his handywork. "There is no more time for discussion," said he. "Let those who wish to stay in the valley come out from the wood, and let the rest hide themselves as quickly as possible in the forest. They will be able to fly with their families; for the strangers do not know how many we are. As for myself, I remain where I was born." A great number assembled round the carpenter with acclamations, accompanied by their wives and children; and all together without a moment's delay showed themselves to the troop of strangers. "We will return to our dwellings," was all the carpenter said to the captive interpreter, and then they advanced towards the little camp.

Many had bows and stone hatchets. "Throw down your arms," said the captive; "throw down your arms, you have no need of them." The invaders who had taken up their position on the shore, dividing into two bodies, were rapidly climbing the sides of the promontory, to the right and left; so that in a few minutes the carpenter and his companions were surrounded by an innumerable crowd, which penetrating the mass of the fugitives, separated them into small parties and took possession of the few weapons which had been retained by some of their number.

The strangers laughed, skipped, and leaned their brows on the breasts of the inhabitants of the valley in token of good will. Thus some hundreds of the natives went down towards the river surrounded by their new guests. They were compelled to get into the boats, and they went back to their houses, which had been completely pillaged. Many of the huts remained vacant, and the new-comers took possession of them, without troubling themselves much respecting the inhabitants and what had become of them.

CHAPTER II.

THE OPPIDUM.

Two centuries later, the land of Ohet had assumed a new aspect, and its name was changed. It was then called the Valley of Avon.

Beautiful fields, affording pasture to flocks and herds, carpeted the slopes of the bordering hill; while in the vale below ripened harvests of barley and rye. The uplands were still covered with forest, and on all sides wooden houses peeped out from the meadows, with their inclosures of palisades painted in lively colours.

The marshes of the rivulet were drained, and at the summit of the promontory was to be seen cutting the sky the talus of an *Oppidum* which commanded the valley and the two streams. Its origin was as follows:—

Not long after the invasion of the fair-haired people, the inhabitants of the valley who had fled into the woods had re-appeared, accompanied by a great multitude of men of the same race, and at dawn had fallen with great violence and loud cries upon the strangers.

The latter, not expecting an attack, defended themselves as best they could; but the younger and more active among them assembled on the promontory, where they waited until night. Then they descended noiselessly, crossed the stream, and fell in their turn upon the men of the ancient race, who thought to repossess themselves of the valley. The greater number were asleep; many had dispersed in search of food and plunder. The young fair-haired men massacred a vast number of them, making no distinction between the old inhabitants who had remained in their homes and those who presented themselves as enemies; the women and children alone were spared.

After a council of the elders, and after having consulted the women, it was decided that in order to prevent fresh surprises, and to protect the inhabitants of the valley, they should form a vast camp on the promontory, where in case of alarm the people of the valley of Avon could take refuge with their families, their flocks and herds, provisions and arms, defy every attack, and resume the offensive at the opportune moment.

The summit of the promontory was therefore cleared; every able-bodied man was required to give one day's work in four till the camp was finished; and those of the old inhabitants who had escaped the massacre, as well as the children and women, had to labour without ceasing at the circumvallations. The women prepared food for the workmen, and the children carried earth in baskets or brought branches of trees which were mingled with the earth.

Following exactly the verge of the plateau, the chiefs of the eight tribes settled in the valley marked out the boundary of the camp, its entrances, its defences, the retreat of the elders, the place for the cattle, that of the huts for the families, and lastly the site proper for the erection of the Némède—the sacred inclosure—the sanctuary of Belen and the dwellings of the Druids.

First, with the aid of strong levers of wood hardened by fire, the stones which obtruded above the level of the plateau were forced out and arranged on the perimeter described; then upon this layer, behind which was heaped coarse gravel mixed with earth, were placed trunks of trees, crosswise, four feet apart. The width of the base was twenty feet. The interval between the trunks was filled with stones, earth, and branches. Then another layer of stones mingled with earth, then three rows of trunks of trees, laid this time lengthwise, bound together with strong bands of green withy, always with gravel between. On this a third layer of stones, more trunks of trees across, overlapping the others, and a topping of gravel, of turf and soil, forming the rampart walk.

Stakes were placed upright, five feet apart, and firmly driven three feet down into the rampart on the outer edge, serving to fix, by means of osier bands, wattled hurdles five feet six inches high, so as to form a continuous parapet pierced with loop-holes.

The rampart rose to a height of five feet. The inclosure completed, the Druids marked out the area allotted to the eight tribes. To each of them was given a circular space of two hundred feet in diameter; the huts were disposed in two rings around the perimeter; in the middle was the paddock for the animals and the hut of the chief.

The general view of the camp is given in Fig. 2, with the rampart, the two entrances, the sunk approaches, defended on the other side by a mound raised with the earth excavated to form these approaches, and the eight circles allotted to the tribes; at A, the Némède and the dwelling of the Druids and Druidesses, surrounded by the sacred inclosure. Wells were sunk in each of the circles of the tribes, and in the inclosure of the Némède.

Fig. 3 gives the section of the rampart with its terrace-walk, A, for the defenders, and, at intervals, the inclines, B, affording an easy means for ascending to the terrace-walk. The entrances were masked by a mound forming

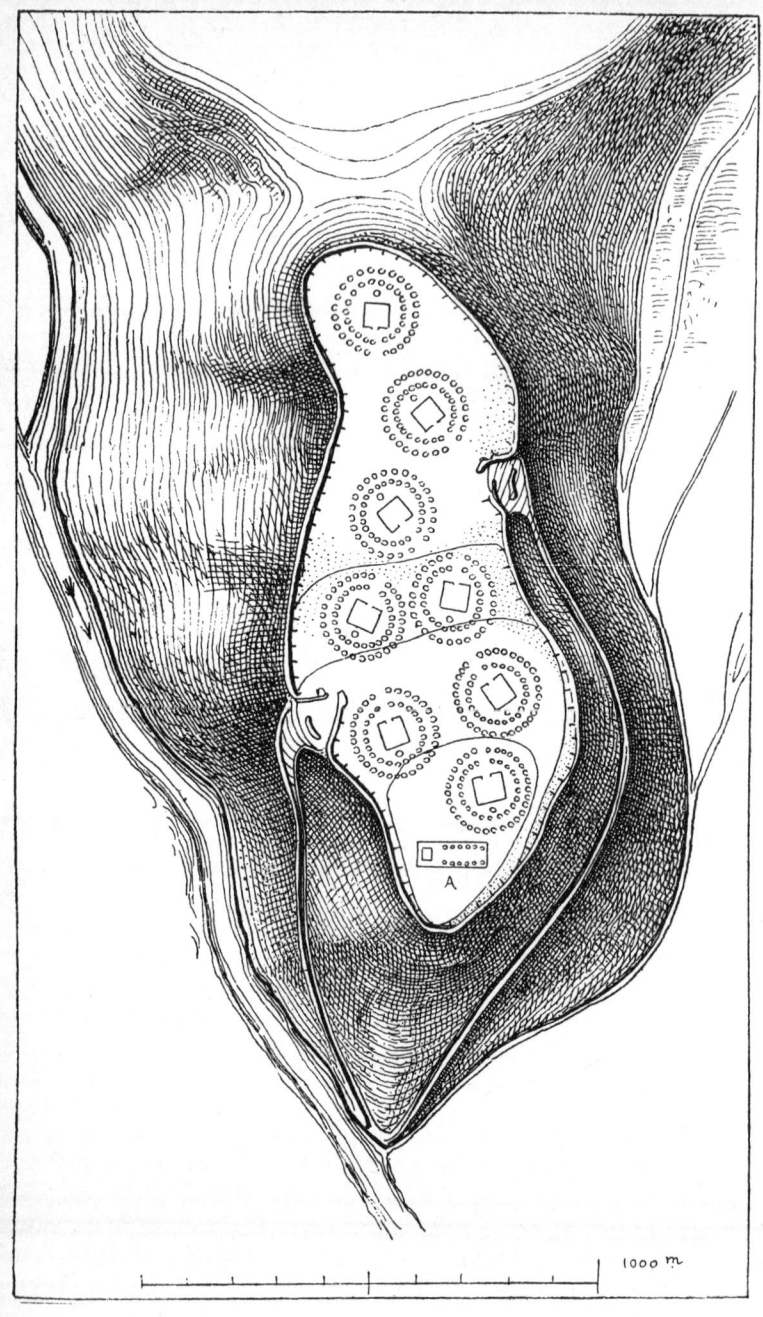

FIG. 2.—THE OPPIDUM.

an advanced work, and leaving two ways out along the ramparts. Fig. 4 shows how these entrances were disposed. The two extremities of the rampart were

FIG. 3.

strengthened by a wider embankment, H, affording space for a numerous assemblage of defenders. Here is shown the screen thrown up outside the cutting; and at K the sunken road with its mound, L.

FIG. 4.

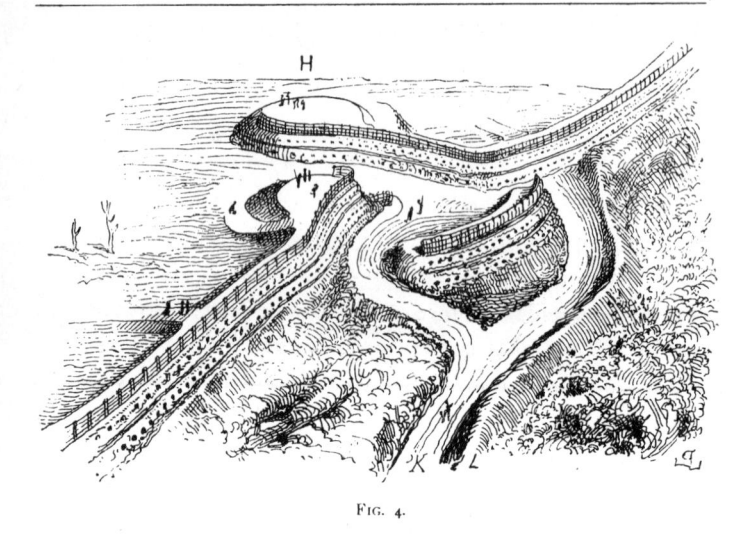

Fig. 5 represents the Némède, with its inclosure and the dwellings of the Druids.

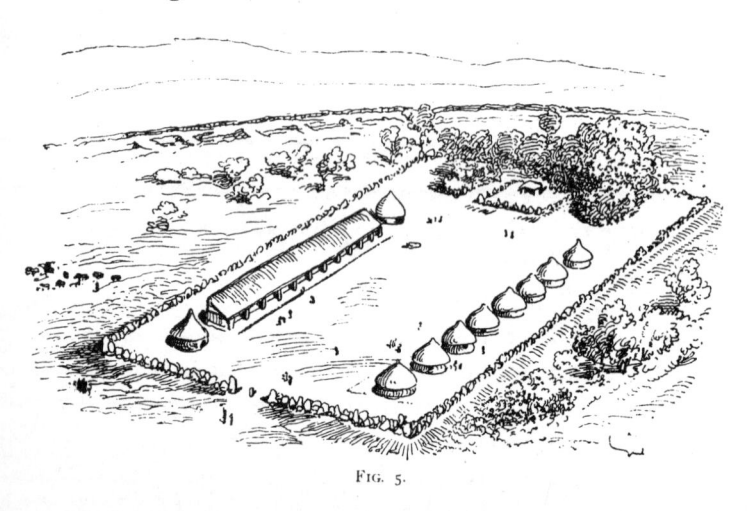

FIG. 5.

The camp finished—except the habitations of the tribes, whose site was only marked by circles of stones—a certain number of young men were put to live there, who replaced each other every day. Arriving there at sunset, they remained in the camp until the beginning of the next night. Those of the former inhabitants of the valley who still lived were forbidden to enter the camp on pain of death.

The tribes prospered, enriching themselves with the produce of the earth and with their cattle. Some, having discovered copper ore in the neighbourhood, manufactured arms and utensils. There were also potters who wrought skilfully in clay. At certain periods of the year, merchants brought to the valley stuffs, salt, spices, and even wine in leathern bottles. They took in exchange articles of bronze, skins, cheese, and corn.

The tribes, not having had any fresh attacks to resist during a lengthened period, left off guarding the camp, which was rarely visited except on occasion of certain solemnities and of assemblies convoked by the Druids. The latter lived by themselves, surrounded by their college, within the vast inclosure which they cultivated, and where their sheep and cattle grazed. The ramparts, whose timber work had decayed, had sunk, and presented only a slight elevation. They were overgrown with vegetation in several places. But in the peaceful state in which the tribes were living, no one thought of repairing these defences.

The inhabitants of the valley had been frequently embroiled with the neighbouring tribes, and had often come to blows with them; but peace was soon restored, for none of these groups of tribes cherished the intention of subjugating its neighbours and seizing their territory.

Nevertheless repose was irksome to them, and their youths would often quit the valley in quest of adventures, and to see the world.

About 389 B.C., a great number of men, attracted by the

seductive eloquence of a Brenn—a chief elected by certain tribes to command distant expeditions—had quitted their hearths in the hope of amassing wealthy spoils in the southern lands beyond the mountains. Two years having passed away, a small number made their appearance again in the valley; they brought with them gold and costly fabrics, and marvellous were the tales they told of the countries they had traversed, and in which they had been incessantly fighting.

They had seen cities environed by strong stone walls, and filled with magnificent public buildings and sumptuous mansions—richly fertile regions, where the vine and luscious fruits of every kind were cultivated.

Among other results of adventure, it was observed that those who returned from these distant expeditions had lost the habit of peaceful industry; and although more than half their comrades had perished by the way, their dreams were still of battles, and plunder, and adventures. They were idle, insolent, and irascible, and even aspired to a kind of lordship over the peaceable families that lived by industry. The latter had at first joyfully welcomed the unhoped-for return of these warriors; and had listened with admiration to the stories of their prowess and adventures recited around the family hearth; but their imperious bearing, their idleness and boasting, were beginning to become intolerable. Every day saw new quarrels arise, which generally ended in blood. The wives of these heroes were still more insolent than the warriors themselves, and presumed to treat their dependents as slaves, such as were those of the ladies in the countries so gloriously traversed by their husbands.

Things being in this state, the tribes of the valley had been summoned to a meeting in the old camp, according to custom, to deliberate on their common interests, and to endeavour to put an end to feuds. The men always repaired to these assemblies armed; the women used to come bringing food and drink; for these meetings were usually terminated by festivities lasting the whole night.

On the morning of the day appointed, the sound of trumpets re-echoed through the valley, and from every quarter the inhabitants might be seen flocking towards the hill. A wooden bridge had long since been built over the river near the mouth of the rivulet. When the chiefs of the tribes, accompanied by the mass of the people, presented themselves at the bridge, they found it occupied by the warriors, whose ranks had been increased by a large number of young men of the valley, and even other warriors, strangers to the tribes.

"It is at the camp and not here that the people meet," said one of the chiefs; "let us pass over." "You shall not pass," replied one of the warriors, "without listening to the conditions we propose." "We have neither conditions to submit to nor conditions to impose," rejoined the first; "the men of this country are free, and the land is theirs, in the valley and on the mountain; let us pass on!" "It will be by force then," replied the warrior, half unsheathing his sword.

A long-continued cry of indignation followed this defiance, and arms began to glitter in the sun among the crowd like flashes of lightning. The chiefs, however, imposed silence, and held the crowd in check. Then advancing in concert to the entrance of the bridge, one of them spoke thus:—"What do you want? Do you not belong to our tribes? Have you not flocks, and wives, and children born in the valley? What conditions do you aim to impose upon us—us who are your equals? Speak! What can you ask for more than you already possess? What wrongs have been done you? Why bring with you men who are strangers to the country, whom we do not know, and who have no claim to an interest among us?" "Answer him, answer him, Sigild," said all the warriors with one voice. Sigild advanced. He was a handsome young man, a native of the valley, tall and slight, with a mild look, and a beard just appearing; his breast covered with a small bronze cuirass which glittered in the sun: his white arms were bare, and adorned with bracelets of gold. He disdained a helmet, and his blond hair, fastened at the top of his head with a long golden pin, fell down over his back; *chases*[1] wrought in bright colours covered his legs; his waist was girt with a kind of scarf, which was gracefully thrown back over the shoulder and left arm. A narrow buckler and a sword hung at his side. He smiled, made a sign with his hand as if requesting silence, and said:—" Friends and brethren, we are all free--all of the same blood; we ought to remain united to conquer those who desire to plunder or to enslave us. Consider, however, that you have among you the élite of the warriors who have conquered powerful nations, and have spread the renown of the Gallic name beyond the mountains. Many have died in battle; but do not those who have returned to you after so many trials, bringing with them a rich booty and having acquired skill in arms, deserve some consideration from you? Inured to war and always ready to shed their blood, are they not more fitted to defend your hearths than men who have done nothing but tend cattle and till the soil? They do not, however, ask you to keep them in idleness, or to consider them as chiefs or masters; their only wish is to defend you. They know to what extent you are encompassed by rapacious and envious men, who, jealous of the prosperity of your

---

[1] *Chases* –a kind of trousers divided down the legs and fastened with bandelets.

valley, are cherishing the most sinister designs against you. They know this because they have seen many peoples of whose existence you do not dream, though they are close to your borders. Lulled by a prolonged security, you are not in a condition to resist a serious attack. Now these warriors—your relations, your brothers, your friends, of the same blood as yourselves—have been considering with painful anxiety this state of repose in which you are living. They have, therefore, formed the intention—they, as men of war, to occupy the camp, to fortify it effectually, to make it a reliable place of refuge in case of invasion, and to defend themselves in it to the death. Is there any wrong in this? As to these warriors, whom you regard as strangers, they are brethren in arms who have fought side by side with us beyond the mountains, but who no longer finding their abodes on returning to their valleys devastated by marauders, ask an asylum with us. Besides, if they do not belong to your tribes, are they not Gauls like ourselves?

"We have wished to say this to you here, and not in the place of rendezvous itself, in the fear lest our intentions should be misunderstood amid so great a concourse. If our proposals, conceived with a view to the common interest, appear to you just, and if you still persist in holding the assembly on the height above, we will go before you to the camp, and will remain there when you return to your habitations.

"As for us, devoting ourselves to those new functions which we are competent to discharge, we will make of this camp a stronghold impregnable to any enemy that might dare to attack us." A long murmur followed this discourse and the chiefs of the tribes looked wistfully at each other.

The most venerable of them, advancing in his turn, replied thus: "Sigild, your words are fair; but the act to which you and your companions are committing yourselves at this moment is insulting, and aims a blow at the liberty of the inhabitants of the valley. You parade before us imaginary dangers, with a view to remaining on that height under the pretext of defending our families, but really in order to separate yourselves from us and act according to your good pleasure. Tell us who will support you and take care of your cattle while you are remaining on the height under arms, waiting for an enemy who perhaps will never make his appearance? Sole masters of the bridge and the two streams, you will be able, if you choose, to debar the inhabitants of the valley from hunting in the woods that extend behind the camp, and from fishing in the waters of the upper stream which furnish the best supply. We shall thus be at your discretion. If the assembly thinks it desirable to strengthen the fortifications of the camp, every inhabitant of the valley will take his share in the work—yourselves with the rest. If it shall be necessary to defend the inclosure, all who are in a condition to bear arms must engage in the defence; for all are equally interested in protecting their families, in repelling an enemy, and not exposing themselves to insult. Come, then, with us to the camp; we will deliberate on all that concerns the interests of the tribes, and you will only have to submit, like ourselves, to the result of our deliberation. As to the new-comers, if they ask for an asylum, you know that it will not be refused them; but they must fulfil the conditions imposed upon foreigners wishing to live among us. Moreover, we shall have to consult the Ovates."

Thrusting back Sigild, who was preparing to give an answer, the first warrior, who had spoken so insolently, advanced to the edge of the bridge in front of the chiefs of the tribes, and putting aside their arms, he said, "No one shall pass; all this parleying is useless; go back to your houses; we will hold the camp."

At these words a thousand voices arose, and, in spite of the endeavours of the chiefs to restrain them, the crowd of the men of the valley rushed forward like a torrent. Swords were drawn on both sides, and the clash of arms was mingled with the cries of the two parties. The imprecations of the women dispersed along the shore, and who were urging the men towards the bridge, were heard above the clamour of the multitude. The party that was endeavouring to obstruct the passages recoiled for the moment, with a view to concentrate themselves on the narrowest point; and, as the warriors had crowded together on the bridge to hear what was being said on both sides, and many had even mounted the wooden parapets, this movement from front to rear threw confusion into the closely-packed mass, and several fell into the river.

At sight of this a shout, followed by an immense burst of laughter, issued from the groups assembled on the shore; and the defenders of the bridge, and those who were advancing to meet them, having no conception of the cause of this laughter, stopped and looked behind them on either side.

But the warriors who had fallen from the bridge into the water, embarrassed by their clothes and shackled by their armour, although able to swim, were being swept down by the current, with a rapidity increased by the swollen state of the river. They were all but engulfed in the rapid torrent. Two boats were fastened to the bank on the valley side; in a moment some of the spectators pushed off in them, and rowing with might and main, and with the help of poles, had soon rescued the half-drowned warriors and brought them to the shore.

Three had lost consciousness; every assistance was

afforded them, and the women especially lavished upon them the most assiduous attention.

The result of this episode was the intermingling of the parties ; the defenders of the bridge had advanced on the shore as far as the middle of the passage, and were surrounding the handsome Sigild, who, with a smile upon his lips, was answering all the questions addressed to him by reassuring words. He might be seen slightly shrugging his shoulders and shaking his head in graceful fashion. An armed struggle was no longer possible, and the war-cry had been exchanged for laughter. A more compact group, however, consisting of members of the two parties, were keeping up a lively discussion along one of the parapets of the bridge, when one of the inhabitants of the valley, to whom the attention of those surrounding him seemed to be directed, mounted the hand-rail with agility, and, fastening his buckler to his shoulder, plunged into the river.

He soon re-appeared, and swimming with vigour and address, gained a footing on the bank at the base of the promontory.

The hurraing on the opposite shore recommenced ; in an instant the two boats were filled by men of the valley, and others crossed swimming, partly aided by the boats, which soon reached the other side. Some vessels towed across conveyed considerable numbers—so many, indeed, that the holders of the bridge saw themselves placed between two hostile bodies, should they persist in their resolution. The laughter was kept up on both sides, and was communicated even to the warriors posted on the passage. The knot of defenders became less and less dense, and if they did not retreat *en masse*—which would have called forth a fresh burst of hilarity—they were gradually retiring. Soon the platform of the bridge was deserted by all but the surly instigator of the strife, whose insolent words had almost occasioned a sanguinary struggle. He indeed was not laughing; when he saw himself abandoned he threw his sword into the river, and making himself a passage through the crowd, he bent his steps towards the valley. The handsome Sigild, surrounded by the greater part of the warriors, was on his way upwards towards the camp, and the whole multitude was following him.

CHAPTER III.

THE FIRST SIEGE.

THIRTY years after the event just related, the valley of Avon still preserved its smiling aspect and was covered with rustic habitations; there might be seen, however, in front of and behind the bridge just mentioned, two groups of houses in pretty close proximity: the first in the direction of the valley, the second on the lower slopes of the plateau. A considerable number of boats were moored on the two banks below the bridge, and were receiving or discharging packages covered with wrappers made of rushes. On the top of the promontory was seen the outline of a rampart made of stone, wood, and earth, but with square towers composed in great part of timber and wattle-work, about a hundred paces apart. Outside the inclosure rose palisades of no great height, in front of a ditch six feet wide by three or four feet deep. The entrances to the Oppidum, which still occupied the place previously indicated, were amply environed outside by stakes connected by branches of trees. At the lower end of the two sunk roads were raised besides two towers of timber and wattle-work.

Grave events had been the cause of these changes.

The meeting announced in the preceding chapter had taken place on the plateau. The uproar and confusion that prevailed threatened a sanguinary conclusion. The warriors insisted on adhering to the programme sketched by the handsome Sigild, and on reserving to themselves the privilege of guarding the camp.

The chiefs of the tribes would not agree to this. The Ovates, the wisest among the Druids, had been consulted. But their responses, of a somewhat ambiguous character, did not satisfy the multitude.

The latter (the Ovates) declared in the first place, that the Némède could not be touched without drawing down the gravest calamities upon the tribes; that the flocks belonging to the college must be allowed to graze undisturbed on the plateau; and that if any peril threatened the inhabitants of the valley, they, the Druids, would be able to give timely warning to the defenders. During this deliverance the handsome Sigild wore his accustomed smile and suavely shook his head in his usual manner, but said not a word. The Druidesses, seated along the inclosure of the Némède, their hands on their knees in a musing attitude, appeared to take no part in the discussion. The men were divided into groups, and it seemed as if no decision would be arrived at before sunset. Hunger and thirst began to be keenly felt, and the women were spreading on the turf the provisions they had brought. At this juncture one of the Druidesses, at the solicitation of her companions, advanced into the midst of the assembly. She was young, tall, and dressed in a long white robe—a kind of dalmatic without a girdle; and her bare arms were adorned with bracelets of black glass. On seeing her every voice was hushed, and surrounded by her companions, who had followed her, she spoke thus:—

"You who are assembled here, who live in peace, thinking you have no enemy to fear, are unable calmly to deliberate and adopt a wise resolution. How will it be when the enemy is upon you? And I warn you that such an enemy is near; he is preparing his arms and reckoning his spoils in the pillage of your flocks and the plunder of your houses; indeed he is already rejoicing in a victory which he deems certain because he knows you are not in a condition to act in concert to resist him.

"Abandon this place, which you are incapable of defending, since you know not how to fortify it; return to your houses, and await in careless ease the hour of peril." Around the young woman, pale with emotion, and who spoke without a gesture or a movement, as if the words she was slowly pronouncing had issued from a statue, the multitude had assembled in a compact mass. A tremulous agitation ran through the crowd like the breeze through the corn. Then, by one of those instinctive movements which sway the multitude, all eyes were turned towards Sigild. The latter, standing in front of the Druidess, who had remained rigid as a statue on the stone that served her as a tribune, had his eyes fixed on the ground contrary to his usual custom, as if he could not endure the fire of all these glances directed towards him.

Through the murmurs of the crowd the name of Sigild could be vaguely distinguished. "Let Sigild be our Brenn!" said a voice. Immediately thousands of voices repeated, "Let Sigild be our Brenn!" It seemed then as if all those who a few minutes before were of opinions widely contrary had but a single thought, a single soul, a single voice.

Sigild was therefore proclaimed Brenn, and the night passed in joyous festivities.

Whether the young Druidess had been informed of the projects formed against the happy inhabitants of the valley of Avon, or whether inspiration or chance had led to the coincidence, only a few months had passed since the meeting in question, when they observed certain strangers roaming about the hills, who speedily disappeared when the inhabitants began to question them; and subsequently a larger number of merchants than was customary, arrived in the valley. They were insolent, endeavoured to embroil themselves with the inhabitants, and uttered menaces when their assumptions were met by reason; and several of them who were expelled from the country threatened to return and avenge themselves.

One day, in fact, the heights that surrounded the valley appeared occupied one after the other by troops of armed men.

Meanwhile Sigild, elected Brenn, had lost no time. He had first assembled around him all his old companions in arms; and many young men who preferred a life of war to the peaceful pursuits of the shepherd or the husbandman had also joined him.

The new Brenn had gold, and on occasions would pay men to work at the Oppidum. Full of respect and deference for the Druids, he had embellished the Némède; and seemed to engage in no undertaking till he had consulted the Ovates. He gave them the produce of his hunting expeditions, and had caused a decree to be made that the fishery above the bridge should be reserved for the college.

The camp was assuming day by day a more formidable aspect, but the Brenn and his men, with the college of the Druids, were the only persons entitled to sojourn there. As on former occasions, every man of the valley was obliged to devote one day in four to the work of fortification; moreover, the inhabitants of the Val d'Avon supplied the warriors with provisions. They were, however, beginning to murmur, and to complain of the exactions of the latter; and things would probably have not long continued on this footing, when the threatened enemy appeared.

The sound of trumpets was immediately heard in the camp: it was the signal agreed upon; and the unfortunate families of the valley might be seen rushing in disorder towards the bridge, driving their cattle before them, and carrying with them on their backs or in waggons their most valued property, with provisions, clothes, and even furniture. The bridge not being wide enough for the passage of the distracted multitude who were thronging towards it, boats were heavily laden with people, and many foundered.

The armed bands that had appeared on the hills, whether as a matter of prudence or because they were waiting for the command to advance, made no haste to descend into the valley, and night came without a single enemy having quitted his post of observation.

This night was a painful one for the inhabitants of the valley. It was autumn, and the cold was already beginning to be felt. They were arriving breathless in the camp, covered with sweat; the sharp air of the night was freezing their limbs. They were calling to or searching for each other in the crowd, and although space was not wanting, it seemed as if this multitude would never succeed in housing itself on the plateau. Fires were being lighted, and the warriors, Sigild's companions, were hastening to and fro on horseback among the distracted crowd, endeavouring to make themselves heard and to introduce a little order into this confusion; for each tribe had had its quarter traced out for it by the wise foresight of the Brenn. But those who had arrived first at any spot were loath to quit it and take up their baggage again to carry it elsewhere. The animals were lowing or bleating, the children were crying, and the women lamenting.

The valley presented a quite different spectacle; animated the night before, lighted up by the household fires that sparkled through the trees, and filled with the sounds of evening, it was now silent and deserted; not a light nor the least appearance of life could be distinguished. A pale fog was diffused over the meadows. At nightfall Sigild ordered the barriers of the camp to be closed, prohibiting, on pain of death, their being opened to any person whatever. Thus many belated families had to await the return of day below the ramparts.

With smiling countenance the Brenn was leisurely traversing on horseback the various quarters of the camp: he was addressing all he met, and his gentle, penetrating voice seemed to restore order and silence wherever it was heard. His words and counsels, and the fatigue that was taking possession of the crowd, had soon caused an appearance of calm to succeed the confusion that prevailed at first. Then the Brenn re-entered the hut he had caused to be constructed for himself on the projecting summit of the promontory, in front of the Némède, and summoned Tomar into his presence.

Tomar was one of the stranger warriors whom Sigild had kept near him after the meeting above mentioned. Had these foreign warriors been forced to quit their native regions in consequence of the devastation of their estates and the ruin of their families, as the Brenn had affirmed; or had they been banished by their countrymen for certain misdeeds? We cannot say. Certain it is that they were devoted body and soul to Sigild, who on his part was in a position liberally to reward their devotion. Tomar was of medium height, and his large head, on a short neck bristling with harsh, thick hair, seemed to move with difficulty. His face also preserved a kind of immobility; and but for his grey eyes, which,

under his bushy eyebrows, seemed to penetrate in every
direction, the man might have been taken for a rough-
hewn image of wood. With curved back, long arms,
always falling down by the side of his body, and legs
heavy and bent, Tomar could nevertheless perform a

SIGILD AND TOMAR.

march of twelve hours in succession without turning his
head. Yet at the end of the journey this automaton-
like being had seen all that was visible through the whole
route, and could give an account of what he had observed
with the most minute exactness and in the most perfect

sequence. He could speak many Gallic dialects, but no one—not even Sigild—knew his past history. Tomar rarely laughed. A travelling merchant had brought an ape into the valley; and witnessing the grimaces of this specimen of the quadrumana, Tomar burst into a fit of laughter. It was almost the only time that he had permitted himself such an ebullition, and if any one wanted to provoke anything like a smile upon his rigid countenance, he must mention the ape.

As his manner was, Tomar entered the Brenn's hut as noiselessly as a cat, and placing himself before Sigild said, "Here I am!" "Tomar, I rely upon thy aid." "Yes." "Thou wilt go out of the camp without a single person—mind, a single person—suspecting thy departure." "Yes." "Thou wilt go to the border of the Sequani; thou understandest? Thou wilt speak to Ditovix; thou understandest?" "Yes." "Thou wilt ask him for five hundred warriors who have nothing to lose." "Yes." "Thou wilt tell him that these warriors will find here lands and wealth." "Yes." "Thou wilt conduct them through the forests, getting all the information thou canst." "Yes." "Thou wilt require three days to go; one day to arrange matters with Ditovix; to assemble the five hundred warriors, six days; to bring them here, four days; altogether fourteen days. The evening of the fourteenth, dating from to-morrow morning, thou and the five hundred warriors will be at a distance of three miles from the camp, towards the north, in the woods. At sunset thou wilt place a pole at the top of one of the highest trees; when the first quarter of the night has expired thou will hoist a lighted faggot on the summit of the pole. Thy warriors will be under arms, and you will immediately rush upon the enemies between us and you. We shall make a sally at the same time, and fall

D

upon them." "The enemies will be there?" "The enemies are sure to be there, because if they wish to besiege the camp they cannot take up any other position. They are sure to be there." "Very well, I set out." "Listen! if you meet any parties of the enemy, say that you have been wronged by us, and that you are seeking vengeance, knowing that we are on the point of yielding to them. They will either accept or refuse your co-operation. If they accept it, the warriors of Ditovix will occupy a part of the enemy's camp, and at the signal agreed on will spread confusion on all sides, while we make a sortie from the ramparts, and fall upon them; if they refuse it, you will pretend to be greatly irritated, but will affect to retire, and at the close of the day you will return to the place mentioned." "But if the enemy occupy that spot?" "They will not occupy it, because we shall compel them to concentrate their forces around us. Stop, here is gold, and a ring well known to Ditovix. Listen further. During the attack, as it will be at midnight, the warriors thou bringest and our men, not being acquainted with each other, might engage in mutual slaughter. Before the battle let each of thy men put on a necklace of grass, and set fire to everything that can burn. That will be easy; the enemy will make himself a shelter with branches: we shall wear necklaces like yours, and will light fires on our side. Next, when making the attack, let all thy men shout 'Sigild!' Ours will answer with the same cry. To ensure the lighting of the fires, take burning embers in earthen vessels; let there be at least one of these to every five men. If the enemy accept your aid, keep as much as possible in separate quarters, so that it will not be difficult for you to make your grass necklaces, and you will have your lighted fires to use, while you will also avail yourselves of the fire made by the enemy. But if through distrust they separate you into small parties, arrange beforehand your signals of attack, and instead of grass necklaces, have the right leg bare. . . . Fourteen days!" "I understand."

Sigild had surrounded the camp with a number of wooden towers placed on the old rampart, which had been strengthened. These towers, whose appearance is shown in Fig. 6, were made of trunks of trees piled one

FIG. 6.

upon another, and framed at their extremities. They projected from the rampart. At their summit was constructed a wooden floor surrounded by a parapet of wattling; and this floor was reached by means of a ladder placed inside the tower. The under story gave shelter to the men charged with the defence of the towers, and who watched from the top. If they perceived any suspicious movement without, it was their duty to give the alarm by blowing a horn. Sigild had fixed the number of men for each tower at twenty. Two of these twenty men remained day and night on the platform, the day and the night being each divided into four parts; there were eight men on duty during the day and eight during the night. Of the four remaining, the first was constituted chief of the tower; the second was intrusted with the stores, and the distribution of food and munitions; the third was to be at the disposal of the chief of the tower, to carry messages and seek for help in case of need; and the business of the fourth was to repair the injuries caused to the defences in the event of an attack.

As the circumvallation measured four thousand five hundred paces, and the towers were one hundred paces apart, there were forty-five towers, including the stronger and loftier ones placed on the two sides of the entrances. Nine hundred men sufficed to guard them. Sigild had taken the precaution of having a store of timber and branches brought within the inclosure of the Oppidum. By his care the wells had been deepened, and a trench dug outside the ramparts, towards the north. In addition to the flocks that habitually grazed within the camp, a great number of cattle had been brought by the fugitives to the plateau. But it would not have been possible to feed all these animals if stores of fodder had not been laid in beforehand. Accordingly, great stacks of grass had been placed along beside the rampart, thatched with reeds.

Between the towers the guarding of the ramparts was intrusted to a thousand men, put under the order of fifty-three chiefs; the two entrances were under the command of warriors of tried courage, and well known to Sigild.

This garrison, consisting of about two thousand men, had long been settled in the camp, and had partly executed the work of its fortification. As to the fugitives, they might have amounted to twelve thousand; and out of this number two thousand at least were able to fight, were provided with arms, and had been habituated to endurance.

In place of the original huts, which had fallen to decay, Sigild had formed a kind of *halles*, or vast sheds. There were eight of these sheds; one for every tribe. In front of each were disposed, at regular distances, circular fire-places, formed with flat stones, and intended for cooking. As soon as the sun appeared above the horizon a confused sound of voices succeeded to the silence which had gradually fallen upon the plateau. But Sigild had not lost time during the night. Orders had been given to his trusty followers; eight mounted chiefs, followed by armed men, went among the multitude of fugitives, and pointed out to each tribe the locality that had been assigned it. Whether through lassitude, or from a sense of danger, the multitude obeyed, and towards the middle of the day the camp had ceased to present the appearance of disorder it exhibited the evening before. Around the sheds, which were insufficient for such a number of families, might be seen men making huts with branches. The larger animals were fastened to stakes, and browsed on the grass which had not been too much trodden; the sheep were folded, and the women were preparing the day's repast; in every quarter the children were running about, and seemed to enjoy this new life. As to the warriors, they silently kept watch on the ramparts and the towers.

In the morning the valley was filled with a thick mist, and the hills were visible on either side above it; upon their ridges was no sign of the enemy, and from the white vapour which hid the valley, not a sound issued. Had the enemy withdrawn? Was it a false alarm?

From the camp the course of the river was scarcely distinguishable beneath the thick cloud of mist which covered it. Towards the end of the first quarter of the day Sigild sent out a detachment of a hundred men, with orders to explore the bridge and the banks of the river and rivulet. If no enemy appeared they were to follow the course of the latter and to reconnoitre towards the north; they were to avoid engaging with the enemy. Ten men were to remain upon the bridge to collect brushwood, and set fire to it the moment they saw the enemy in the valley. Gradually the fog dispersed, and at noon the sun shone out in all its splendour through the whole extent of the valley. Nothing broke the silence, the air was still, and in the distance, cattle that had been forgotten were seen quietly grazing. Many of the fugitives wished to leave the camp and return to their houses, with a view to remaining there, or to fetch articles which they had been unable to bring away. Sigild doubled the posts at the gates, with orders not to let any one go out. He went from one to another, trying to make the people understand that the enemy, far from withdrawing, was only waiting an occasion to seize the unwary who attempted to return to their homes. "They are in ambush," he urged; "they hope that you will relapse into security and will become their prey without a struggle; for though they covet your goods, they are still more anxious to get posesssion of your persons: they will carry you off to sell you, your wives and your children, as slaves among the nations beyond the mountains." Despite this warning, however, a great number were crowding towards the points of exit, and the armed men had hard work to keep the multitude back, when there arrived at the eastern entrance fifty of the warriors sent by Sigild to reconnoitre. They were covered with mud and sweat. When interrogated by the Brenn, they said that about three thousand paces from the camp, towards the north, among the woods, and although they were proceeding cautiously, they saw themselves all at once surrounded by the enemy; that many of them had been killed or captured; that they owed their escape only to their knowledge of the neighbourhood, and that they effected it by rushing into a narrow ravine filled with underwood and decayed trunks of trees, and leading down to the rivulet, not far from the camp. " Your chief is killed?" said the Brenn. " We do not know." " You left him behind you!" " We had orders to avoid any engagement." "You have not abandoned your arms?" " We have our arms." " Go and take rest." In an instant the entrances were clear, and the crowd returned in silence to its camping grounds.

Sigild then went to the northern end of the camp; he looked long through the depths of the forest; then he summoned to this front five hundred armed men from the tribes, besides those who were at their post; he stationed them behind the parapet, and ordered them to keep silence. He went into each of the towers raised on that side, and spoke in a low voice to each of the chiefs. Then all at once a shout arose from the southern side of the plateau. The Brenn mounted his horse and rode off hastily in that direction; but on his way he was told that the bridge was on fire, and that the ten warriors stationed there were coming in by the western gate.

"You have seen the enemy?" said Sigild, when the ten warriors made their appearance. " We have seen them: they were advancing in a strong body towards the bridge, endeavouring to screen themselves behind the reeds and willows." Then Sigild selected a hundred men from among his best warriors, and posted them on the slopes of the plateau outside the western gate, ordering them to pile up underwood and trunks of trees in the sunken road, to keep behind on the banks, and not use their bows and slings till they saw the enemy near the barricade; and if they attempted an assault on this point in a considerable body, to retire within and occupy the ramparts, helping those intrusted with their defence. In reality, however, the Brenn did not anticipate any serious attack on that side, which was difficult of approach. He thought the enemy would not attempt an assault with a river at their back, even should they succeed in crossing it. His attention was once more directed to the north. On this side, in fact, the camp is separated only by a slight hollow from the adjacent plateau, which widens and affords space for the gathering of a large number of troops, and a secure retreat in case of failure. He had also ascertained that the enemy already occupied the wide, forest-covered plateau.

Sigild again rode through the whole length of the camp at a walking pace, uttering here and there words of encouragement whenever he encountered looks of alarm. His calmness, his frank and agreeable expression, reassured the most timid. Night fell by the time he reached the ramparts on the northern side. Silence still reigned in the woods. When it was quite dark, some boys were let down by his orders over the parapet, loaded with bundles of straw and dry grass; their instructions were to untie these bundles in the ditch sunk at this point at the foot of the escarpment. Then with the help of poles held down to them the children climbed back again. Sigild allowed only a few small fires to be lighted, screened by the height of the rampart, and all awaited the issue. The Brenn walked about conversing in a low voice with some of his trusty men, and the warriors standing around the smouldering fires, which threw a red glare upon them, exchanged only a few low and hurried words. Now and then a laugh escaped, but it was immediately stifled. The guard of the rampart had orders to keep a good look out, and if they perceived the enemy, to raise no cry. They were to give the alarm only by throwing clods of turf on the fires. They were not to show their heads above the wattle parapet. The night was clear, but there was no moon.

At the middle of the first quarter of the night one of the chiefs came down from the rampart walk and approached the Brenn.

"The enemy are coming," said he.

"What proof hast thou?"

"I heard the cracking of dead branches." Sigild ascended the rampart surrounded by several warriors. "To your posts!" he said, in a low voice. That very moment some clods of earth fell upon the fires, scattering a shower of sparks.

Sigild and the watchmen had observed certain forms of a whitish appearance that seemed to be creeping towards the counterscarp. Some of them let themselves down into the ditch, and pushing one another up scaled the escarpment; they succeeded in reaching the wattling. Hearing no sound inside, they turned round and helped up others. When about fifty were at the top of the escarpment, poles were handed to them furnished with hooks, which they fixed into the wattling: then those who had remained on the counterscarp pulled the poles with all their force.

The wattling gave way, and the assailants rushed on to the rampart walk. Thrust back by the swords of the defenders, the greater number rolled down to the bottom of the fosse. Then, in accordance with the orders of the Brenn, flaming brands were thrown among the straw placed at the bottom of the ditch; it took fire, and, spreading a bright light, brought into view a broad front of enemies. From the summits of the towers the slings and bows discharged a shower of stones and arrows upon them. Many of the defenders were preparing to cross the debris of the wattling and get down the escarpment to throw themselves upon the enemy, but the Brenn stopped them, threatening with death any who should quit the rampart. The surprise had failed, and the ranks of the enemy wavered and retired out of range of the missiles.

The Brenn, however, caused the wattling to be repaired as far as circumstances allowed, and doubled the ranks of the defenders on the rampart, as well to present a firm front to the assailants as to hold back the men of the foremost rank whom the enemy should seek to pull down into the ditch. Besides this, he formed between each tower small bodies of twenty men, who were to hasten to the weak points and to hurl down any of the assailants who should gain a footing on the rampart. Then he sent some of his trusty men on horseback to the eastern and western fronts, to convey intelligence, or to give warning in the event of attacks being made on several points at once.

Scarcely were these measures taken when the enemy were seen returning in considerable strength to the ditch; with loud cries they rushed up the escarpment. They were warmly received, and the ditch was being filled with the dead and wounded, facilitating the passage of those who followed, especially as many bore fascines. After two attempts the assailants gained a footing on one of the ramparts; but the reserve bodies attacked them in front, while the men from the towers issuing right and left took them in flank.

Whether the lighted straw had not been quite extinguished, or the besieged had thrown more burning brands into the ditch, some fascines took fire, burning the wounded, who uttered the most dreadful cries.

The attack languished, and at length the leaders of the besieging host gave the signal for retreat.

A certain number of the assailants had remained alive in the power of the besieged, and Sigild gave orders that they should be guarded and not put to death. As to the wounded lying within the ramparts, they were killed.

Towards the middle of the night fires were seen to be lighted in the woods, about a thousand paces from the camp. The besieged had lost a few men only, but the ditch was filled with the enemy's dead and wounded. The groans of the latter were the only interruption to the quiet of the night.

Sigild slept not; he kept half the warriors on vigorous guard during the third quarter of the night, and the other half during the last quarter.

Those who were not on guard slept around the fires. The Brenn, when the assault was over, had sent messengers to the chiefs of the eight tribes to acquaint them with the happy result of this first engagement.

At break of day the Brenn had the prisoners brought before him. Two or three of them spoke the language of the valley, but with a foreign accent.

Clothed in drawers laced around, and a tunic of undyed wool, with a broad strap which served them for a girdle, they looked not unlike some of those merchants who occasionally came into the valley to barter yellow amber and bronze for corn, cheese, tanned hides, and wool. "Why do you come to attack us?" said Sigild. "We have been driven from the lands we have inhabited from the most ancient times, by hordes from the north. These men have killed many of us, taken away our wives, and murdered our children: the stronger among us have combined together, and crossing a wide river on rafts, we have travelled onwards towards the setting sun, seeking a home. Two days' journey from this spot we were told that this country is good and can afford sustenance to many; so we have come hither.

"When our chiefs saw that you shut yourselves up in this place, regarding us as enemies, they told us we must first make ourselves masters of the camp. We obeyed. We are only doing to you what has been done to us." "Why not have sent some of your number to ask of us what you required?" "I do not know." "You have come as enemies, and as enemies we have received you. How many are you?" "A great many." "Go seek your chiefs and tell them that if by nightfall their entire host have not quitted the land of Avon, the captives we have made here shall suffer." "I will not go." "Why?" "Because our chiefs will not leave this land. Put us to death; for if any of your party have fallen into the hands of our men, they are doomed to death to avenge our comrades killed this night." "Good." Sigild ordered that the captives should be fettered till he had decided on their fate.

The Brenn was very anxious that the enemy should take up a position towards the north, opposite to the weak point of the Oppidum. Accordingly he was continually reconnoitring on the eastern and western fronts as far as the river and the other side of the rivulet, to prevent the besiegers from establishing themselves in either quarter. Upon the steep sides of the plateau, opposite the burnt bridge, Sigild had placed a small camp guarded by two hundred men. The reconnoitring parties, which he sent out in large numbers, had orders to bring back into the camp all the fodder and strayed cattle they could find, engaging the enemy only when they encountered them in small bodies.

But the invaders did not seem to be contemplating another assault. They took up their quarters in the woods to the north and on the slopes of the hills, right and left, leaving between them and the camp the river and the rivulet; marauding parties might also be seen in the valley, foraging, and pillaging the deserted dwellings. On the other side of the destroyed bridge they formed a wide palisading strengthened by barricading of timber; and two days afterwards they had constructed a floating bridge on the river, formed with trunks of trees fastened together and kept in place by a kind of dam made with piles of timber fixed in the bed of the river and inclined up the stream.

It was evident that the besiegers were in no hurry; that they were living upon the provisions left in the valley; and that it was their intention to reduce the besieged by famine.

In fact the inhabitants of the Val d'Avon had been able to carry with them only a small quantity of provisions. They had their cattle, but these being badly fed and crowded together were dying in great numbers; the cows ceased to give milk, and the store of forage was rapidly diminishing.

On the sixth day of the investment, the chiefs of the tribes proposed to the Brenn to cut their way through the enemy's lines while their men still preserved their strength entire, and not to wait till the utter failure of provisions should place them at the mercy of the invaders. Of course the Brenn opposed this proposition, declaring that the day of deliverance would come, and that they must have patience. Nevertheless it was of great consequence to him that the enemy should concentrate his forces on the northern side. Accordingly, one evening at nightfall, he collected two bodies of men, one at the eastern, the other at the western gate. He had observed that the enemy used to prepare their morning meal just before noon, and that of the evening at sunset. After the evening repast they were heard singing and shouting.

When the opportune moment arrived he divided each of his bodies into two. The first two halves were to march along the ramparts parallel to one another till they reached the woods; there they were to rush on the two flanks of the besiegers' outposts; they were not to prolong the attack, but to fall back with all speed to the northern salient of the Oppidum. An issue would be open at this point. In the meantime, the two other halves would unite, provided with stakes, before this salient, where, with the aid of palisading, they would make an advanced work (Fig. 7). and then fall back one hundred paces to the right and left.

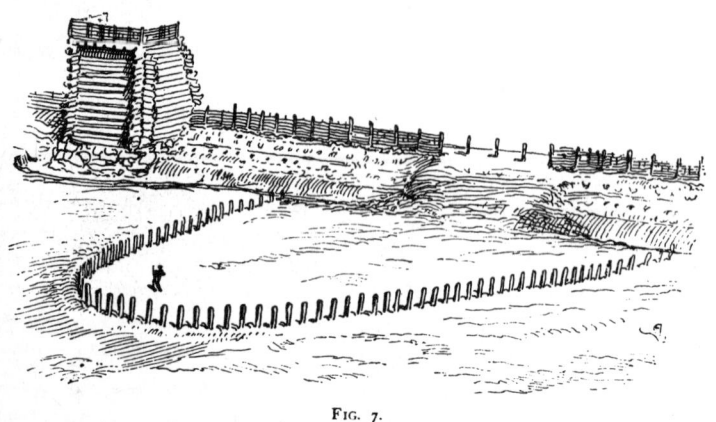

FIG. 7.

The men who guarded the north front had orders to cut an opening in the rampart twenty paces wide, and to throw fascines and clods of turf into the ditch, and have wattles ready to close the opening instantly.

The first two detachments, therefore, set out in silence; that on the western side left a little before the one on the east, so as to arrive at the same time on the enemy's flank. The two other detachments preceded them, and stationing themselves at the northern extremity of the Oppidum, drove in their stakes according to the instructions given, and then fell back to right and left. A fine autumnal rain was falling, and the ground was slippery. Some time elapsed before the two detachments found themselves in sight of the enemy's camp. The besiegers had no outposts; but their army encamped in front of the Oppidum, and at a distance of about six hundred paces from it, was intrenched behind barricades of timber; the intrenchment presented an extended front. Their men might be seen around the fires, talking loudly, singing, and drinking cider and mead, of which they had found abundance in the houses of the valley. An attack on this front was not to be thought of; they must get round it. So the two detachments separated farther and farther from each other, and advanced with the greatest difficulty along the bogs and under the woods in momentary fear of being seen by the enemy. At length the one which was manœuvring on the right reached the end of the front, got under cover, and awaited the signal, which was to be given by the one on the left by the blowing of a horn; for the Brenn had calculated that the former would reach the extremity of the front before the latter.

The time, however, was getting on, and Sigild, who had advanced with several warriors on horseback along the verge of the wood, still heard nothing. He sent two of his warriors to ascertain where the two detachments were; they had great difficulty in making their way through the wood, while the enemy's fires, which they saw in the distance through the trees, only added to their difficulties, by preventing them from seeing the ground they were riding over. The right front of the enemy towards the river formed a lengthened curve, and the left detachment kept advancing parallel with the front without finding a point of attack.

Midnight had passed when this detachment found itself at last before an opening left in the barricade, but this opening formed an interior angle, which rendered the attack very hazardous. The detachment waited until all was silent in the camp. The fires, fed only at irregular intervals, cast here and there a fluctuating light, and fewer shadows were passing before the braziers.

One of the warriors sent by Sigild was approaching; he considered that the attack on this point should not be deferred, and that the enemy must be surprised during his first sleep.

One of the men gave the signal agreed upon, and the troops rushed through the opening, slaying all before them with terrific shouts, scattering the fires and forming in triangle, so as to prevent the enemy from getting round them. They did not proceed very far, for at the cries of the assailants and of the wounded, men were seen to rise up on every side and hasten towards the point of attack. The little troop then closed, and ceasing to advance, turned and fled back towards the Oppidum, following the verge of the wood along the steep banks of the river. A long-continued shout was then heard on the enemy's left; the attack had begun on that side also.

Whether the enemy, which had started in pursuit of the left detachment, had succeeded in getting round it, or whether the detachment itself lost its way in the darkness, it was unable to regain the plateau in time, and continued to follow the course of the river.

As to the troop detached on the right, being less distant from the Oppidum, directly it found itself pressed by a numerous body of the enemy, it retired in good order, and went direct to the angle of the intrenchments, as had been arranged, hotly pursued by the crowd of besiegers. At the same time most of the enemy's forces that had started in pursuit of the left detachment were coming on the ground.

The Brenn had anticipated the contingency of the attack which he had arranged not succeeding in every point. Despite the darkness, he saw that his people were not in advance, as they ought to have been, of the hostile warriors who were making their appearance on his left; he therefore quickly retired within the outwork of stakes which had been formed by his orders, and commanded the straw fires to be lighted.

The two detachments in ambuscade to the right and left outside the rampart had orders to refrain from attack till a signal agreed upon had been given. At the barrier of stakes, then, there arrived at the same time the right detachment in flight, that portion of the enemy who were in close pursuit of them, and those who were looking for the errant left detachment.

A great number entered pell-mell into the triangular space formed by the stakes. It became the scene of an indescribable *mêlée ;* those who were defending the wattling which closed the breach dared not make any openings for their brethren-in-arms whom they saw engaged with the enemy. The Brenn struck into the midst of the crowd trying to rally his men. He succeeded in cutting his way up to the wattling, against which he leaned his back; and the warriors of the right detachment being encouraged by his example, presented a head to the enemy, whose numbers, however, continually augmented. A few minutes more and they would have been swept down by the multitude of the assailants; the last comers were urging on those in front of them, and the wattling and the warriors who defended it would have been borne down by the tide. The Brenn, with his long sword, was making a circle of dead and wounded around him. Then shouting over the parapet to give the signal, the sound of trumpets arose above the yells of the combatants. The enemy seemed to hesitate for a moment; then, closing into a compact body, they rushed upon the barricade, which gave way as if swept by a torrent.

At the same instant loud shouts were heard on each of the enemy's flanks; the two troops in ambuscade attacked the confused column outside the rampart. . . .

The combat did not cease until daybreak. Those of the enemies who had succeeded in penetrating into the Oppidum were killed or captured. The triangle of broken stakes was strewn in every direction with the dead. The enemy, disconcerted by the two simultaneous flank attacks, and finding himself cut in two, was no longer able in the darkness to concert an assault, and retired. Nevertheless, those who had been taken in the outwork and at the gap of the Oppidum fought obstinately to the last, and the captives who were driven before the Brenn were all more less severely wounded.

Sigild was covered with blood and dirt; his great black horse had been killed in the last *mêlée*, and he himself had been trampled on.

He ascended the nearest tower, and saw that the enemy remained not far off; they were forming a contravallation of barricading three hundred paces from the Oppidum. Their attitude was threatening, and it was to be feared that they meditated another attack. The Brenn, therefore, had the gap immediately repaired and the parapet strengthened with strong stakes about two feet apart. Besides this, he sunk a second ditch with intrenchment in a concave line, within the northern salient of the Oppidum. This intrenchment could not be seen from without. He contrived an egress at either end against a tower. The object was attained; the enemy was concentrating himself in front of the weak salient of the Oppidum, and was drawing nearer. The defenders, however, ignorant of the motives which had induced the Brenn to attempt the hazardous sortie of the previous night, shook their heads and appeared anxious. If two or three hundred of the enemy had been killed, they had lost nearly as many.

The women whose husbands were dead were filling the camp with their lamentations. Yet it was essential that Sigild should possess the confidence of his brethren in arms till the *dénoûment* he had prepared should arrive. He called together the chiefs of the tribes. "You see plainly," said he, "that we cannot break through the lines which inclose the camp. The enemy are very numerous and daring, and not to be disconcerted. Besides, can we think of leaving here the aged, the women, and the children to become their prey! It is very certain that even if a troop of brave warriors could cut their way through such a host of enemies, the women, the aged, and the children could not follow them.

"My object in the sortie of last night was to force the enemy to concentrate all his forces towards the north; which he will be all the more disposed to do, as it is the weakest point of the Oppidum. When we have thus drawn him to that side, obliging him to withdraw from the hill-sides, we will go down on a dark night into the valley, cross the river by a bridge which I shall have in readiness and which fifty men will be able to put in place, and fly towards the river. When we find that we have no more provisions left than we are able to take with us, friends with whom I am in communication will guide us to some neighbouring tribes of our race, and who will give us a hearty welcome, because they want help in cultivating the broad lands they possess. You may therefore bid the tribes and the warriors take courage: every contingency is provided for. But if the plan is to succeed, we must not allow the enemy a moment's peace while we remain here."

Having nothing better to suggest, the chiefs of the tribes appeared to put faith in Sigild's words. His confident air, his good looks, the energy he displayed, and the care he took to make himself acquainted with everything, continued to secure for him the sympathy of the unfortunate refugees.

In the little camp above the burnt bridge he had, in accordance with the plan stated, some light rafts made which could be readily fastened together. He went frequently to see the work, and appeared to attach great importance to it. He ordered that the captives who were badly wounded should be killed; the others taken in the last engagement were supplied with food in abundance. Confined in a sort of pit surrounded by stakes, they could not observe what was going on in the camp. Well guarded in the daytime, they were by Sigild's orders scarcely watched during the night, on the supposition that some would contrive to escape and would make the enemy believe that there was no scarcity of provisions, which was exactly what happened. One night, three of the stoutest captives succeeded in getting out of the pit, and gliding along the ramparts, regained the besieger's camp. Then Sigild had the others killed.

Of the warriors not engaged in guarding the ramparts, the Brenn had formed four corps of three to five hundred men each; and at certain times of the day and night he sent them down by one or other of the gates to harass the enemy on one side of his camp, or at both sides at once. Neither party suffered much loss in these skirmishes, whose only result was to keep the besiegers in constant suspense, to weary them and oblige them to concentrate their forces. It was also evident that the enemy were preparing for a general assault. They were seen accumulating faggots, cutting long poles, and making wicker screens.

On the morning of the fourteenth day of the siege only a few scattered parties were seen on the surrounding hills, while in the valley the palisading formed opposite to the ruined bridge and the raft bridge were alone still occupied by a considerable number of troops. "It is certain," said Sigild, to the chiefs of the tribes, "that the enemy is preparing to attack us. We must resist this assault with vigour, and then we will take advantage of his exhaustion and disorder to carry out our plan of flight." The besieger's preparations appeared formidable, and the camp opposite the northern salient of the Oppidum presented a busy scene. Sigild on his part neglected no means of resistance, though he calculated on the arrival of the troops summoned to their relief in the evening. He had the towers well supplied with stones and darts: on the ramparts he strengthened the wattle parapet, and increased the number of inclines for reaching it easily.

Both sides were preparing for a decisive conflict. The intrenchment made behind the salient was well manned, and the Brenn trained his men to pass out in a body through the two egresses formed at the extremities of the intrenchment, so as to take the assailants in flank.

That day, however, passed without fighting. At sunset the Brenn ascended one of the towers, and attentively examined the horizon. His attendants thought he was watching the movements of the enemy; he was, in fact, waiting for Tomar's signal. The night passed, and no signal appeared.

Repressing all signs of the serious anxiety that had oppressed him through this tedious night, the sun had no sooner arisen than the Brenn disposed his men at the points he thought likely to be attacked.

The enemy had formed in two large bodies three hundred paces from the Oppidum; they had accumulated in front of them an immense quantity of faggots, beams, and wattles. The sun was already high above the horizon when they began to move. First came a line of warriors under cover of wicker shields, which protected them from darts and stones.

In this way they reached the counterscarp of the ditch, despite of missiles from the towers. There they fixed the wicker shields, and behind these a great number of the enemy bearing faggots gradually posted themselves. Then over this screen they threw a great quantity of these faggots into the ditch. When they judged that there were enough of them, they threw flaming brands upon them.

The besieged had no means of counteracting this kind of attack. They showered darts and stones in abundance upon the assailants, but only wounded a few of them; nor did they seem to mind these missiles. The wind blew from the north-west. The faggots were soon kindled, and the smoke and sparks blinded the defenders Three of the towers took fire, as well as the wattling of the ramparts.

Sigild, calm and unmoved, had withdrawn his men behind the second intrenchment. "The enemy," said he, "will not be able to pass till all is consumed; that will take time; let him mount the rampart and cry victory.

Then will be our time for action." In fact, the green wood burned badly, and produced much smoke; the besieged threw bushes and chips on the red-hot faggots to feed the fire, and it continued burning. The enemy were becoming impatient; the besieged looked on cheerfully. About the middle of the afternoon, however, the fire went out at some points; the besiegers threw earth and trunks of trees into the ditch, and, perceiving no defenders, thought that the ramparts being intenable were abandoned. With shouts they rushed on to the slopes, leaped the half-consumed wattling, and meeting with no resistance, descended in a close body into the camp (Fig. 8).

FIG. 8.

There they were greeted by a sudden shower of darts and stones; but they unhesitatingly rushed upon the intrenchment, which presented only a slight elevation and a shallow ditch, thinking to carry it easily.

But the intrenchment was strong, and furnished with thick pointed stakes. The assailants, urging forward and aiding each other, gained its ridge; they were received with swords and pikes, and fell back dying upon their comrades; others filled their places. The bodies of the wounded, which in some places gradually filled up the ditch, afforded them a passage. Many of the enemy had succeeded in throwing themselves into the midst of the defenders, and in opening deep passages among them which were instantly occupied by the most daring. The deep front which the Brenn had formed behind the intrenchment was broken. Then it was that he unmasked the two egresses at the extremities, sending out from both the troops of chosen warriors, who, keeping close along the deserted rampart, fell upon the dense stream of assailants. So compact was the crowd, and so great the pressure against the intrenchment, that they had scarcely room to move. The two detachments above mentioned were mowing away before them to enable them to advance. But the enemy kept pouring in, and the space regained was immediately filled with fresh assailants, who, disregarding the attacks on their flanks, pushed furiously on to the centre.

The bodies of the slain and the faggots had filled the ditch for the length of a hundred paces, and the loosened stakes formed but a slight protection to the defenders. The noise of the attack brought a great number of women hurrying to the spot. They might be seen with bare arms, raising stones above their heads, and hurling them with shrill cries against the breasts of the assailants, or despatching the wounded that had fallen inside the intrenchment with the culinary wooden pestles used for pounding herbs and flesh in hollow stones. A shout was raised, the crowd of assailants opened, and a hundred men were seen steadily advancing, bearing on their shoulders an enormous trunk of a tree, and surrounded by warriors armed with axes. This column overthrowing all in its passage, whether friend or foe, made a wide lane in the intrenchment, strewn with dead and wounded. The beam was already more than half way through on the inside of the defences when the women ran in, and rushing like she-wolves on the flanks of the column, passed between the warriors, and clung to the legs of the bearers. The enormous beam swayed, toppled over, and bore down in its fall both assailants and defenders by its vast weight. Sigild profiting by the confusion, then dashed into the breach, followed by a troop of warriors which he had not without difficulty kept in reserve. In his return he cut himself a passage through the crowd of assailants. Seeing this movement, the warriors who had issued from the two ends of the inner intrenchment redoubled their efforts. Others rushed on to the rampart-walk by the side issues of the intrenchment, and fell upon the enemies within or without the rampart. The latter, cramped within this narrow space, and with their centre broken through, were unable to use their arms. Some fell and were suffocated. Those who were on the projecting part of the rampart began to turn and fly into the midst of their advancing comrades, who not seeing what was taking place behind the rampart, were for compelling them to return to the battle.

The crowd fell into confusion, and disregarding the voice of the chiefs, accumulated in such masses in the ditch, the escarpments and the rampart-walk, that it could act only by its weight, and offered itself to attack without power of defence. Most threw down their bucklers which hampered their movements.

Sigild kept advancing, and all the warriors not engaged in defending the intrenchment formed behind him in a column which became denser each moment. As soon as they were outside the intrenchment, these warriors turned about and threw themselves on the bulk of the assailants, who were separated into two masses. Caught as in a pair of pincers by Sigild's band, and by those coming from the terminal egresses of the intrenchment, they were slaughtered without resistance.

In vain did the chiefs of the enemy sound a retreat. The bulk of assailants, who were massed between the rampart and the intrenchment, could neither advance nor recede. Very few succeeded in rejoining their companions.

Fatigue alone stayed the defenders; it was no longer a combat but a massacre.

Although the warriors of the Val d'Avon had suffered considerable loss, the success of the defence had intoxicated them, and they were eager to take advantage of the disorder of the enemy to sally forth from the Oppidum and fall upon them. Sigild was obliged to swear to them by the most terrible of oaths, that their vengeance would be more effective by delay.

He told them, moreover, that the enemy were very numerous, and that the losses they had suffered had not weakened them to such a degree as to render them contemptible; that they were burning for revenge, and that to attack them in their camp was to give them the very opportunity they desired. The authority of the chiefs of the tribes of the Druids had, however, to be appealed to, to keep the warriors within the Oppidum.

Night fell on the narrow battle-field covered with the dead and wounded. The Brenn took re-possession of the ramparts, had the wattle parapet hastily repaired, the enemy's wounded put to death, and his own carried into the middle of the camp, where they were consigned to the care of the women; then he ascended one of the unburnt towers of that front, hoping to perceive Tomar's signal. But the night was hazy, and the fires of the enemy three or four hundred paces distant were scarcely visible.

It was evident that Tomar could not have lighted his

fire, or if he had lighted it, it was impossible to see it through the haze.

The warriors after the laborious day, chilled by the autumn fog, were sleeping around their fires. The cries of victory had been exchanged for a death-like silence, broken only by the groans of some of the wounded who had been forgotten.

The Brenn was considering whether it would not be wise to follow the plan which he had indicated to the chiefs of the tribes—to leave the camp before daybreak by crossing the river on a line of rafts, before the enemy had time to effect a fresh assault. Provisions would certainly fail them soon. But how move this multitude! The warriors needed rest. "One more day," he said to himself; "and if I have no news of Tomar, I still must consider it." Then he went out and ordered to the point attacked a body of warriors some hundreds strong, who, having guarded the unbroken part of the ramparts during the assault, and having taken no part in the conflict, were fresh and vigorous. Some women even mounted the towers. He enjoined all of them to give the alarm vigorously if they saw the enemy approaching the ramparts, so as to rouse the sleeping warriors. He despatched several of his trusty friends to the other fronts of the camp, with injunctions to watch the approaches, and to send out scouts through the gates to ascertain any movements outside, and to light fires a little way from the ramparts, so as to illuminate the immediate vicinity. He proceeded towards the southern extremity of the Oppidum, and saw that the little camp above the bridge that had been destroyed was guarded; but also perceived through the mist the fires of the enemy in the valley opposite this point.

It was midnight, and Sigild, exhausted by fatigue,

returned to the northern side and retired to rest beneath one of the towers. Some of his friends kept watch outside around a large fire.

The Brenn was sleeping, when a hand placed on his shoulder awaked him. By the light of a resin torch he saw Tomar standing by him. " Is it really thou, Tomar ? " said he, thinking he was dreaming. " It is I." " Alone ? " " Alone here ; the warriors are down there ; the fog rendered the signal useless : I am come." " Hast thou been seen ? " " Thy warriors sleep, no one has recognized me ; a woman told me thou wert here." " Why a day late ? " " Ditovix has assembled a thousand warriors." " Ah ! Ditovix is with them." A cloud passed over the brow of the Brenn. " He is a noble fellow," said he, after a pause. " Thou knowest that we were attacked yesterday ? " " I know it ; I saw the field of the slain. The enemy are numerous ; they cannot turn back, to-morrow they will make another attack—they are resolved to succeed." " And then ? " " Then Ditovix is to fall upon them before midday, when he knows the conflict is begun." " Well ? " " If I do not go back to Ditovix, or if he hears nothing from you, he will make the attack." " Remain with us, then ; thou art sure that we shall be assailed in the morning ? " " I passed along the enemy's camp—they are preparing for a fresh assault; and there are warriors following the course of the river to attack the west side also."

There was not a moment to lose. Sigild called his friends together, and informed them that a final effort must be made—that the enemy, harassed on their rear by neighbouring tribes, must either get possession of the Oppidum that very day or perish. Tomar was represented as having passed the previous day in the besiegers' camp, and become acquainted with the position of affairs.

No one doubted the veracity of Tomar, who, so far from exaggerating, never told a quarter of what he knew.

Sigild scarcely had at his disposal, after the various assaults that had taken place, three thousand men in a condition to fight, deducting the troop stationed opposite the burnt bridge. He divided his forces into three bodies, one of about twelve hundred men to defend the northern ramparts, the second of eight hundred posted on the western rampart, and the third of a thousand men which he kept in the centre of the Oppidum under his own direct command.

At the other posts around the Oppidum he placed men unaccustomed to fight and unprovided with arms, but who were yet able to offer some resistance if the enemy should present themselves. Women were posted in the towers away from the points of expected attack. Their only duty was to hurl stones at the assailants.

The day broke slowly owing to the thick vapours obscuring the sky; nevertheless the warriors, encouraged by the words of the Brenn and by their success the day before, awaited the enemy full of ardour. The Druids, informed by Sigild of the arrival of help, traversed the camp announcing that the hour of deliverance had come, and that the souls of those who should fall were secure of the most glorious future. The Druidesses, with dishevelled hair, fastened sacred boughs to the wattling of the ramparts.

A body of the enemy about two thousand strong now became distinctly visible opposite the western front of the Oppidum, with the river at its back. Towards the end of the first quarter of the day, this troop climbed the escarpment and stopped an arrow's flight off. It then divided itself into eight parties, each of which, provided with faggots, procceded towards one of the towers. The assailants were received with a shower of arrows and stones. They advanced nevertheless without wavering, and heaped up the faggots at the foot of the towers, not without considerable loss on their side; for the besieged hurled on them over the parapets large pebbles and trunks of trees.

The assailants tried several times to set fire to the faggots, but the wood was damp, and the defenders threw baskets of wet earth on the incipient flames.

The assault on the western side had continued for some time, when a vast number of the enemy threw themselves on the northern salient, whose towers were partly destroyed.

As on the previous day, they rushed in such a compact mass upon the salient, that they were not long in effecting a breach.

Sigild then sent out five hundred men by the western gate to take the assaulting column in flank, whilst he proceeded with the five hundred of the reserve body straight to the salient. By the time he had reached this point the enemy was already within the rampart, and his forces were sheltered behind the intrenchment.

On seeing the heaps of the slain with which this quarter was strewed, the fury of the enemy appeared to be redoubled, and they swept along like a flood through a wide breach. Thinking themselves at last masters of the Oppidum, they fell in disorder upon the troops led by Sigild. This body, disposed crescent-wise, formed as it were a second intrenchment, which the assailants vainly endeavoured to break through.

The five hundred men who had gone out by the eastern gate had reached the left flank of the throng of besiegers, when a tremendous shout arose from the enemy's camp.

Horsemen came galloping at the top of their speed

towards the Oppidum. The attacking host wavered. Assailed on their flank they made scarcely any resistance, and a movement of disorderly retreat became more and more clearly manifest.

Those who had gained a footing within the rampart, seeing themselves no longer supported, or rather forced on by new-comers, turned and fled with all haste towards the wood.

Sigild perceived that Ditovix was making his attack; then, collecting his warriors and summoning all the men from the various parts of the defences, he formed a dense column, and overthrowing the assailants who were betwixt him and the rampart, passed it and rejoined the warriors already outside: "Now," cried he, "forward! the enemy is ours; let not one escape."

The wretched besiegers, hemmed in between the warriors of Ditovix and those led by Sigild, although twice as numerous as the forces of their opponents united, became utterly disorganized, no longer thought of defending themselves, and rushing now to one side, now to the other, met death everywhere.

Many attempted to fly towards the river or the rivulet; but at an intimation from Sigild, Tomar, who had remained in the Oppidum, sent the warriors posted on the ramparts in pursuit of them.

The assailants on the western front, seeing the disorder into which their party had been thrown on the plateau, had got down towards the banks. On that side the warriors poured forth by the western gate, broke the bridge of rafts, and fell upon the enemy hemmed in by the river.

Those of the besiegers who did not meet their death that day, perished of cold or hunger in the endeavour to escape pursuit. A thousand, however, were taken;

among others those who guarded the palisade in the valley. They were slain in the Némède in presence of the Druids and Druidesses. Most of the bodies were thrown into the river, and for several days the dwellers on the banks of the river found corpses entangled among the reeds.

CHAPTER IV.

THE COST OF DEFENDERS.

DITOVIX and his warriors had done their duty bravely; the tribes of the Val d'Avon regarded them as saviours, and when the unfortunate besieged went back to their devastated homes, they cheerfully divided the little that remained to them with the new-comers.

In the enemy's camp were found provisions, the fruits of pillage, and upon the bodies of the slain a little gold, and arms; and all this was equally distributed. But winter was approaching, the fodder that had been collected was dispersed, the animals lost or consumed, the stores of grain destroyed. The means of subsistence had to be procured from the merchants, and the allies to be fed. Scarcity prevailed in this valley, so prosperous a month before. Its saviours were exacting, and began to ask where was that wealth and plenty which had been promised them.

Quartered in the Oppidum with the warriors of Sigild, the followers of Ditovix assumed a domineering air on the strength of the service rendered to the inhabitants of the Val d'Avon, and whose importance they were incessantly magnifying. Quarrels arose continually, and it needed all the influence which Sigild had acquired among his people to moderate their angry feelings.

Ditovix abstained from interference in these disputes. When assistance had been asked—he would say to Sigild,

—his men had been promised wealth of all kinds; how could he remonstrate with them if they were left to die of want?

Ditovix had brought a thousand warriors to aid the inhabitants of the Val d'Avon; and, in spite of the losses suffered during the action, a month after the dispersion of the enemy's army the number of these auxiliaries was found to have unaccountably increased.

The Druids then interfered; they represented to Ditovix that though he and his warriors had saved the families of the valley from total destruction, they were reduced to poverty; that if they died of hunger the same fate would befal his men, since there was nothing left to give them; and that in the common interest it was necessary to come to some understanding.

Then Ditovix adopted a different attitude. "I should be willing to take my warriors back," said he, "but I cannot. They would refuse to follow me, and would give themselves up to excesses of all kinds. I can scarcely prevent their proceeding from murmurs to violence. I had to promise much to induce them to come, and they must be satisfied. Fighting has been their constant occupation—for the most part in the countries beyond the mountains. They are not fitted for tilling the soil or tending cattle. What do you propose?"—"What do you ask?" said the Druids. "I will call together the leading men among them, and explain the state of things; and will let you know what they want."

Ditovix and Sigild consulted together, for both saw the necessity of securing the same advantages for the warriors of the valley and the auxiliaries, if they would avoid a collision. The two chiefs called in some of the principal merchants who frequented the valley, to induce them to furnish supplies in consideration of certain guarantees very advantageous to them.

Matters being thus concluded between Sigild and Ditovix, they called their adherents together, and had no difficulty in getting them to accept the conditions on which they themselves had agreed.

These conditions were as follows:—The Oppidum was to be placed under the guard of the warriors of the vale and the followers of Ditovix exclusively of all others. Their number amounted to nearly three thousand. The inhabitants of the valley were to give them one day in four to help them in executing the works necessary for defence or for building their dwellings. A fourth part of their crops and of their cattle was to be contributed by every family of the vale for the maintenance of the three thousand warriors. As Sigild and Ditovix took upon themselves to supply the wants of the people during the scarcity, all the merchandise was to be deposited beneath the promontory near the bridge; and the inhabitants were to receive and exchange it there, being forbidden under the severest penalties to treat directly with the merchants.

Harsh as these fiscal arrangements were, they were obliged to accept them. Ditovix, loaded with valuable presents, quitted the Oppidum, leaving his followers, who accepted Sigild for their Brenn. The bridge was quickly restored, and there arose at either end dwellings and storehouses for the merchants and their merchandise.. The chiefs of the warriors levied a toll on all the exchanges; they had the monopoly of the market, as they bought up all the produce that was exchanged.

Notwithstanding the pressure of fiscal burdens, nay, even as a result of it, the inhabitants of the Val d'Avon secured a larger return from their land than formerly, and they had a greater number of cattle. Their commerce became more extensive, and the population increased. Many merchants came to live in the town built at the two extremities of the bridge.

Thirty years therefore after the siege we have just described, the valley had become highly prosperous; though the inhabitants smarted under the domination of the warrior caste, and considered a quarter of their substance and of their labour a great deal too much to give to men who lived in idleness, and whose chiefs displayed an ostentatious luxury. Often, it is true, these warriors would undertake some expedition, from which all did not return to the valley; but those who came back safe and sound took care to enforce the payment of past dues, and would then spend days in eating and drinking, and were more exacting than ever.

They recruited from among the youth of the valley, and even from among foreigners, for it was of importance to them that their numbers should not diminish.

Gradually the remembrance of the events which had led to this state of things faded from the minds of the population. The grandchildren of the followers of Sigild and Ditovix regarded the privileges accorded to their ancestors as a birthright; while the tillers of the soil, and the shepherds and craftsmen of the vale, became accustomed to submission, and finally adopted the conviction that they had come into the world to serve and support the men who inhabited the Oppidum.

CHAPTER V.

THE SECOND SIEGE.

Two centuries and a half had elapsed, and the Val d'Avon had become the centre of a numerous and wealthy district of the Lingones. At the base of the Oppidum, extending on both sides of the river, was a town—a mercantile *depôt* of some importance; for as the river is navigable below the promontory, many boats coming from the Sequani ascended thus far, laden with merchandise brought from the south, and returned freighted with horses, tanned hides, ironwork, smoked and salted meat, timber, grains, cheese, &c. &c.

The Oppidum was then partly covered with habitations and gardens belonging to the descendants of Sigild and Ditovix's warriors. Its ramparts, oftentimes repaired, were in imperfect condition; earthworks were to be seen there, with a few towers of dry stone walling—principally on the north side. The part of the town on the right bank was uninclosed, but that which stood on the southern slopes of the promontory was surrounded by dry stone walls which reached the ramparts of the Oppidum. A *tête de pont*, built of the same materials, appeared on the right bank nearly contiguous to the houses of the part of the town built on that side (Fig. 9).

It must not be supposed that this town presented the aspect of our modern cities. It consisted of a series of inclosures of wood or dry stone walls, surrounding

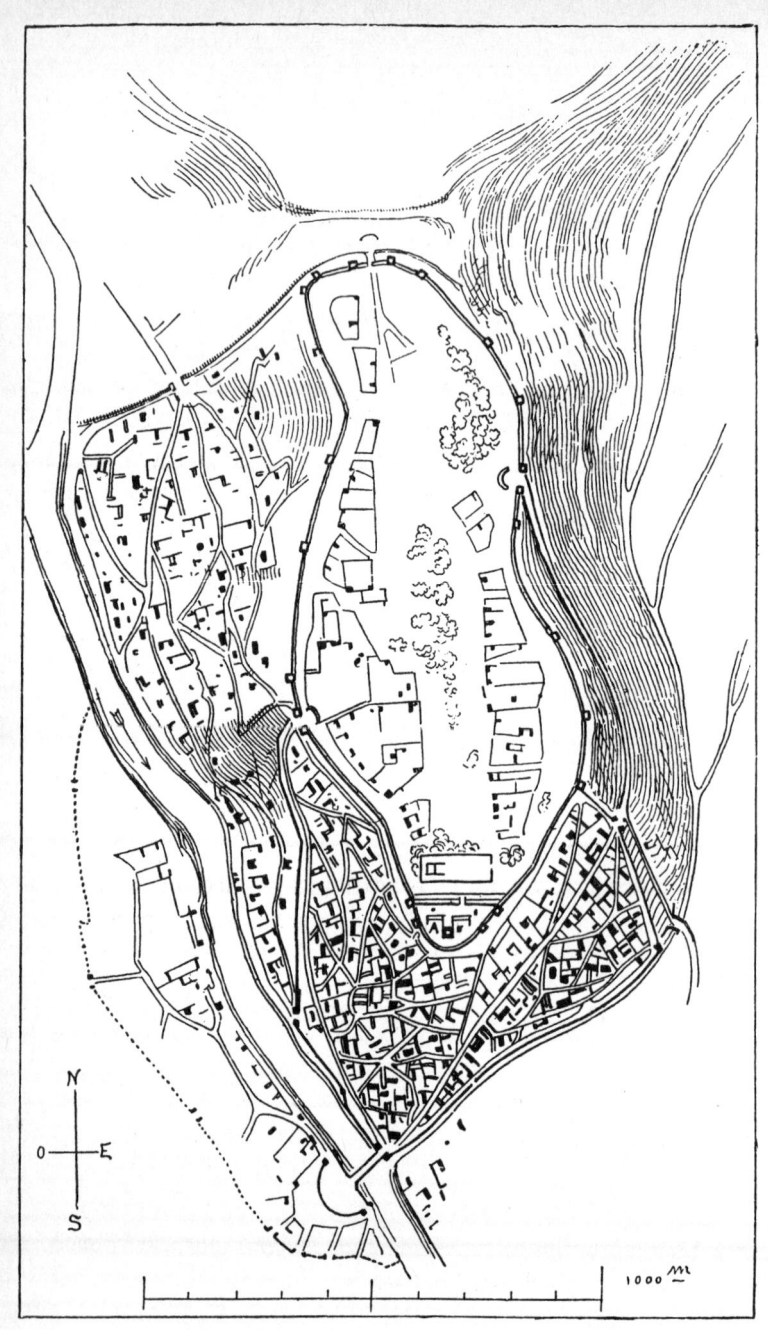

FIG. 9.—THE TOWN AND CITÉ D'AVON (WAR OF THE GAULS).

gardens, in the middle of which were built the houses—wooden buildings thatched with straw or reeds.

On the southern point of the Oppidum, however—behind the Némède and commanding the valley—there rose a structure of wood and stone, which was conspicuous above the rampart (at A). It was the dwelling of the chief of the warriors and his Ambactes,[1] who were numerous.

His name was Catognatus: rich by inheritance, he also farmed the tolls and taxes over a wide district of the Lingones, having thus greatly increased his wealth. By his liberality he had gained numerous partisans, and was always surrounded by a troop of cavaliers equipped and fed at his expense. By family alliances he had acquired considerable influence, extending even among the Ædui, and took part in the wars which that people were waging against the Arverni. He was able to muster five or six thousand warriors among his own adherents and those of his Ambactes.

When Cæsar set out in pursuit of the Helvetian emigrants who persisted in passing through the Roman province to spread themselves in Gaul, the Ædui had promised to supply his troops with corn.

The Helvetians, and close upon their track the Romans, had already passed the Avar,[2] and the promised grain had not arrived. The fact was, that certain persons of influence among the Ædui were opposed to the Romans, and, fearing that if once they got a footing in Gaul they would aim at subjugating it, were using every effort to prevent the fulfilment of the promises made by the magistrates of the principal city of the Ædui.

Catognatus was one of the chiefs most actively opposed to the Romans, and had friends among Cæsar's auxiliaries who informed him of all that was going on in the Roman

---

[1] *Fideles*—warriors devoted to the chief.   [2] The Saône.

camp. On his side he communicated to the Helvetii whatever information he received respecting the movements or position of the Roman army.

Cæsar having become acquainted with these manœuvres through Liscus, took his measures accordingly; and after having in great part annihilated the emigrant horde of the Helvetii, when the scattered remnant sought refuge among the Lingones, he first sent couriers to prohibit the latter from aiding or sheltering the fugitives: then, after allowing his troops three days to recruit themselves, he pushed on again in pursuit of the Helvetii. These quickly submitted; but Cæsar had not forgotten the share which Catognatus had had in the matter of supplies promised by the Ædui, and while he was treating with the latter with a view to relieve part of Gaul from the tyranny of Ariovistus, he despatched a legion and some auxiliary troops to assure himself of the disposition of the Lingones, to seize Catognatus and the Helvetii whom he had harboured, and, if necessary, to chastise the inhabitants of the Val d'Avon—*i.e.*, if they persisted in holding to their chief.

Catognatus, who had his informants in Cæsar's army, was soon warned of the danger that threatened him.

He had, in fact, given an asylum to some Helvetian fugitives, thereby raising the number of his men to nearly six thousand, supposing the warriors of the Val d'Avon willing to make a stand against the Roman troops. Assembling his Ambactes, therefore, and their principal retainers, he urged on their consideration the inconsiderable size of the Roman army; the fact that it was already distant from the frontiers of the province, and had been weakened by preceding conflicts; that though it had defeated the Helvetii in the open field, the issue would have been different if the enemy had been posted behind intrenchments; that they ought not to suffer the Romans to busy themselves with their affairs or differences, since they, the Gauls, did not interfere with the affairs of the provinces; that the Romans might justly prohibit the Helvetii from passing through Roman territory, but that they infringed the independence of their neighbours and allies when they presumed to keep order among them without being formally requested to do so; that he knew, moreover, that the Ædui, devoted though they seemed to the Romans, were only waiting for an opportunity to chastise their presumption; that Cæsar was going to divide his forces, and that if the men of the Val d'Avon resisted the troops sent against them, this would be the signal for a general rising which would be fatal to the Roman armies. He told them also that they ought to remember that their ancestors made the Romans tremble even in Rome, and that it was disgraceful to submit to the dictation of those whom they had formerly conquered.

Catognatus also adopted the stratagem of sending emissaries to the houses of the people under the guise of travellers. They professed to have seen Cæsar's troops, and to have found them half-starved and utterly destitute; they affirmed that the best of them had been obliged frequently to retreat before the Helvetii; that they were reduced by three-fourths, and that the remainder of their army was composed of raw recruits and of auxiliaries, who were only waiting for an opportunity to return home.

These reports, spread through the valley, were still more efficacious than Catognatus's discourse; for the Gauls have always been inclined to lend a willing ear to representations that flatter their desires, without inquiring whether they are true or false. If any of the older men shook their heads and said that it would be as well to know what was asked of them before assuming a hostile attitude, they were treated with contempt. Catognatus, seeing all the people inclined to resist, had trunks of trees mingled with earth and pebbles heaped up before the weaker points of the Oppidum.

They re-dug the ditch before the walls of the left bank and surrounded with palisades the part of the city that had remained unprotected on the right bank. In addition to this, Catognatus had a cutting dug at a hundred paces from the Oppidum between its northern salient and the plateau. These works, hastily undertaken, were still unfinished when the arrival of the Roman troops was announced. The infantry were advancing in good order in the valley on the left bank, while the cavalry followed the hills on the same side. Not a man quitted the ranks to go and pillage the houses, and neither songs nor shouts were heard. The helmets of polished bronze worn by the legionaries were shining in the sun, and, seen from a distance, the troop resembled a long fiery serpent uncoiling in the meadows.

From the elevated tower occupied by Catognatus the slightest movements of the Romans were visible. They soon deployed along the rivulet, their left being against the river and their right protected by the cavalry on the hills. The lieutenant, Titurius, then sent an envoy into the city. He was commissioned to announce to the magistrates that the Romans appeared as friends, but that since Catognatus had given an asylum to some of the Helvetii, and had notoriously exercised his power to prevent the Ædui from furnishing the supplies promised to the army commanded by Cæsar, and which had come into Gaul with the sole purpose of hindering the Helvetii from devastating,—that is, strictly in the character of allies,—they must deliver up the said Catognatus and the

Helvetian refugees to the lieutenant Titurius without delay: that if this was done the Romans would only demand provisions for ten days,—a reasonable requirement, as between allies; after which they would return to the Ædui.

Catognatus, surrounded by his principal Ambactes, was present in the assembly of the magistrates when the envoy delivered his commission. Seeing them hesitating, he replied to the summons as follows: " Here is the object of your search. I am Catognatus; I have afforded an asylum to certain of the Helvetii, who are my friends, and whose hospitality I myself have shared; I am allied with the Helvetii as I am allied with the Romans. If the Romans had been beaten by the Helvetii, and any of them escaped from massacre had taken refuge here, would they consider it honourable for me to give them up to their enemies, had they come here in arms to demand them? If such was the usual conduct of the Romans, I should blush to be their ally. To the vague accusation respecting the influence I am alleged to have exercised over the policy of the Ædui, I have nothing to reply. The Ædui act according to their own good pleasure, and it is not for me to interfere with them. The Romans should demand satisfaction of the Ædui if they have not fulfilled their engagements. As to myself, the Romans have asked nothing of me, and I have promised them nothing: what business have they here? If they had a message to send me, was it necessary that the bearer should be escorted by a legion? Is this how allies should treat each other? Go and tell the legate that we are at home here; that if he comes as a friend we shall treat him as a friend; but that if he presumes to dictate to us and treat us as children, we shall answer him as men who know how to act for themselves." " He is right! he is right!" was the unanimous exclamation of the Ambactes; and overwhelming the envoy with insults, they thrust him out. Catognatus had to interpose to prevent the crowd from tearing him to pieces.

Titurius was instructed to show the greatest possible consideration for the inhabitants, that the neighbouring peoples might not be irritated; and to adhere scrupulously to the terms of the demand transmitted by the envoy—simply to require the surrender of the Helvetii and Catognatus.

On the other hand, his orders were to accomplish the expedition with all possible despatch, as Cæsar had but a few legions with him. The legate, therefore, refrained from investing the city and the Oppidum, and, as he had no reason to fear the immediate arrival of help to the enemy, he judged it best to direct all his efforts to the plateau, hoping to take the fortress by a vigorous effort. It was, however, to be feared that if the Oppidum was taken by assault, Catognatus and a part of the Helvetii might succeed in escaping.

At night, therefore, the legate was devising a plan by which, with the eight thousand men or thereabouts of which his force consisted, he might at the same time prevent all means of escape from within, and make a vigorous attack upon the Oppidum, when a centurion came to tell him that some of the inhabitants requested a private interview with him.

The inhabitants in question were magistrates of the lower town. . . . . Falling at Titurius's feet, they told him with tears that it was with no good will they submitted to the dominion of Catognatus and his warriors; that the demands presented that day to the assembly by the envoy were nothing but reasonable, since the Helvetii had entered Gaul only as marauders, and that Catognatus had used his influence to embarrass the march of the Romans their allies, who had come to destroy the Helvetii; that they the magistrates had no authority over the warriors, and very little over the populace, enthralled as they were, and deceived by the agents of Catognatus; that this chief and his men had taken refuge in the Oppidum, and the part of the town situated at the extremity of the promontory, abandoning the part built on the right bank; that, in fact, they entreated the legate to occupy that part of the city with his troops, who would be well received, and who, they hoped, would not give themselves up to any excesses, since they were treated as friends.

Titurius raised them, and, speaking kindly to them, promised to do what they asked; but, fearing treachery, stated that he must keep them as hostages. The magistrates surrendered themselves to his disposal, declaring that his troops would find the gates open, the posts unoccupied, and the inhabitants in great excitement, but by no means hostile, if they were well treated.

On their arrival, the Romans had instituted a ferry on the river below the town. A reconnoitring party despatched immediately reported that the egresses were in fact free, and that no one appeared behind the walls.

Titurius therefore invested all the egresses, and towards midnight a thousand men selected from among the auxiliaries were in possession of the lower town, without any sound of disturbance or sign of disorder. In the morning the Gallic warriors posted at the head of the bridge saw the Romans before them, and were vehement in their abuse of the inhabitants, threatening to burn the town as soon as they had driven away the Roman troops. Meantime, the Romans demolished several houses adjoining the head of the bridge, and made use of the *débris* to form a semi-circular intrenchment of contravallation, ending against the river at its two extremities. Titurius established some posts along the rivulet; and on the larger stream above the city he constructed a bridge of boats guarded by two posts at either end. This accomplished, he removed with the bulk of his troops to the northern part of the plateau.

Next day he examined the position, after having filled up a part of the intrenchment; but Catognatus had done away with the egresses of the northern front, and completed the rampart at this point. The assault was vigorously repulsed. This success emboldened the besieged, and they began to overwhelm the legate with sarcasms. Seeing that he could not take the Oppidum by storm, in presence of a determined and numerous body of men, he resolved upon a regular siege.

Although the cutting dug by the defenders between the Oppidum and the plateau was only a bowshot from the rampart, in a few hours it was almost entirely filled up, consolidated, and levelled. Then Titurius had a great number of trees felled in the woods extending along the northern plateau, and brought in front of the camp.

This wood being duly prepared, an *agger* was commenced fifteen paces from the ramparts, in spite of the darts and stones hurled by the besieged.

This *agger* consisted of a terrace about a hundred paces long, ten feet high and twenty deep, with a gap in the middle twelve paces wide. From the two sides of this interval extended at right angles two galleries (*vineæ*), solidly constructed with trunks of trees and covered in; these galleries were about a hundred paces long. The *agger* was made of trunks of trees piled up, mingled with earth, with inclines for reaching the summit. This was a work of some days; and as during that time the Romans made no attack, and thought only of protecting those engaged in it from the missiles thrown from the ramparts, the besieged did not cease to ridicule them (for they were within hearing), asking them if they were in-

FIG. 10.

tending to build a city and pass the winter there. But one morning the warriors of the Oppidum saw a wooden tower rising at the extremity of the two galleries. This tower, the woodwork of which had been prepared beforehand, was set up within the day; its summit rose more than ten feet above the top of the towers of the rampart (Fig. 10).

The Gauls contemplated this structure with uneasiness, although they did not comprehend its importance; so Catognatus resolved to set fire to the works during the night. With this view he had placed on the ramparts, behind the wattling, barrels filled with pitch, grease, and dry sticks; then he placed two bodies in readiness to go out by the eastern and western gates, provided with vessels full of resin, tow, and grease. These troops were to make their way along the outside of the defences, and simultaneously attack the flanks of the besiegers, while the men posted on the ramparts were to remove a portion of the wattling, and to roll the barrels, after setting them on fire, against the *agger* whose front was raised on the counterscarp of the ditch.

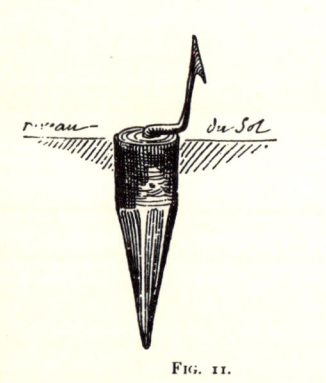

The Romans had been able to see these preparations from the summit of the tower; moreover, they stationed a strong guard on the flanks of the plateau every evening. The legate at nightfall had these points protected by stakes, and had a quantity of *stimuli* (Fig. 11) driven into the ground outside. About the third hour of the night the besieged issued noiselessly from the two gates and came within half a bowshot of the Roman posts. At a signal given from the interior, the two bodies rushed at once on the besiegers' flanks. But even before they

FIG. 11.

could reach the palisades, many of them, wounded by the *stimuli*, fell uttering cries of pain. Those who reached the besiegers' posts, thinned by the darts showered upon them, and hesitating on seeing so many of their party fall, were more inclined to fly than to continue the attack when they saw themselves in their turn taken in flank and rear by the besiegers. The defenders on the ramparts, whom the darkness of the night prevented from seeing clearly what was taking place, and not knowing whether the confusion arose from the flight of the Romans or of their own men, dared not discharge stones and arrows.

Meanwhile the lighted barrels were being rolled in front of the galleries, which had already begun to take fire. By the glare of the flames they could see the Roman soldiers mount on the terrace carrying baskets full of wet earth, which they threw on the barrels; and the defenders killed or wounded many of them. At this moment some of the fugitives who had taken part in the two sorties, re-entered the camp calling out that they were pursued by the Romans.

Catognatus had barely time to send troops to defend the two egresses and to protect the retreat of his men. He himself took up a position in the centre of the Oppidum with a chosen band, that he might be able to assist the quarter that should be most closely pressed. Aided by this diversion the Romans, less harassed by darts from the rampart, were able to extinguish the fire. They took advantage of the last hours of the night to advance the tower along the galleries by means of rollers, as far as the edge of the *agger*, and in the morning the warriors of the Val d'Avon were not a little surprised to see this ponderous wooden structure commanding the whole rampart and the towers of the defences.

At dawn, showers of stones and arrows hurled from the top of the besiegers' tower prevented them from approaching the defences, and two catapults swept the part of the Oppidum in front of it with enormous missiles, which, hissing through the air, killed or shattered to fragments all they encountered. Two *onagri* overwhelmed with stones the scaffolding set up by the defenders on their front to attack the *agger*, and smashed it in pieces.

Fig. 12.

A bridge was soon let down on the rampart from the face of the tower, and the Romans, advancing in good order, took possession of the defences (Fig. 12).

Catognatus and his retainers, to the number of five or six hundred, had not expected this turn of events, and had taken refuge in the stronghold built beyond the Némède, at the southern part of the Oppidum.

When the besiegers, whom no one thought any longer of resisting, were drawn up in force on the rampart, and had occupied the towers—killing those who occupied them rather as refugees than as defenders—they separated into three large bodies: the two wings marched along the inner side of the rampart, taking one after another the towers upon it, and entered the enclosures and houses, killing those who endeavoured to resist. The centre troop, drawn up in the form of a wedge, marched right on and swept the plateau. The unfortunate defenders fled, and crowded together along the side of the Némède. Many endeavoured to gain the stronghold, but the entrances were closed and the bridge destroyed. Catognatus was thus abandoning the greater part of his followers and leaving them to the mercy of the enemy. The warriors of the Val d'Avon threw away their arms, and with outstretched hands implored quarter of the Romans. Titurius then stayed the slaughter, and told the defenders that if they gave up Catognatus and the Helvetii who had taken refuge among them, their lives should be spared. Pointing to the lofty fort beyond the Némède, the besieged replied that it was not in their power to surrender Catognatus, who had taken refuge there with a small number of his followers, but that they would immediately deliver up the Helvetii still among them. The legate wishing to act with mildness, according to Cæsar's instructions, contented himself with this assurance. The Helvetii were immediately delivered up, and the people of Avon, disarmed and stripped of their warlike accoutrements, were sent back to the valley, with the exception of a hundred hostages. The few chiefs, however, who had remained among them, having been put in fetters, were to be kept, with a view to being placed at Cæsar's disposal. As to the Helvetii, who numbered five or six hundred, Titurius kept some as hostages; the rest, having been disarmed, were ordered to return to their country by the most direct route: provisions for the journey were distributed among them.

The buildings of the Némède and its grove prevented Catognatus from seeing what was going on beneath its walls, but as he no longer heard war-cries nor the clash of arms, he concluded that his men had surrendered. As for himself and his retainers, knowing that they had no mercy to hope for, they prepared themselves for defence, and resolved to sell their lives as dearly as possible.

A deep ditch partly cut in the rock separated the stronghold from the Némède. The defences consisted of an enclosure, made in Gallic fashion, of trunks of trees alternating with layers of stone surmounted by wattling. A large quadrangular tower, constructed in the same way, enclosing four stories, and terminated by a roof of reeds covering a crenelation, served as a place of retreat. Within the enclosure were wooden huts for the garrison; as the tower, which was only twenty paces wide by twenty deep, and whose walls were thick (about three paces), could barely contain a hundred men.

Titurius reconnoitred the approaches. The ditch interrupted all communication with the Oppidum, and ended against its ramparts. Towards the south, the stronghold rose immediately over the escarpment, which on this side was so steep that no ditch had been required. But a palisade on the outside, fixed in a mound, prevented approach to the base of the stronghold. As stated before, the walls of the upper town occupying the southern slopes extended to the rampart of the Oppidum. But these walls had been abandoned by the warriors of Catognatus who had taken refuge in the stronghold. On quitting the upper town they had set fire to the bridge, seeing which, the Romans posted opposite the head of the bridge had passed this latter without meeting any resistance, and had succeeded in extinguishing the flames. The bridge was promptly repaired.

The legate, therefore, effected a communication with his troops in the northern quarter, who were then occupying the upper town, and completely invested the stronghold. Time pressed, and as he had already lost twelve days before the Oppidum, haste was necessary.

In the first place, he sent one of the Gallic prisoners to hold a parley with the defenders of the stronghold. He promised to spare their lives if they would give up their chief, and the Helvetii that might be among them. If, on the other hand, the attack was once commenced, they must expect to be all put to the sword.

The messenger was received by a shower of stones, and returned bleeding to the legate, who could no longer hesitate. The order was given to fill up the ditch, and to speed the work; the centurions, employing threats and blows at need, compelled a good many of the vanquished to carry faggots and earth. Protecting themselves with mantelets, the Romans suffered only trifling loss, for the besieged had but few missiles. Besides, Titurius had brought up the engines of war, demolished those parts of the wall of the Némède which might embarrass the operations, and posted the best slingers and archers on the flanks, so that the rampart of the stronghold, riddled with projectiles, was scarcely tenable. At night the filling-in of the fosse was consolidated by timberwork, on which were spread brushwood and turf.

At the first hour of the day a cohort advanced in slow

march on the ground thus made, forming the *testudo* (Fig. 13).

Some of the defenders endeavoured to resist; but they were few in number, and exposed to the projectiles which the auxiliary troops of slingers and archers incessantly discharged upon them in an oblique direction. The rampart was soon taken; but darts, stones, and flaming balls

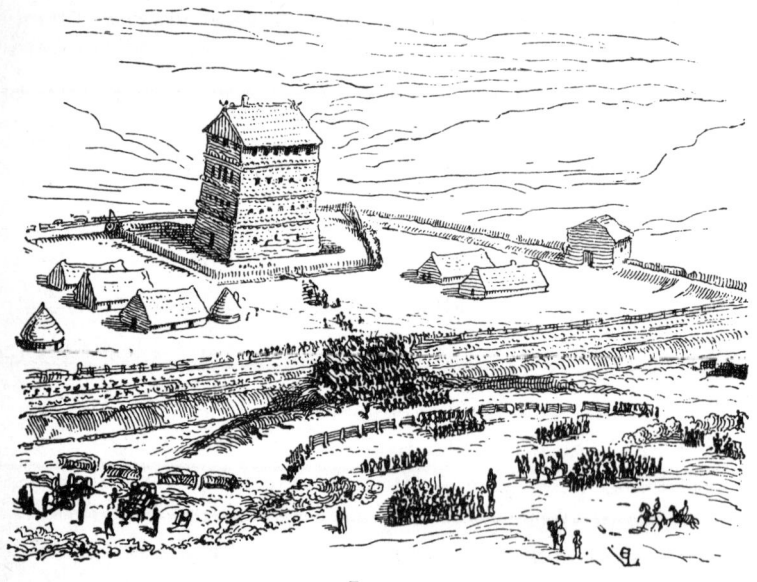

Fig. 13.

of pitch and tow were hurled upon the assailants from the tower, and if they attempted to approach it, planks and pots filled with gravel. It was necessary, therefore, to set up screens on the rampart even; for to abandon that would have revived the courage of the defenders. Here the Romans lost several men, and many were wounded. To set fire to the tower was scarcely possible; for constructions of timber mingled with stone do not readily take fire.

Titurius, however, placed one of his catapults so that the projectiles thrown by it should reach the roof of the tower; and when satisfied that this object was attained (it was towards sunset), kept up a continuous discharge of burning missiles—consisting of darts wrapped in tow saturated with oil and tar—on the roof, which soon caught fire. The legate made sure that as the floors of the tower were of timber, the roof when it fell in would communicate the fire to the ground story; and in fact, the roof had not long fallen in when a dense column of smoke, accompanied by sparks which appeared as if issuing from a vast chimney, shot forth from the summit of the tower.

Catognatus, and those of his followers who had crowded into the stronghold, despairing of maintaining it, then opened a concealed aperture, which gave egress on the sides of the upper town; and without bucklers, a sword in one hand, a flaming brand in the other, rushed with terrible cries on the Romans, who were keeping guard outside the palisading on that side, and who, surprised by this column of warriors, opposed but a feeble resistance, and made an attempt to rally and fall upon the flanks of the fugitives. It was night, and the slopes were steep, occupied here and there by houses and palisading enclosing gardens. The Romans were ill-acquainted with the ground, and often got into places whence there was no exit.

Catognatus and his followers, reduced to about two hundred men, rapidly descended the paths with which they were familiar; and in passing threw their brands upon the thatched roofs, or into the barns filled with hay and straw. The inhabitants rushed out in bewilderment, not knowing whence the attack came. Seeing parties of Romans passing by seeking egress, entering the gardens and the houses, and breaking through the gates and barricades to reach Catognatus and his men, they cried "Treachery!" and threw stones at them, thinking their object was to burn and massacre. The women, with dishevelled hair, threw themselves in their path, covering them with abuse; others hurled furniture and whatever came to hand upon them from the windows. Rendered furious by these obstacles, by the failure of their pursuit, and the attacks of the inhabitants, and seeing it was useless to reason with these terror-stricken people, the Romans killed all they encountered.

Hearing this outcry, and seeing the sky lit up by the flames, the legate guessed what had happened, and sent two cohorts over the ramparts on the town side, with injunctions to march with orderly pace down the paths, rallying the Roman troops, and driving the inhabitants before them. At the same time, he sent a centurion, by the bridge of boats which he had formed across the river above the town, to warn the Roman detachments that could be got together in the lower town and at the gateway of the bridge, not to let any one pass out from the upper town.

Catognatus, with most of his warriors, had in fact got as far as the bridge; but he found it guarded by a body of Romans. He attempted to cut his way through them; but as the bridge was somewhat long, the enterprise was hazardous. The commander of the guard, an old soldier, had marshalled his men at the first alarm, seeing that this passage must be defended at any cost. Barricading the entrance with all the materials they could collect, they awaited the fugitives behind their bucklers. When Catognatus presented himself and—uttering the war-cry—sought to force his way through, he was met at close quarters with a shower of darts. The whole foremost rank of the fugitives fell right and left: the others, rendered frantic by despair, passed over their bodies and threw themselves upon the front of the Romans, who had now taken to their swords. A fearful struggle commenced, lighted only by the gleam of the conflagration. The Romans, having the glare in their faces, aimed badly, while the Gallic warriors knew where to strike.

The column of fugitives began to melt before the Roman front, whose gaps were immediately filled up. Then came up the centurion, with fifty men whom he had rallied. Seeing themselves supported, the Roman guard took the offensive, and pressed on to the platform of the bridge, hewing down the remnant of the defenders of the Oppidum like bushes in a thicket. Not one of these warriors drew back; all met their death in the pass through which they had thought to make their way.

It was with great difficulty that order was restored in the upper town, and only when they saw the Romans extinguishing the fires did the inhabitants begin to understand what had happened.

Next morning the body of Catognatus was found lying on the bridge; his head was sent to Cæsar, and the expedition being terminated, Titurius led back the legion and the auxiliaries to their quarters among the Ædui.

CHAPTER VI.

THE PERMANENT CAMP—FOUNDATION OF A CITÉ.

SIX years after the events just related, the siege of Alesia being terminated, Cæsar gave orders for the establishment of a permanent camp on the plateau of Avon—the site of the Gallic Oppidum.

As the plateau was near the road connecting Chalons-sur-Saône with Langres, Cæsar judged it desirable to have at this point, which was naturally favourable for defence, a safe retreat for a numerous body of troops, more especially as the road passed through somewhat disturbed countries. The camp was to be sufficient in case of need for two legions and some auxiliaries—about twenty thousand men. Now, as the site of the Oppidum was much more extensive than was needed for a force of that strength, it was determined that the camp should be placed on the southern part of the plateau, whose level was elevated some few feet above the northern point, and which was separated from this extremity by a wide ditch.

Fig. 14 gives a plan of the arrangement. A ditch thirty feet wide and seven feet deep divided the plateau obliquely from W.N.W. to E.S.E. At A was placed the Prætorian gate, and at B the Prætorium. At D was the Decuman gate. The two lateral gates, F, E, fronted east and west respectively. The sunken roadways of the Gauls had to be altered and made into metalled roads; they started right and left of the bridge, C, and followed the acclivities

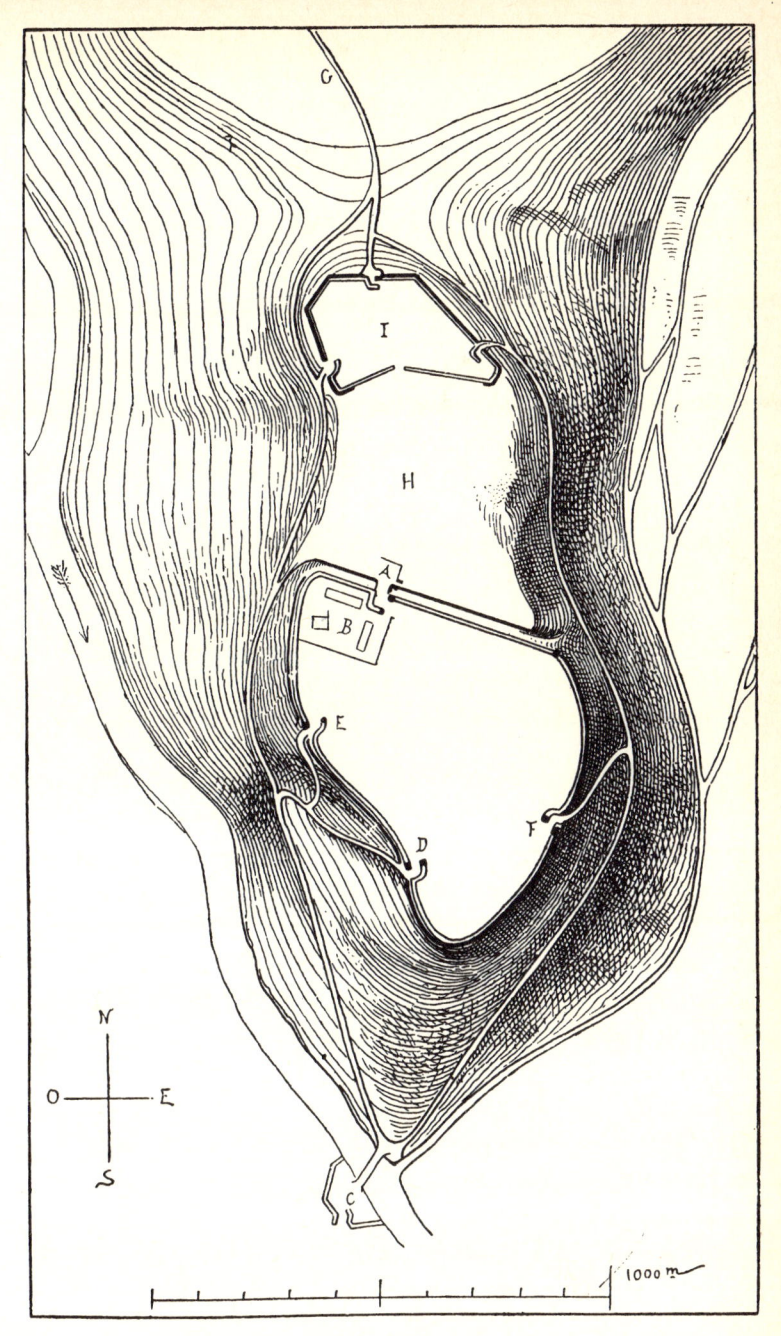

FIG. 14.—THE ROMAN PERMANENT CAMP.

of the plateau, rising till they branched off at O into the road from Chalons to Langres. From these two lateral military roads there was an ascent to the gates E, D, F, the *place d'armes*, H, and the two side entrances of the small advanced camp, I, on the south point of the plateau. Thus the outer circuit could be traversed without difficulty.

The ramparts of the town occupying the southern declivities of the promontory were destroyed, and the inhabitants obliged to settle on the other side of the river, either to the south-east or to the south. The head of the bridge, C, was repaired.

The gates of the camp had good *claviculæ*, each with two towers constructed of dry walling, earth, and timber work (Fig. 15).

At regular intervals along the *vallum*—which, except the front on the N.N.E., exactly followed the edge of the plateau—were erected towers, or rather watch-towers, of timber. In addition to the supply from the wells within the limits of the camp, the Romans collected the water of the springs on the northern plateau, by means of pipes made of trunks of trees bored lengthwise and joined end to end. This channel followed the roadway G, and conducted the water into six good cisterns, hollowed out in the rock and lined with cement. There was a cistern under the Prætorium, and two for each of the legions.

On the western side palisades connected the smaller camp with the ditch sunk near the angle of the Prætorium; while on the eastern side of the plateau its escarpment rendered this precaution unnecessary.

The engineer entrusted with the setting out had disposed the fosse in an oblique direction, as shown in Fig. 14, so as to present a larger front to assailants who, having taken the smaller camp, should present themselves on the *place d'armes*, H. The projecting angle was well defended by the Prætorium, and the obliquity of the *vallum* enabled the defenders making a sortie by the Prætorian gate, and by that marked F, to take the enemy almost in rear, and to drive them over the eastern declivity of the plateau.

The rampart walk of the *vallum* was raised three feet above the level of the camp, and was furnished with a cresting of stakes with wattling to retain the earth of

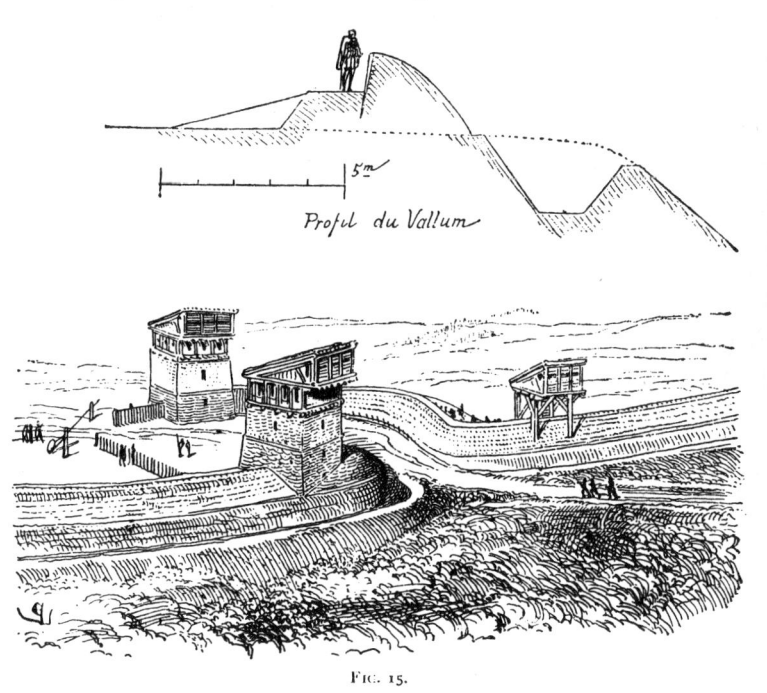

Profil du Vallum

Fig. 15.

the parapet (see Fig. 15). The fosse was twelve feet wide and seven deep, and was continued all round the camp, even on the sides where the declivities were steep.

The Némède was demolished. The Druids had it re-erected on the plateau in front of the camp, to the south, at the entrance of the wood. The inhabitants of the

Val d'Avon were enjoined, under penalty of seeing their town destroyed, to abstain from injuring these intrenchments while unoccupied ; they were even charged to keep them in repair, and to supply provisions to the troops who should be quartered there to protect the country against the invasions of the barbarians ; for as Gaul was then tranquilized internally, and brought under the Roman sway, there was nothing to fear, except the attacks of the Germans, who were continually threatening the north-eastern provinces.

The camp was in fact occupied several times by Roman troops, and new works were successively planned and executed there. The country was fertile, and the position excellent, viz., between the large towns Chalons-sur-Saône (Cabillonum), Langres (Andrematunnum), and Autun (Bibracte). The camp received the name of *Aboniæ Castrum,* the town being thenceforth called Abonia—a name which it retained until the fourth century.

It was from Abonia that Vindex set out with a party of troops, which he assembled in the plains of the Saône, to rouse Gaul in revolt against Nero, and to give the empire to Galba. After the death of the Gallic hero, Galba wished to testify his gratitude to the towns and countries that had declared in his favour : and Abonia then acquired the title and rights of *civitas,* and enjoyed a long peace.

From the reign of Titus onwards, the camp was no longer appropriated exclusively to the troops. At the time when the Oppidum had been converted into a permanent camp, the whole of the plateau, its slopes, and part of the ground situated to the north, had been considered as *Ager Romanus.* It was what we should now call " crown land,"—*Ager Publicus.* The inhabitants, therefore, could not possess or build upon this land, or, if permitted to occupy a part, it was as usufructuaries, not as freeholders.

This Roman law, which dated from the time of the Republic, and which at first affected all provincial soil, was never rigorously applied. Its enforcement would have been difficult, and the populations of the provinces, as well as those of Italy, solicited and easily obtained the *jus Italicum*, which consisted in the full possession of the soil, with liberty to use, to sell, and to transmit it by way of inheritance. When the imperial government was definitively established, the emperors favoured the development of the principle of private property; because the great landholders were then the only persons who could be considered as forming an aristocratic class, privileged, it is true, but, on the other hand, bearing the burden of special functions—such, for instance, as that of urban magistrature, then very onerous. It must be observed that the civic rights accorded by Rome extended not only to a town, but to the whole of the territory pertaining to it.

As the Vale of Abonia possessed the *jus civitatis*, and the site of the camp remained unoccupied, the inhabitants petitioned that ground so well adapted to habitations should be restored to civil uses. It was then determined by the Emperor Vespasian that the *ager publicus* of Abonia should be colonized. Colonization under the Roman empire meant the division solemnly made by the *agrimensores*, according to certain religious prescriptions, of a part of the *ager publicus* into shares.

These shares were unequal, and, although apportioned by lot among the colonists—that is to say, among the native inhabitants and the foreigners who presented themselves as applicants for their possession, it always happened —by what means we are unable to say—that the allotments fell according to the rank or fortune of the individual. The ancient Oppidum was therefore colonized.

The remains of its ramparts soon disappeared; the wide fosse, which separated the large camp from the smaller one, became a road terminating by sloping paths in the level of the plateau; a theatre rose on the eastern declivity; water was brought in abundance, by a fine aqueduct of masonry, to baths constructed at the southern point, and to all the new habitations which soon arose on every side, surrounded by gardens. A temple, dedicated to Augustus, was erected on the site of the ancient Prætorium, on the very spot where stood the shrine of former days, and a second sacred edifice dedicated, say some, to Hercules—which is doubtful—took the place of the ancient southern stronghold. A forum and a basilica occupied the middle of the plateau. The *villæ* spread beyond the circumvallation, and extended over the two declivities, east and west.

The lower town continued to be occupied by the merchants, craftsmen, boatmen, and the poorer class; it extended along the two shores down the river. The bridge previously mentioned was rebuilt with stone, and a second bridge of timber was thrown across half a mile further up the stream, at the continuation of the sunken way by which the plateau was divided.

CHAPTER VII.

THE FORTIFIED CITÉ.

THREE centuries of peace had caused the disappearance of the last vestiges of the ancient ramparts which surrounded the permanent camp of the Romans, then occupied by the cité of Abonia. But for many years the incursions of the Germans had disquieted some of the neighbouring countries. They had made their appearance among the Remi several times, and although they habitually presented themselves as defenders of the empire, or were actually called in by one party or the other during the civil discords by which Gaul was then rent, their conduct was that of enemies, not of allies. Finding the country attractive, they spread gradually among the eastern provinces, robbing, pillaging, and burning among the friends who invited their aid, as well as among the enemies they were going to attack. At their approach the rural districts were deserted, and the uninclosed towns hastily fortified.

Reims, Langres, and Autun had repaired their defences. Sens had walled itself round with the materials of its chief public buildings. The vale of Abonia, which at that time contained about twenty thousand inhabitants, followed their example; and pulling down their public edifices and the deserted temples of the city, the urban population formed ramparts around the plateau and a fence around the lower towns.

The works, however, undertaken in haste, were of no great account, and fortunately the Germans did not think of assailing them; but in the year 359, Julian, having assumed the purple, betook himself to Gaul to drive out the barbarians. The siege of Autun raised, he passed through Abonia, found its situation excellent, and arranged the plan of a fortress, which after the battle of Strasburg and the defeat of Chnodomar, was carried into execution. Abonia thus fortified formed part of the second line of strong places established by Julian between Reims and Lyons, in anticipation of fresh invasions by the Germans.

Gaul, although her sons had furnished the Roman army with its best soldiers for three centuries, had become unaccustomed to war at home. The Roman legions no longer consisted of troops such as those commanded by the Vespasians, the Tituses, and the Trajans. Composed principally of barbarians, they wanted cohesion, were not sustained by patriotism, and deposed their chiefs on the slightest pretext.

The latter, moreover, too often appointed by a court governed by intrigue, were for the most part incapable, or eager to enrich themselves rather than to conquer the enemy. For these troops, composed of heterogeneous elements, and having no faith in the valour of the chiefs placed over them—for these populations, accustomed to peace and the well-being it secures—ramparts were necessary, behind which the defence of the territory might be organized; for in the open field, such was the terror inspired by the Germans that a prolonged resistance could not be reckoned upon. Julian, however, had shown that the troops in the pay of the empire, if well commanded, were still in a condition to fight the barbarians; but Julian was a philosopher; he understood his times, and could not shut his eyes to the unsound

FIG. 16.

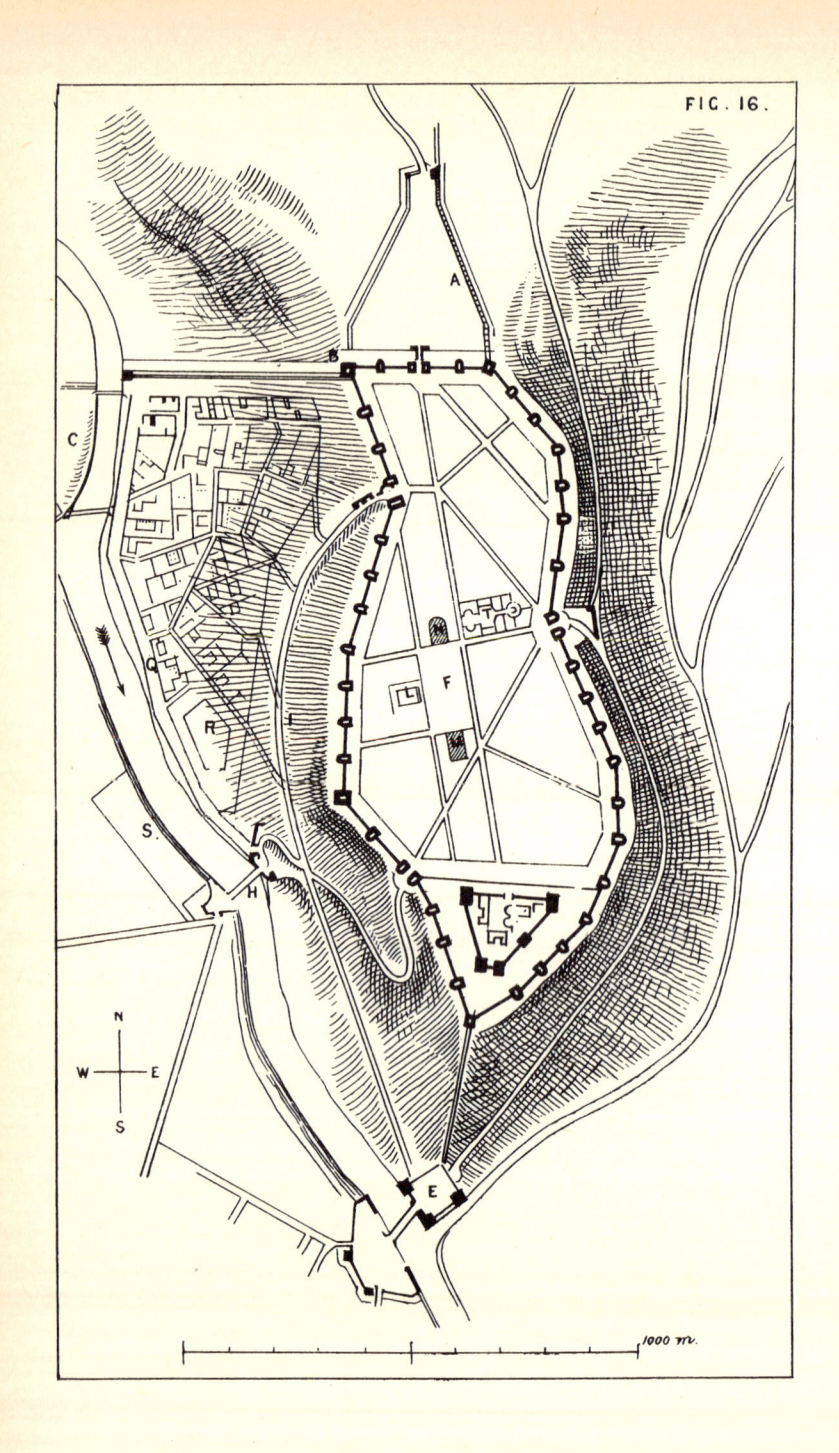

THE GALLO-ROMAN TOWN CITÉ JULIANA.

state of the imperial government, or at least believed the evil to lie so deep that he attempted to stay its progress by a return to paganism, hoping perhaps in this way to restore youth to the worn-out body.

Julian had then about him Byzantine engineers who were very skilful in the art of fortifying places. This branch of knowledge is often developed among nations in proportion to the decay of military organization in the field. The conqueror of the Germans had caused the fortifications of Autun to be repaired and completed.

Those of Abonia, which were less extensive, were carried out with completeness according to an entirely new plan, since there existed no traces of the ancient fortifications: the engineer Philostratus sent by Julian was therefore left to his own discretion.

He began by clearing away the slopes of the ancient Oppidum along the verge of the plateau, thus removing some of the villæ that had not been destroyed at the time when the arrival of the Germans was expected (see Fig. 16). After having carefully studied the conformation of the ground, he perceived that the front of the city towards the north was weak, inasmuch as this front was most accessible to attack on account of the neighbouring plateau, whose level was but little below that of the site. He determined, therefore, to fall back, so as to get a more extended front. The front thus adopted was three hundred and fifty paces long.[1] Outside of this front he had a fosse sunk twenty feet wide in the bottom,[2] so as entirely to divide the tongue of land which connected the promontory with the northern plateau. This fosse terminated at the two declivities east and west. At each end the bottom of the fosse was furnished with palisades, and there was a

---

[1] A pace was equivalent to three feet.
[2] The Gallic foot was the *pied du roi* (thirteen inches).

descent into the fosse by means of a flight of steps contrived in one of the towers, as will presently be shown. Outside the fosse he formed a *vallum* about four hundred paces in length, with an outwork containing a guard-house and a watch-tower. The Roman road to Langres came to this point. On the eastern side, the aqueduct which brought water to the city followed the *vallum*, and was crenelated (*vide* A). A gate was opened in the north front, flanked on the outside by two cylindrical towers. At the north-west angle arose a square tower high enough to afford a distant view of the valley at the bottom of which runs the river, and of the plateau; another square tower was built at the north-east angle, and between these two towers and the gate two other towers; so that between each tower there remained a space of about eighty feet.

Philostratus remarked that a daring besieger might run in towards the west, between the river and the city, and attempt an assault towards the salient of the west front, which commanded a rather gentle escarpment. From the square tower, B, to the river, and set back a little, so as to be flanked by the western face of this tower, he formed a *vallum*, with a square tower at its extreme end, commanding the water-course. Further back was constructed a wooden bridge, connecting the two banks, and passing over the island of sand, C. Along the two escarpments the engineer followed almost exactly the sinuosities of the edge of the plateau, but placing the gates in the re-entering angles. Two gates were disposed on the western front, and one on the eastern, very near the situation of the ancient entrance to the *Oppidum* on that side. These three gates were each flanked by two towers, like those on the north. The inclosure of the city, formed of a rampart rising twenty feet above the level of the ground, including the battlement, and nine feet thick, was thus strengthened by thirty-six towers, without reckoning those of the gates. At the southern extremity, on the site of the ancient retreat of Catognatus, was erected a *castellum*, or stronghold, separated from the city by a battlemented wall, and about one hundred and eighty feet away from the ramparts. At the southern extremity of the rampart, a square tower had to be built of greater height than the others, to overlook the vale of Abonia. Beneath this tower an egress was contrived, abutting on a massive wall, following the declivity of the ground, and crenelated on both sides; from the summit of which a descent could be made into the work, E, commanding the junction of the rivulet with the river, and the stone bridge constructed there. Upon the other bank was built a vast *tête de pont*. The eastern gate was furnished with an outwork commanding the road, G; on the northern flank of the north-west entrance a guardhouse commanded the vicinity of the gate. The approaches were improved, and a wooden bridge was thrown across at H, with a *tête de pont* and work commanding the confluence of roads at that point. Building was prohibited on the western declivities—once occupied by houses and gardens—within a distance of one hundred and ten paces from the ramparts, or the military road, I; that is, habitations were allowed to remain or to be built outside the military bounds.[1] Inside the city, through the confusedly-grouped clusters of ancient houses, Philostratus had new roads cut,[2] with a view to establish a communication between the gates, and to facilitate the defence. At F was placed a forum, with a temple to Apollo at I (for Julian had caused a little Christian church, previously

---

[1] The dark line indicates the habitations preserved, the red line the tenements rebuilt on the sites left unoccupied after the clearing necessary for the fortifications and their approaches.

[2] These new roads are indicated by red lines.

built in the city, to be demolished). A basilica was built at M, a *curia* at N; and at T baths were erected. In the lower town, quay-walls, Q, kept the river within bounds; a vast market was disposed at R, and an emporium for merchandise at S. The town, or rather its suburbs, extended on the right bank, east as far as the middle of the island of sand, C, and south, to the lower side of the large *tête de pont*. These suburbs were simply inclosed by a *vallum*, as a safeguard against a sudden attack; for being commanded by higher ground they did not admit of defences adapted to resist a long siege.

These works occupied several years, and were executed with resources drawn partly from the imperial treasury, but chiefly from municipal imposts. Abonia was wealthy; but it suffered long from the burdens imposed upon it to render it secure against the incursions of the barbarians. Philostratus, moreover, had authority to make requisitions and levy dues, and he largely availed himself of it.

The undertaking completed, this cité, thus transformed by the order of the emperor who had saved Gaul, received the name of Juliana. The valley alone preserved the name of Abonia.

It may be desirable to give a few details explanatory of the defences. Fig. 17 gives the section of the rampart between the towers.

Its terrace, raised to an average height of fourteen feet above the ground-level of the plateau, had a flight of steps between the towers five feet wide. The merlons were six feet high, and the sill of the embrasures was three feet above the footway.

The rampart was constructed with two faces, of courses of small square stones, with courses of brick at intervals. The masonry between the two faces was of coarse rubble concrete. Outside, along the verge of the plateau, a fosse ten or twelve feet wide protected the base of the rampart and followed the projections of the towers. A narrow covered way was led along the counterscarp to facilitate surveillance and allow the patrol to go their rounds. Fig. 18 gives the plans of the northern gate with its two

FIG. 17.

towers, at A on the ground level, at B on the level of the curtain battlements. In one of these towers was constructed a stair, C, leading down to a postern, D, and in each of them other flights of stairs, E, which afforded easy access to the higher stories. The gate, divided into two archways for entrance and exit, was surmounted by a gallery, G, at the level of the rampart-walk, forming a crenelation. The road crossed the fosse, F, over an arch, *a*, and a wooden platform, *b*, which could be easily re-

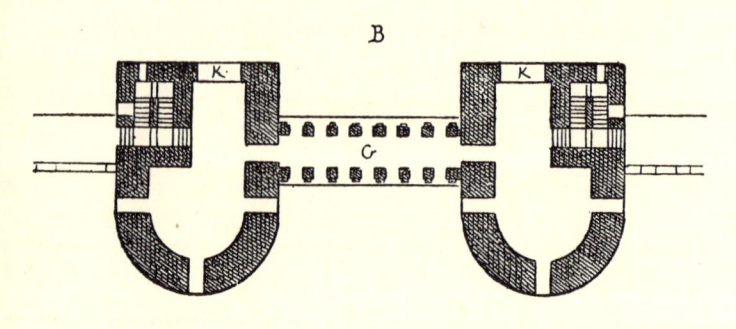

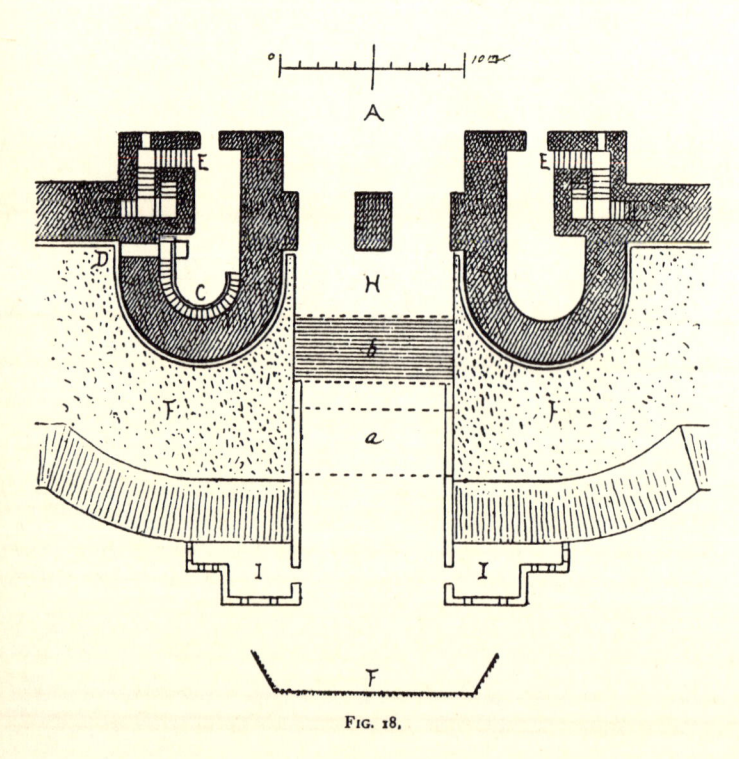

Fig. 18.

moved in time of siege; and then upon the platform, H, a

screen of woodwork was to be erected, completely masking the two archways. Outside the bridge, the stonework of which was battlemented, two small uncovered posts, I, defended the approaches, and a palisade, P, obliged all comers to make a circuit in order to cross the bridge. Fig. 19 shows this gate in perspective. Below the roof-

FIG. 19.

ing was the crenelation, which constituted the effective defence of the towers. Moreover, at the level of the first story three openings were made, which in time of war were furnished with screens, and which afforded front and side views. Munitions of war were hoisted to the higher stories by means of pulleys suspended in the round-arched openings, K (*vide* plan of the first story). The other gates were constructed on the same model, the outworks alone being different, according to the disposition of the ground.

Fig. 20 gives a general view of the great *tête de pont* on the south, the *place d'armes* and the battlemented wall ascending to the square tower on the south angle of the cité, and the *castellum*. The square towers were not covered by roofs but by platforms, so as to allow catapults or *onagri* to be placed upon them.[1]

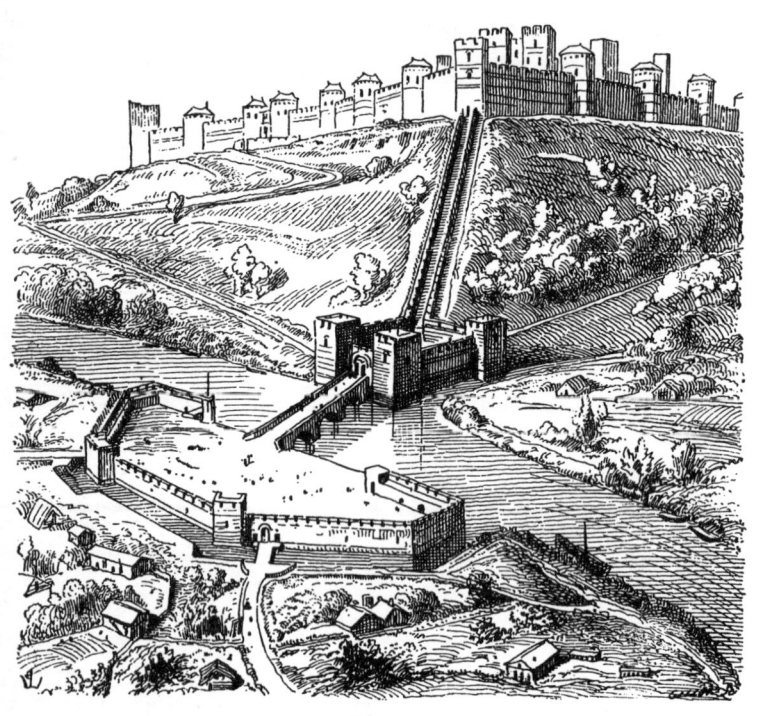

FIG. 20.

With this design quadrangular towers of the kind described were raised at the salient angles of the defences, which were weak points, but which, on the other hand,

---

[1] The catapults could discharge bolts six feet long and very heavy. The *onagri* hurled stones of sixty pounds weight to a maximum distance of two hundred and fifty paces.

facilitated the discharge of missiles over a more extensive field. In case a front was attacked, propulsive machines were set up behind the curtains on earthworks or wooden platforms.

The city thus strongly fortified was in a position to resist and defy the attacks of the barbarians, who, at that period of their history, were unable to undertake the siege of a stronghold well planned and defended.

CHAPTER VIII.

THIRD SIEGE.

WHETHER the Burgundians crossed the Rhine at the solicitation of the Gauls, or to find more fertile settlements, or because the emperor Honorius had granted them a territory on the left bank of the river, certain it is that about the year 450 they were occupying the banks of the Saône, and had pushed their way northwards to the neighbourhood of Langres and Besançon, westwards as far as Autun, and southwards beyond Lyons. Having entered Gaul as allies—as auxiliaries of the tottering empire—they treated the inhabitants with a degree of consideration which was not shown by the Franks and other tribes that were gradually invading the west. They had indeed gained concessions of lands and gifts of herds; but they were living on a footing of equality with the Gauls, and their presence resulted in a partition of property with the new comers rather than subjection to their sway. The establishment of the Burgundians on Gallic soil may be compared with that of those colonies of veterans whom Rome sent out formerly to various territories, whose position was similar to that of the original inhabitants, and who in the second generation were confounded with them.

Gondebald, the third king of the Burgundians since their entrance on Gallic soil, was sovereign in the year 500. At that time the territory of this kingdom extended from Basle to Lorraine and Champagne, included the district round Macon, reached as far as the frontiers of Auvergne, and skirting the High Alps, followed the course of the Rhone to the shores of the Mediterranean. Juliana, including the city and fortress, with the district appertaining to it, was therefore clearly in Burgundian ground. The war undertaken by Clovis against Gondebald, and the defeat of the latter near Dijon, had indeed resulted in reducing the extent of Burgundy on the north-west; but Autun and even Dijon and Langres still remained in the hands of Gondomar, the second son of Gondebald, since Childebert and Clotaire came and besieged him in the first of these three cities. Gondomar had been elected king of the Burgundians, after his eldest brother Sigismund had been deposed and condemned to monastic seclusion at Orleans by the sons of Clovis. Gondomar put his tenable places in a state of defence, collected an army, and after a battle with the Franks in Dauphiny, and in which Clodomir perished, resumed peaceable possession of his kingdom. Ten years later Clotaire and Childebert made a fresh attempt to destroy the menacing power of Gondomar. They wished to associate Theodoric with them; but as he was occupied with a war in Auvergne, he refused to accompany them. The two sons of Clovis therefore directed their forces in 532 towards Burgundy, and sat down before Autun, in which the king of the Burgundians had shut himself up.

The cité was on the point of being taken; Gondomar succeeded in escaping with some of his troops, and took refuge in the cité Juliana, as one of the best munitioned strongholds of his kingdom, and the key to all the mountainous and wooded part of Burgundy.

He was hoping to keep the troops of the Franks there till winter, and then to take advantage of the rigour of the season in that district to assume the offensive, with the aid of auxiliaries promised from the East.

In fact, Clotaire and Childebert having taken Autun about the middle of the summer, led their army before the cité Juliana; for they could not think of pursuing their conquest while leaving this place on their flanks or behind them.

Gondomar, having entered it about a fortnight before the arrival of the Franks, had caused the defences to be repaired and provided with all that was needed to sustain a long siege.

The lower town, the cité, and the vale, contained at that time a population of about forty thousand souls, among whom might be reckoned at least ten thousand persons capable of bearing arms. Many had even become practically acquainted with war. For since the time of Julian Gaul had been the theatre of incessant struggles; and though the country surrounding Juliana had remained comparatively tranquil, its inhabitants, both Gauls and Burgundians, had been present at more than one engagement, especially since the definitive invasion of the men of the North. These barbarians, long the auxiliaries of the empire, had themselves learned the profession of war in the Roman school, and were making use of the military engines adopted by the imperial armies.

Among the Franks, however, as among the Burgundians, the Roman standard of discipline was not attained, and these troops had not the firmness and tenacity which still distinguished the best soldiers commanded by the generals of the empire. On the other hand they were often brave even to temerity.

The cité Juliana was well stored with provisions and munitions of every sort when the army of the Franks presented itself. Gondomar had not thought it possible to defend that part of the town situated on the right bank of the river of Abonia; for it was open, the habitations having been built beyond the line of Roman intrenchments, and the latter being commanded on the western front. He had contented himself with keeping the two *têtes de pont;* one, the smallest, up the stream, covering a wooden bridge; the other, the largest, a stone bridge. As soon as the enemy's approach was announced, Gondomar set fire to the foot-bridges spanning the river across the islet of sand.[1]

The troops of Childebert and Clotaire debouched by the northern road and the western plateau, above the part of the town that had been abandoned. These troops therefore formed two bodies, separated by the river. Gondomar was a man of astuteness rather than a soldier; but he had with him a certain Clodoald, a veteran of long experience in arms, and who knew how to inspire confidence in the soldiers, as much by his bravery as by his rude and simple manners. Severe towards himself as well as towards others, and gifted with herculean strength, he used to punish every act of disobedience with his own hand, inflicting one unvarying penalty—death. In spite of, perhaps on account of this inflexibility, Clodoald soon became the idol of the city; while he was among them they could not doubt of success. He confounded the Franks with the Germans in the implacable hatred which he had vowed to the latter. Gondomar placed all the forces at his disposal under his command.

The defences of the cité Juliana were just as Philostratus had left them; intact and massive, they defied all attack by main force. To take them a regular siege was necessary. The army of the Frank kings consisted of about forty thousand men when they had laid siege to

[1] See Fig. 16.

Autun, and, deducting losses and desertions, it counted scarcely more than thirty-five thousand men on arriving before the city. It was, however, expecting to be reinforced. The body which presented itself on the northern plateau consisted of twenty thousand men, and that which appeared above the lower town of fifteen thousand. The lower town was nearly deserted; all the able-bodied men had taken refuge in the city, and had sent the women, children, and old men to the eastern hills.

The main body of the Franks was therefore able to enter the lower town without striking a blow, and naturally enough, began to pillage it. Clodoald observed from the ramparts the disorder thus occasioned. At nightfall he despatched a thousand men to the *place d'armes* at the south of the plateau, and reinforced the post that defended the *tête de pont* on the right bank. The Franks engaged in plundering the town had scarcely taken notice of the large *tête de pont* placed on the extreme right, but had given special attention to the smaller one opposite the wooden bridge. Towards the third hour of the night, Clodoald had the gates opened, and led forth his men in silence. The Franks had scarcely kept a guard at this point. Surprised by Clodoald's attack, they went up again to the lower town, uttering cries of alarm.

Many had encamped between the *Emporium*[1] and the *tête de pont;* the Burgundians passed round them, and attacking them unawares, drove into the river those who were not massacred. At the same time Clodoald set fire to the whole quarter. The wind was blowing from the south, and the habitations situated on the banks of the river soon presented a mass of flames. When, the Franks having rallied, their forces were on the point of taking the offensive, the Burgundians had already re-entered the *tête*

[1] See Fig. 16.

de pont, and were re-ascending the plateau. The Franks had lost from four to five hundred men in this skirmish, while of the besieged not more than twenty men had been put *hors de combat*. This commencement brought joy to the city, and those who from the top of the ramparts saw their houses in flames, endured their ill-fortune patiently, thinking of the vengeance they might reasonably anticipate.

Experienced in war as he was, Clodoald would not allow this ardour to cool. On the morning which followed this night so fatal to the Franks, he formed two bodies of two thousand men each, well armed with *angons, francisques*, and *scamasaxes* (for throughout Gaul at that time these weapons were common to the Franks, the Gauls, and the Burgundians, with some slight variations). He ordered a body of about five hundred men to issue by the eastern gate of the southern *place d'armes*, to cross the rivulet, and make a show of intending to pass the river below the stone bridge of the valley, by means of light boats which four men could carry on their shoulders. These boats had been stowed away in the *place d'armes*. At the same time, one of the two bodies was to assemble in the northern outpost, which had not yet been attacked, and make a vigorous sortie. Clodoald himself, with a body of a thousand men, was to pass the eastern gate of the city, skirt the ramparts and the outpost, and come to sustain the attack and take the enemy in flank. The five hundred men furnished with boats were to limit themselves to such a pretence of crossing over as would be sufficient to attract the Franks to the spot; then the second troop was to pass the great *tête de pont* and act as the occasion might suggest, either attacking the enemy on the march, if he followed the descent of the river, or keeping back the Franks coming from the lower town. A body of a thousand men were to fall upon the troop presenting itself on the banks of the river, and cut them to pieces or drown them.[1]

This plan well explained to his lieutenants, the movement commenced about the fourth hour of the day. The two Frank kings had taken the command: Childebert of the troops encamped on the north, Clotaire of the body encamped on the west in the lower town. A bridge of rafts had been early constructed five hundred paces above the isle of sand, to establish a communication between the two bodies.

It must be observed that after taking Autun, the two chiefs did not expect any serious resistance in the rest of Burgundy. On the strength of the reports that had reached them, they were persuaded that Gondomar had been killed, that the garrison of Autun constituted his best soldiers, and that the other strong towns would be defended, if at all, only by inexperienced men.

The event of the preceding night, however, caused them to reconsider their judgment; and at the moment when the sortie on the north was taking place, the two chiefs were planning to take the *tête de pont* by a vigorous effort, and at the same time to attack the northern outpost.

The Franks are inclined, even more than the Gauls, to take for truth what they desire to find so; and the two kings were under the persuasion that the garrison within the city was small in number, and would be disconcerted by these two simultaneous attacks. Things were in this position when the Frank chiefs received the news that the line of investment on the north was attacked.

By the term "line of investment" must not be understood a disposition of their forces presenting a complete analogy with the strategic arrangements of modern times.

[1] See the plan, Fig. 16.

This line consisted of a body of men, one thousand strong, grouped somewhat confusedly behind a barricade of trees and brushwood, four hundred paces from the northern salient. A second body followed, consisting in great part of cavalry, dispersed in the woods at a hundred paces from the first line, and masking the encampment of Childebert, surrounded by the bulk of his troops.

At the first alarm the two kings mounted their horses, and, hurrying along with them those who were equipped for fight, hastened to the field of action. The cavalry of the second line dashed forwards to aid the first, separating into two squadrons to attack the enemy on his flanks.

Recovering from their first surprise, the Franks, protected to some extent by the barricades, were keeping their ground against the attack. A hand-to-hand conflict was commenced, but the Burgundians, as the more numerous, were beginning to outflank the enemy's line, when the Frank cavalry came up, and in their turn fell upon the two wings of the attack. The Burgundians were compelled to give ground, and were obliged to avail themselves of the barricades of branches and brushwood not to be outflanked. Their position, however, was becoming untenable, when Clodoald came up on the enemy's left flank. The Franks were panic-struck, for the troop conducted by Clodoald was marching in good order after the Roman fashion, in echelons, so as not to allow the cavalry to outflank their right wing. The left of the Franks took to flight, and their example was followed in turn by every part of the line. The Burgundians dashed forward in pursuit of them, but Clodoald, advancing to the front, brought his whole force to a stand, though not without difficulty.

The fugitives, on the other hand, found themselves confronted with the main body of Childebert's army. Full of wrath, and upbraiding them with their cowardice, he compelled them to go back; and a body of ten thousand men soon presented themselves in sight of the Burgundians through the woods. The order for retreat was given; and they returned in good order, not re-entering by the outpost, but marching along the east front, under the protection of the ramparts. Childebert's irritation was such that he immediately sent a thousand men to seize upon the outpost, thinking it would be feebly guarded, since the defenders were outside the city; but the attack had been foreseen, and the Franks lost a hundred men in this fruitless attempt.

On the southern side, the sortie of the Burgundians had been more decisively successful. The state of affairs was such as Clodoald had foreseen. The Franks, expecting the enemy to cross the river so as to outflank them on the right, had sent a thousand men to meet the Burgundians. The lieutenant of Clodoald had then sallied out from the great *tête de pont* with his two thousand warriors. Drawing up half his force in a square, on the river side, with his front towards the lower town and his right supported by the *tête de pont*, he had dispatched the other half in all haste against the Frank troops on their way to oppose the passage.

This troop, taken in flank and thinned by the darts hurled at them by the Burgundians in their boats, was broken up, and fled in utter confusion. The Franks remaining in the lower town, now learning that Childebert's army was attacked on the north, were uncertain whether they should march towards the southern side to support the troop lower down the river on the right bank, or betake themselves to the bridge of rafts to assist Childebert's army. This indecision rendered the attack on the

Burgundians drawn up in square near the great *tête de pont* inefficient, and permitted the two thousand men who made the sortie to return without serious loss. The sortie on the north encountered more trying fortunes; it had left in the woods more than two hundred dead, and brought home as many wounded.

The Franks had lost in these two conflicts more than six hundred men, without reckoning the wounded. Far from yielding to despondency, however, both chiefs and soldiers were full of rage, believing they should take the city in a few days, and that they had before them a garrison quite disposed to capitulate, so depressed did they suppose the Burgundians to have become by the capture of Autun: in twenty-four hours they had lost more than a thousand men, without having even approached the ramparts.

The wounded Burgundians remaining in their hands were decapitated; and their heads, stuck on long poles, were ranged in a line at a hundred paces from the advanced work. This, however, did not constitute a countervallation sufficient to protect them from the sorties of the besieged. It was therefore decided that the army on the north side should dig a ditch at two hundred paces from the advanced work, which should extend from the river valley to that of the rivulet; the ditch to be about two thousand paces long, and behind this ditch, with the earth dug out and barricades (of branches), an intrenchment was to be raised. They could thus in the first place obviate any attack of the besieged at this point. In the second place, it was resolved to seize the great *tête de pont*. The only communication with the outside then left to the besieged would be the valley of the rivulet; but this valley was almost impracticable, full as it was of bogs and marshes; so that the inhabitants of the city could attempt nothing on this side. As to assistance from without, it was deemed out of the question then to expect any; in any case, to prevent the besieged from issuing by the eastern gate, a well-guarded work should be raised in front of it; next, to prevent the besieged from getting provisions, the country on the left bank of the river should be devastated. As regarded the aqueduct, it was discovered and cut off.

These measures resolved upon, the besiegers set to work without loss of time. But Clodoald, who had been present at more than one siege, knew by experience that a garrison which had no expectation of help from without, has but one means of safety, viz. to allow the besieger no respite, especially at the commencement of the investment, when the enemy had not yet been able to complete his works and effect a close siege. Without knowing exactly what the army of the Franks had in contemplation, he knew its numerical force, and did not doubt that it commanded the services of some Latin engineers, as such was the case at the siege of Autun. Clodoald therefore divided his troops into eight bodies. The inclosure[1] being defended by forty-four towers, eleven hundred and eighty men were required to guard them, reckoning twenty-five men for each of the thirty-six towers of this inclosure, and thirty-five for each of the eight towers of the gates, or seventy men for each gate and its works. The post of each tower, it must be understood, was, in conformity with the military usages of the time, intrusted with the guard of the neighbouring curtain. The guard of the northern outwork required two hundred men; for the *place d'armes* on the south, and the *têtes de pont*, five hundred men; to garrison the stronghold (*Castellum*) one hundred men; to watch the rampart on the north descend-

[1] See Fig. 16.

ing from the angle of the city to the river, and to guard its banks, six hundred men. Total for the ordinary guard of the defences, two thousand five hundred and eighty men. He distributed this first body so that the best troops occupied the *place d'armes*, the *têtes de pont* and the advanced guard, as well as the front on this side. Clodoald constituted a second body of a thousand men, held in reserve in the middle of the city, to hasten at need to one or several of the points attacked. He had about six thousand men left, which he divided into six bodies of a thousand men each, thus distributed: two in the part of the town situated between the cité and the river, two in the neighbourhood of the northern gate, and two near the eastern gate. These six bodies were to be ready to make a sortie whenever the order was given.

Clodoald retained under his own direct command the thousand men in reserve lodged in the middle of the cité. Then he provided for the wants of the garrison and the inhabitants living within the walls. A great quantity of provisions had been brought into the town by means of requisitions and according to Roman usage. These provisions were stored in the stronghold. The flocks and herds were driven to graze on the slopes of the plateau on the south and east. Timber in considerable quantity had also been laid in store. It was ranged along the interior of the curtain walls. In addition to its walls the town had vast cisterns, supplied by the aqueduct. This being cut off, Clodoald had the rain-water from the roofs collected in channels which led into these cisterns. Moreover, in the part of the town situated between the ramparts and the river there was a fine spring capable of supplying all the upper part of this quarter.

Clodoald looked carefully to the lodging of his troops. Many of the soldiers had their families in the town; he would not allow the defenders to lodge in their houses. He had the public buildings arranged to receive the seven thousand men who did not habitually occupy the ramparts. Those who were charged with the guard were well lodged in the towers, the public buildings of the quarter, or outside the ramparts. Clodoald, as has been said, enjoyed the full confidence of his troops before the arrival of the Franks; but after the successful affairs of the first day, his men considered him as a kind of Providence, and blindly obeyed him. Accordingly, these arrangements were readily accepted and carried into execution. In details he had adopted the composition of the Roman cohort, and every chief of a corps was responsible for the execution of the orders he received under pain of death. As for the inhabitants, they were obliged to lend assistance whenever required; a refusal was capitally punished.

Gondomar, whom we have scarcely had occasion to mention hitherto, inhabited the *Castellum;* and Clodoald manifested the greatest respect for him, acting as he said only according to his instructions; but for the garrison, the veritable chief was Clodoald.

Having provided for what was most pressing, namely the organization of his force, he had two *onagri* placed in the outwork the day following the engagements, and these *onagri* began to hurl stones of sixty pounds weight on the Frank workmen engaged in the contravallation, two hundred paces from the salient, with such effect that the besiegers were forced to put back their fosse fifty paces out of range. The following night, Clodoald sent out a thousand men by the eastern gate, who, defiling by the road along the rampart, went and destroyed the first works of the Franks, and re-entered immediately; at the same time another sortie, effected through the south gate of the great *tête de pont*, surprised several men of the Frankish outposts. Their heads, fixed on stakes, were placed at the extremity of the northern outwork, as a response to the proceedings of the Franks. That very night, the enemy attempted to cross the river, aided by the islet of sand, in order to attack the ramping curtain on the north from behind; but they were unable to land, the quays being well lined with troops. Many of them were drowned.

Things were proceeding rather unfavourably for the army of the Frank kings; it was accompanied, however, by an able Latin engineer, who had given proofs of his skill, especially at the siege of Autun. Childebert, exasperated by the success of the besieged, poured forth menaces against his own men as well as the enemy. He had not deigned to listen to the advice of his engineer, who since the arrival of the army before Juliana had been urging him to encamp on the north, and not to invest the town till he had reconnoitred its approaches. Consulted after the preliminary checks, Secondinus—that was the name of the Latin engineer—admitted that it was difficult to withdraw, since the army was engaged around the place; that the first thing to be done was to make it impossible for the besieged to make a sortie; and to effect this result—the latter being unable to issue without danger except by the eastern gate, and the *têtes de pont*—it was necessary to raise works in front of these points of egress, so as to close them completely; that it was hazardous and of little advantage to try to seize the great *tête de pont* by a direct attack; but that it was necessary to occupy the western quarter below the ramparts, and therefore to cross the river; that then, by the same blow, the *têtes de pont* and the ramping wall on the north would be lost to the besieged, and the southern *place d'armes* endangered.

Thereupon, trees were felled in the forest on the plateau, and the timber-work of the houses of the lower town brought away. A moat, filled from the river, surrounded the works of the great *tête de pont;* but those of the smaller one no longer possessed any; the fosse had long been filled up, and the besieged had neglected to sink it afresh. The south wall of the *Emporium*, which joined the northern shoulder of that smaller *tête de pont*, was crenelated, and in the hands of the defenders, including the square return on the road coming from the west. Thus half the area of the Emporium was commanded in its length by this wall.[1] Astride on this western road, Secondinus erected an *agger* which rested against the river, fifty paces from the square return, and on this agger he fixed up a work of framed timber, which commanded the enemy's rampart (Fig. 21). Around the great *tête de pont*, he contented himself with raising a contravallation, which cut off the two roads. Before the eastern gate of the city, the operation presented great difficulties, because of the steepness of the slope of the plateau. Every night, the besiegers' works were thrown down by the defenders, who had the advantage of the dominant position. Secondinus, after several unsuccessful attempts, was obliged to confine himself to forming beneath the ascent of the plateau a work of earth and timber, forming an arc of a circle, as in the accompanying sketch (Fig. 22).

The besiegers could reach this work, which was out of range of the plateau, by a road descending gently towards the western arm of the rivulet.

These works had not been executed without attempts on the part of the besieged to destroy them, nor without considerable loss on the part of the Franks. A fortnight, however, after the enemy's arrival, they were completed, and strongly guarded.

[1] See Fig. 16.

The enemy's troops were thus disposed around the cité:—The large encampment on the north plateau was occupied by twelve thousand men; the defenders of the

Fig. 21.

great contravallation on the same side numbered two thousand. The body lodged in the lower town consisted of six thousand men; the guard of the work opposite the small *tête de pont*, five hundred; that of the contravallation around the great *tête de pont*, one thousand two hundred; the work raised at the bottom of the plateau facing the east gate contained one thousand two hundred men. Total: twenty-two thousand nine hundred men. There remained, deducting for losses since the commencement

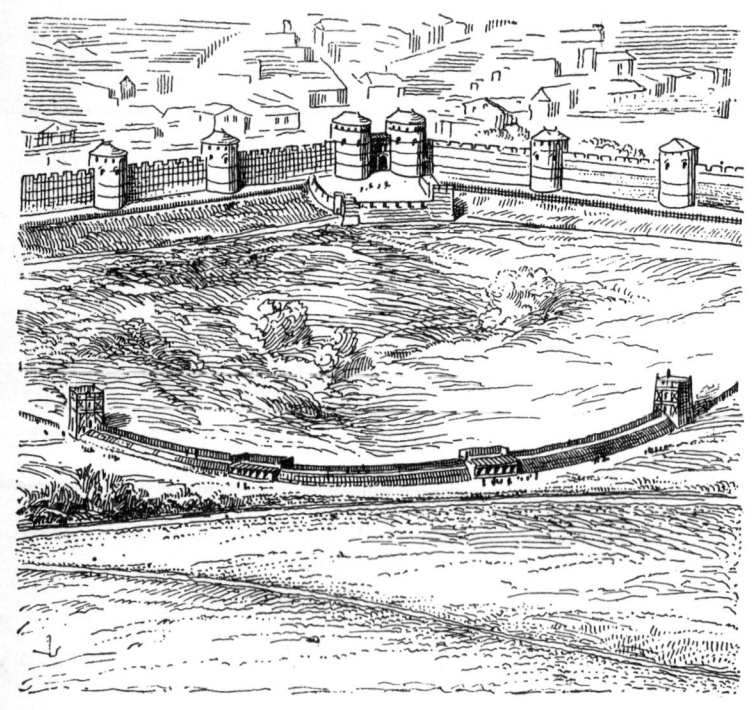

FIG. 22.

of the siege, about ten thousand soldiers, who scoured and devastated the country, collected provisions and forage, and formed a reserve corps, ready to make a fresh attempt when the propitious moment arrived.

These preparations rendered it clear to Clodoald that the enemy since his first checks was acting with method, and preparing for a decisive action. He had quickly perceived that his attack would be directed to the weak points of the fortress,—that is to say, the northern salient and the banks of the river opposite the western bend of the cité; he had therefore strongly barricaded

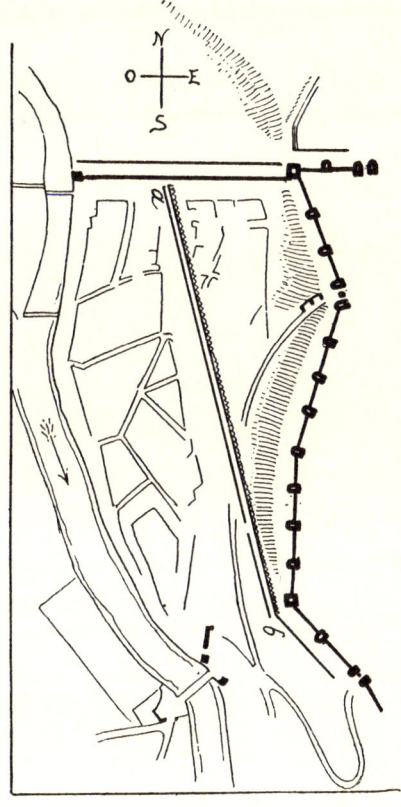

FIG. 23.

all the roads of the town leading to the quay, and had strengthened the latter with a *vallum*.

In addition to this, two hundred paces behind the square tower on the river, to the north, he had run another vallum, *a, b*, through the houses and gardens, following the slopes of the plateau in an oblique direction, and

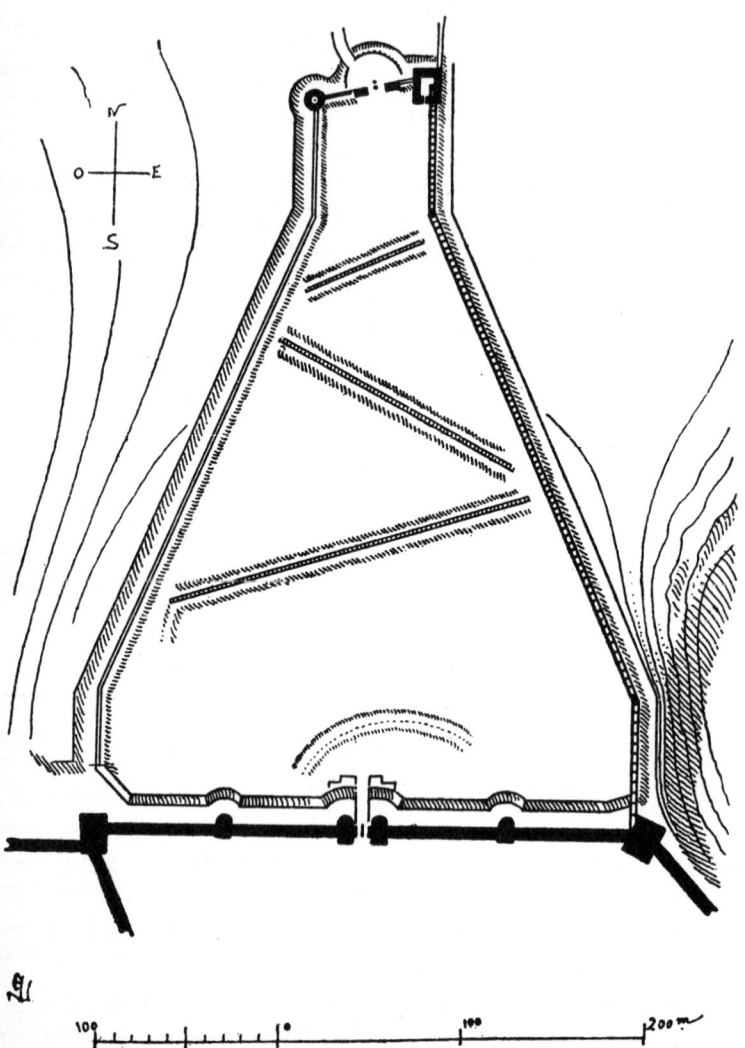

FIG. 24.

joining the south-west gate (Fig. 23). The habitations had been left as a mask in front of this entrenchment;

a few houses and fences only had been cleared away to give a free space outside.

Clodoald could not attempt anything before the northern salient, the enemy being there in front of him in force; but within the salient itself he sunk ditches with retrenchments of earth and stakes, as shown in Fig. 24. These works being low and masked were invisible to the enemy outside. Every night he sent out of the city, by the postern which led to the bottom of the wide fosse on the northern front, spies who rendered him an account of the operations of the enemy.

At the end of the third week from the beginning of the siege, his spies reported a considerable degree of activity in the large camp; that faggots were being got ready, that the soldiers were preparing their arms, and that war-engines were being mounted. One of these spies, who crossed the river below the town and observed the attitude of the enemy encamped on the west, brought a similar report. Clodoald judged, therefore, that the besiegers were on the point of attempting a grand effort on the west and the north.

On the morning of the twenty-third day of the siege, in fact, four *onagri* planted on the work opposite the small *tête de pont* swept the latter with stones so effectually that the defenders were scarcely sheltered behind the parapets, and could not work the engines placed at that point. At the same time, boats laden with inflammable materials were launched in the river above the wooden bridge. These boats, impelled in the direction required, were arrested by the piles of the bridge, and were not long in setting it on fire (Fig. 25). The defenders of the small *tête de pont*, seeing that their retreat was going to be cut off, abandoned the work, which was soon occupied by the Franks. Retired within the *place d'armes* behind the bridge, the besieged could do nothing but watch the fire.

At the same time, shielded by wicker mantelets, a numerous troop of the enemy were advancing boldly against the north-east and north-west flanks of the

FIG. 25.

northern salient. Filling up the fosse with faggots, the assailants rushed in a dense column against the rampart. The conflict was furious. Thanks to the stonework of the aqueduct the enemy were unable to break through the north-east flank; but they succeeded in gaining a footing[1] on the opposite one. The besieged were obliged to abandon the salient, retiring from one retrenchment to

[1] See Fig. 24.

another, and with but slight loss, whereas the assailants had more than two hundred men killed on the rampart and in the ditches.

At nightfall Clodoald with the three thousand men of his reserve corps issued suddenly by the central gate—the bridge of which, strongly barricaded, had remained in his possession—and fell upon the enemy: he killed a hundred more, but was unable to retake the work. Moreover, he anticipated another attack, and was not mistaken. Towards midnight the Franks took possession of the island of sand with the help of rafts, and there entrenched themselves in front of the quay. They were within bowshot, and arrows were discharged on both sides, but with little result.

The loss of the advanced work had only the effect of animating the besieged, who were for immediately retaking it. Clodoald had to calm their ardour by promising them to do better than retake it; adding, that just then he had another enterprise in view, and that the enemy was going to give them a fine opportunity of beating him.

Clodoald strengthened the defences of the northern front, which could not be taken by storm; placed a strong body in the outwork of the eastern gate, with orders to defend it to the last man; and sent down as large a number of troops as they would hold into the two *places d'armes* south and south-west. He strongly manned the oblique entrenchment descending to the edge of the water, and placed there a chief on whom he could depend, with special instructions.

The next day passed without fighting. The Franks were engaged in intrenching themselves within the outwork against the north front, and destroying the *vallum*. They were bringing to the island timbers, fascines, earth, and stones, and were beginning to fill up the small arm with these materials. Sheltering themselves with wicker mantelets, they threw stones into the water, then fascines, in which large pebbles were inclosed to make them sink between the stones, then when these materials began to rise above the surface; they laid trunks of trees upon them across the stream, and between these fascines and clods of turf. The besieged could scarcely do anything to hinder these operations. Two *onagri* sometimes hurled stones at the workmen; but they, well shielded and always in motion, were seldom struck. Towards evening the embankment was barely twenty feet from the quay wall, and the water — rather low at that season — ran through the sunken fascines without endangering the stability of the dam. The Franks continued all night working at the consolidation and enlargement of the causeway; then they brought timbers and ladders, and raised on its extremity about fifteen feet from the quay wall a stage of timberwork prepared beforehand. At daybreak the besieged perceived on the stage the end of a kind of bridge, furnished with a wicker mantelet, moving slowly forwards towards the edge of the quay (Fig. 26). Secondinus had the platform of a bridge framed ten feet wide: this platform, laid on rollers which rested on the inclined beams, was propelled by soldiers, aided by levers, and drawn by two cables wound on capstans fixed in advance. The men with the levers were screened by sheets of thick canvas stretched before them, which stopped the darts. All this time two catapults and two *onagri* showered long darts and stones on the *vallum* of the quay; while slingers and archers rendered it impossible for the defenders to show themselves.

The chief who commanded the latter, following the instructions of Clodoald, drew his men gradually away in the direction of the houses; and when the rolling bridge attained the ridge of the *vallum* of the quay, not a single Burgundian remained behind this defence. The Franks rushed with loud shouts on the platform, threw down the wicker parapet, and spread themselves in great numbers

Fig. 26.—The Attack—The Movable Bridge intended for Crossing the Small Arm of the River of Abonia.

over the deserted and silent quay. Dreading some ambuscade, they were in no hurry to ascend the slopes of the plateau, gentle though they were at this point, or to venture along the roads whose barricades appeared not to be guarded. They drew up along the quay in good order until they numbered about four thousand men. This did not take long; for as soon as the first few had passed from the stage to the *vallum*, the besiegers had placed beams across on which they laid logs, brushwood, and turf, and the bridge had thus attained a width of nearly thirty feet.

A second body of considerable strength ready to sustain the first was assembled on the island, and a third body was approaching on the opposite bank.

Secondinus was one of the first to reach the left bank, and he augured no good from the apparent inaction of the besieged. He desired that any advance should be made with caution, and not until a *tête de pont* had been erected with stakes and *débris* taken from the neighbouring houses. An exploring party sent into these houses found that they were deserted, while behind the barricades erected where the roads opened on the quay there were no defenders.

He therefore ordered these barricades to be cleared away. All this took up time, and the Franks began to murmur loudly, asking if they had been sent across the river merely to guard the shores. Their chiefs insisted that the besieged had abandoned this part of the cité, as they had the lower town, that they had retired behind their walls, and that if advantage was not taken of their retreat, they would regain courage and come and attack the Franks in the night; that it was essential to occupy the ground vacated by them without loss of time, and take up a position beneath the walls, seizing in its rear the smaller *place d'armes*. Secondinus shook his head, and persevered in ordering measures of safety. Towards midday one of the Frank chiefs, still more impatient than the rest, called his men together and declared that there had been too long a delay, and that the slopes must be occupied. " Let the brave follow me, and those who are afraid remain here and find themselves sheltering-places!" and he and his followers made for the summit of the plateau. His example was quickly followed, and by various paths through the houses and gardens more than two thousand men ascended the slopes.

Arrived at the *vallum* formed on the slant, they were received by a shower of stones and darts. But soon recovering the surprise, and urged on by their chiefs, the Franks sprang up the escarpment. Their position, commanded as it was by the besieged, was unfavourable, and the first assault failed. They had to rally in the shelter afforded by the habitations and hedges left by Clodoald outside the *vallum*. Hearing the shouts of the onslaught, the troops left near the passage hurried in their turn up the hill. Secondinus then judged it expedient to get over a thousand men from among those who had remained in the island, giving excellent reasons for keeping them at that point.

Seeing the reinforcement ascending the hill, the first assailants separated into three large parties, and at the word of command advanced anew against the *vallum*. The fall of the foremost did not arrest the new comers, who passed over their bodies. There were moments when the intrenchment seemed to be carried, for its ridge was crowned by Frank soldiers; but the defenders—independently of those who guarded the *vallum*—had also divided into compact bodies, which, in readiness behind, fell on the assaulting columns when their heads appeared above the ridge. Thus the conflict presented a series of captures and recaptures of the *vallum*, and it appeared as if the same turns of fortune would be repeated as long as the assailants and defenders were able to form bodies of soldiers. Many fell on both sides, for they fought hand to hand.

Then it was that Clodoald, who held the smaller *place d'armes* on the south-west, led forth a thousand men in good order, keeping along the river; he ordered those who occupied the large *place d'armes* to pass on between him and the *vallum*, and to fall on the assailants in flank. From the right shore the Franks perceived this movement of Clodoald, and hurried towards the island to attack him and support those of their party who were on the left shore. But Clodoald had the start, and advanced by a direct road, whereas the enemy had to make a détour. In a few minutes, therefore, he came upon the body of Franks which, at the instance of Secondinus, was guarding the passage. He attacked it most vigorously, and cut down the first he met with. The Franks resisted, however, and, covering the embankment, formed in a square, with their right against the river. Fresh assailants passed over to the embankment, and took up such a position on the left that Clodoald's troop was on the point of being surrounded, and to free itself was obliged to make a movement in retreat, not without much loss—abandoning the left shore in order to reach the slopes and choose more advantageous ground.

The second troop of Burgundians was then advancing on the flank of the besiegers, who were furiously storming the *vallum*. The assailants, attacked in flank, almost in rear—by reason of the direction of the *vallum*—gave way and ran down towards the passage, pursued by the Burgundians. Seeing himself thus supported, Clodoald assailed the foe with renewed energy. At that juncture came Gondomar sallying out from the western gate, with fresh troops to reinforce the defenders of the *vallum*. Seeing the enemy flying in all haste towards the passage, he concluded that his force was strong enough to press them vigorously, and, following the southern ramping wall, and then turning to the left, he attacked the enemy on the shore opposite the island. The Franks, thus attacked in front and on both flanks, with a narrow passage behind, offered a desperate resistance; but their very numbers were unfavourable to success, and they were overwhelmed with missiles hurled by Burgundian slingers posted in the houses on the slope.

When night came not an enemy remained alive on the left shore; many had sought to reach the island by swimming, and a considerable number had also effected their escape by the embankment; but more than two thousand five hundred bodies remained along the *vallum* and about the entrance of the passage. Clodoald had faggots and straw heaped on the movable bridge, which soon caught fire as well as the stage. The besieged lost a thousand, and Clodoald was wounded.

The Burgundians had kept the western portion of the town, but they could not take the offensive in that quarter, since dense masses of the enemy presented themselves there.

During the same day the Frank kings had made a feint of attacking the north front of the city; but the ramparts and the towers erected on this front could only be taken by a regular siege, and the Burgundian troops assigned to that quarter were more than sufficient to defy a serious attack.

Retired within their tent, Childebert and his brother accused one another of the failure of their operations, but ultimately agreed in throwing on Secondinus the blame of their defeat. The latter, summoned into their presence, had to undergo the bitterest reproaches. "If," replied the engineer, "your troops were disciplined—if they had not persisted in attacking the quarter, on which we had fortunately gained a footing, at haphazard—we should still be on that shore, and should have been able to-morrow to seize the whole of that region; not that I think it necessary to attack the cité on that front, but because we could thus have prevented any sortie, and might without risk attack the northern front and take it—which would only be an affair of time.

"Not being in possession of the western quarter, all our siege works may be destroyed in a vigorous sortie; for the besieged are audacious—they have shown themselves so; and the ramping wall which descends to the river from the west corner will always put our attack on the north front of the cité at the mercy of a vigorous effort.

"This ramping wall has no visible gates, but it will be easy for the besieged to make outlets if there are not already some hidden ones; and then under favour of night he can fall on the right flank of the attack, burn our works, and render the siege much longer and more uncertain in its issue. Each of our chiefs insists on commanding; and, brave though they all are, before a cité so well fortified and defended, blind bravery only involves you in useless perils. Obtain from them, therefore, an implicit obedience to your commands, and remember that your illustrious father owed his victories to the rigorous discipline which he succeeded in maintaining." This firm language did not fail to make an impression on the two kings, who, repressing their anger, began to deliberate coolly on the situation. It was decided to seize the great *tête de pont*, still in the hands of the besieged; to keep a strict watch on the shores of the river; and to attack the place along the whole extent of the northern front, comprising the ramping wall.

The two kings decided that the chiefs of the various corps should obey Secondinus, whom they intrusted with the direction of their operations. The chiefs were assembled, and received from Childebert's own mouth the order not to engage in any enterprise except such as Secondinus should sanction. But these Franks had no liking for the Roman, as they called him, and received the admonition with a bad grace. Many raised objections, declaring that the slow proceedings of the Roman were the cause of their failures, and that if they might have their way the cité would soon be in their power. Childebert and his brother began to feel their resolution failing at these representations, and looked to Secondinus to reply. Addressing himself then to the chiefs who had accused him, he said: "Let those of you who have a plan of attack to offer, speak; let them explain by what methods they propose to force walls defended by men inured to war and well commanded; and if they can exhibit a plan superior to mine, I am ready to follow them like the humblest of their soldiers. But the kings and the whole army, before being called upon to advance, have a right to demand that their lives be not risked in an enterprise without definite purpose, and not presenting any chance of success." To this speech there was no response. "You, who spoke," said Childebert then to one of the chiefs, "what do you propose?"—"We took Autun by main strength; we invested the cité, made a breach in the wall, and entered it."—"Yes," replied Secondinus; "but Autun is not a cité built on the summit of escarpments like this; we were able to attack it from the level on two of its fronts, without having a river in the rear. Its walls, good though they were, were but ill defended, and our simultaneous attacks on two opposite points disconcerted the besieged. Here there is but a single front that can be attacked from the level; all the others crown escarpments, that could be easily defended, even without walls. Only two courses, then, are possible : either to invest the place so closely as to force it to surrender through want of provisions—which may be a tedious process, for the besieged are well provisioned, and the Frank army, which dislikes inaction, will melt away during such a blockade—or to attack the only vulnerable side, and concentrate all our forces on that point.

" By proceeding regularly, this front will be in our power in three weeks. Then we shall be able to invest the *castellum* closely, leaving a numerous body to prevent any sortie. It must surrender eventually, and in the meantime the kings will subdue the rest of Burgundy, without being delayed here." Many of the chiefs responded, proposing irrational plans of attack—appearing such, indeed, to the assembly; for though all agreed in blaming the conduct of the siege hitherto, no one could suggest a consistent plan of operation. Every proposition was therefore received with murmurs or ironical laughter. Seeing this, Childebert made a formal declaration that he and his brother were determined that Secondinus should be obeyed in all points, since no one had a desirable plan to propose; and the assembly separated. The two kings, remaining alone with the engineer, urged him to contrive for securing an immediate success that might cause the recent failures to be forgotten and restore confidence to the army.

" The difficulty," replied Secondinus, " is to obtain such a success, without risk, with troops that do not strictly follow orders. What secures success in siege warfare is patience, assiduous labour, and rigid discipline; but your men are not patient, are not fond of digging, and are undisciplined. They prefer getting killed in an assault under unfavourable conditions to the safe, though painful, labour which in the course of some days would secure the capture of the place without much loss."

Third Siege. 139

Meantime the Frank army was reinforced by a body of about two thousand men, sent by Theodoric, who, having terminated his expedition into Auvergne, was reckoning on gaining some advantage from the war going on in Burgundy. These two thousand men were robust, but ill-armed, and little fitted for active war; but they were able to render great services in siege works. They were placed directly under the orders of Secondinus, who set them to work immediately, promising them a large share of the booty when the cité was taken.

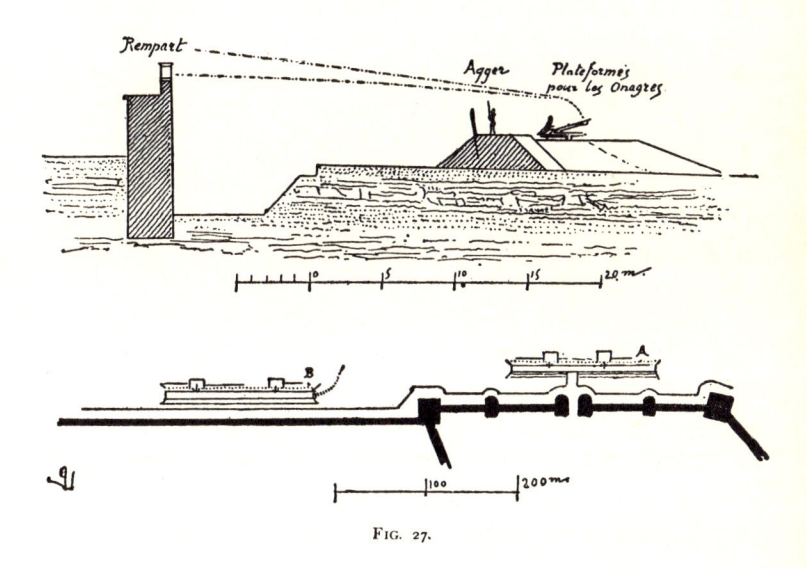

FIG. 27.

We have seen that the northern salient had remained in the power of the Franks. Secondinus raised an *agger* at this point, in front of the gate of the cité; and on the declivity of the plateau another *agger* opposite and on the counterscarp of the fosse of the ramping wall (Fig. 27). The ridge of these works did not reach the level of the footway of the cité walls, but yet rose high enough to allow great stones to be discharged on the battlements by means of onagers, and to render the situation perilous to the defenders. The especial object of this was to occupy the besieged. Under shelter of these two earthworks, Secondinus had two mines commenced, one at the point A, the other at B, which, carried under the bottom of the dry ditches, were to penetrate beneath the walls. Clodoald, who had been rather severely wounded, was obliged to confide the superintendence of the defence to his lieutenants, who informed him of the besiegers' operations, and who believed that the Franks were going to raise timber works to command the walls, destroy the battlements, and throw bridges across. Nothing, however, favoured the supposition that such was the intention of the Franks, who limited themselves to furnishing the earthworks with screens to protect their engines. This apparent inactivity was a constant source of anxiety to Clodoald, who knew, through his spies, that the besiegers had received reinforcements. As he was unable to take the lead, he dared not direct his lieutenants to undertake any fresh sorties, and was obliged to content himself with recommending the most scrupulous vigilance. Trusting, moreover, to the solidity of the Roman walls and the rocky site of the plateau, he scarcely believed that mining could be rendered efficient; yet, in anticipation of such a contingency, he ordered that trusty men should be set to listen in the lower stories of the towers, and at the base of the walls opposite the face of attack; then he had platforms prepared behind the rampart to receive six machines, which discharged stones in abundance on the earthworks of the besiegers (Fig. 28).

The Franks, on their side, were working vigorously at their two mining galleries, not without great difficulty, for they had at several points very hard rock to pierce. The excavated earth was heaped up within the earthwork, and could not be seen by the besieged. Till they reached the fosse the noise of the work could not be heard from the cité; but when the miners had arrived

FIG. 28.

below the fosse, the men on guard in the town heard the sound of pickaxes dully reverberating through the night. Clodoald, informed of this, immediately gave orders to countermine, starting from the interior base of the rampart, and in the direction of the sound. On both sides, therefore, the miners were at work; but this did not prevent the projectile engines from being worked all day by both parties.

In a fortnight the besiegers' tunnels were near enough for the workmen to hear the blows of the pickaxes in the rock. Clodoald was then in a condition to leave his dwelling; he examined what had been done, stopped the work, and listened attentively. He judged that the enemy's miners were digging obliquely under the wall,

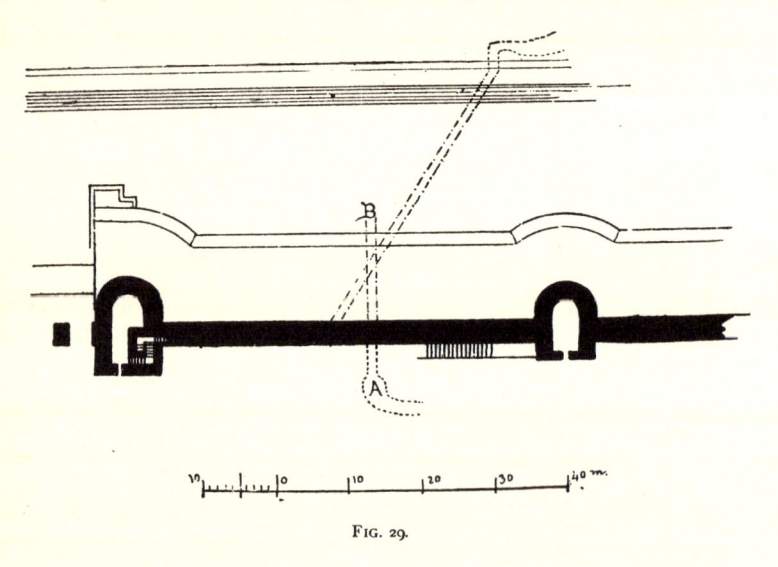

Fig. 29.

near the north gate (Fig. 29), while the countermine of the besieged followed the direction A B.

He thought he also perceived that the enemy's tunnel was on a higher level than his own. This seemed favourable to the plan he was intending to adopt, and with a view to greater safety, he sunk the floor of the countermine-tunnel still lower. On visiting the base of the ramping wall he heard no noise at this point, although his lieutenants said they had heard mining towards the upper third of the wall during the preceding days. The countermine-tunnel was also commenced opposite to the place where they thought they had heard the enemy's miners. Clodoald ordered a suspension of the work till the besiegers' operations were clearly understood.

Next day, on the north front, it became evident that the countermine-tunnel was crossing that of the enemy, for the steps of the pioneers were heard above the ceiling.

Clodoald then had the ceiling shored up along the sides of the tunnel, and ordered that the layers of stone forming the ceiling should be noiselessly removed by levers and crow-bars, so as to render it as thin as possible below the point where footsteps had been heard.

When this had been done to the extent of leaving only a very thin layer of rock, Clodoald had dry faggots, resin, tar, and all the inflammable materials that could be got, heaped up in the countermine tunnel; then, promising the most skilful of his miners a large reward on succeeding, he told him to break down this crust, and as soon as he perceived an opening, however small, to set fire to the faggots, retiring towards the entrance.

In fact, a few minutes after the order had been given, the miner appeared at the entrance of the shaft, followed by a thick smoke. He reascended quickly, and this opening was stopped with planks and earth.

From the hole made below the floor of the besiegers' gallery the smoke was rising into the tunnel, and suffocating the miners. They tried to stop up this orifice, but the necessary materials were not at hand; and the flame soon mounted high, as the hole produced a draft. The heat burst the stone to pieces, and the opening was becoming larger. The mining gallery was soon so filled with smoke that it was no longer possible to stay there and some of the miners fell suffocated before they could gain the somewhat distant mouth of the tunnel.

The stir caused among the besiegers beyond the earthwork proved to Clodoald that the operations had been frustrated, and the mine rendered untenable. He then stopped up the entrance to the countermine, and when the smoke was dissipated, he resolved on examining the state of things for himself. The faggots were burning rapidly by reason of the draft, and the flame was roaring through the hole, which was becoming larger and larger. Fresh faggots were thrown on the fire with pitchforks; the limestone was cracking incessantly and falling in large slabs.

Secondinus had heard the counterminers at work, but had not been able to ascertain the direction they were following, as they were excavating under the limestone bed in a clayey sand. He thought the galleries would meet some time or other, and that then there would be a struggle in the tunnel. Anticipating this, he had screens in readiness, hoping thus to remain master of his own gallery, and even to gain possession of the countermine.

The event disconcerted his projects; no further progress was possible there. Along the ramping wall, Secondinus's miners had reached the sand, and were consequently no longer heard. He sent all his workmen, therefore, to this quarter, and had his galleries deeply excavated according to the plan (Fig. 30). Thanks to the yielding nature of the soil, this operation was completed the following night. The galleries were well propped and shored with dry wood taken from the houses of the lower town. Faggots smeared with tar were placed among these props, and at dawn were set fire to.

Clodoald's anxiety had brought him once more to this front of the defence, when a cracking noise was heard. . . .

A wide piece of the wall, above the oblique intrenchment made by the besieged, immediately split, bent forward, and fell *en masse* outside into the fosse. Clouds of smoke and dust arose, and the exulting cries of the Franks were heard from the cité.

There was not a moment to lose: weak as he still was from his wound, Clodoald assembled all his men within

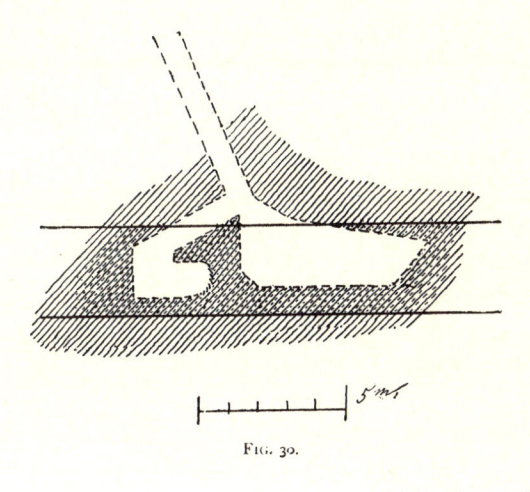

FIG. 30.

call, and sent for a reinforcement. With the soldiers—about two hundred in number—who had hastened together at his first summons, he mounted to the summit of the crumbling wall (Fig. 31) to meet the assault.

When the dust and smoke were somewhat dispersed, he could see the Franks, about two thousand in number, drawn up on the earthwork, prepared to scale the ruins. Happily for the defenders, an engine mounted on the platform of the square tower at the angle of the cité[1] was quickly turned by those serving it, so as to discharge heavy stones on the van of the attack, killing or wounding many men at every volley; which forced the Franks to retreat until mantelets

[1] See B, Fig. 16.

L

were brought up. This delay enabled the besieged to assemble on the breach, and to heap up fascines there—for the besiegers on their side were discharging a quantity of stones on this point—and to place planks so as to ascend to the summit of the crumbling wall more readily.

FIG. 31.

All this occupied but a quarter of an hour, when the Franks ascended the *agger* once more, protected by the mantelets, threw fascines into the space between the head of the wall and the slope of the *agger*, and rushed forward resolutely to the assault.

The position of the besieged was disadvantageous, for they had behind them the escarpment produced by the thickness of the fallen wall, and a ground deeply creviced by the fall of the masonry; while this fallen wall gave the besiegers a slope of slight inclination, and of easy access.

The assault was vigorous and vigorously met, but the people of the cité had only a thin front to oppose to a compact assaulting column; and towards midday the Franks remained decidedly masters of the breach (Fig. 32.)

Clodoald had died in the fight, and with him more than a thousand Burgundians.

The Franks on their side had sustained heavy loss, and the breach was literally covered with dead bodies. Either from fatigue, or because they feared some surprise, the besiegers allowed the remainder of the enemy's forces to re-enter the cité without pursuing them.

They now possessed all the western part of the town lying between the river and the slopes of the plateau. Outside the cité the Burgundians occupied only the southern *place d'armes* and the great *tête de pont:* the smaller *place d'armes* of the bridge previously burned, being uninclosed on the side of its access, and not united with the ramparts, was evacuated.

The Franks had no personal knowledge of Clodoald, and learned only from prisoners that this brave captain had been killed in the assault. They had his body sought for, and his head, fixed on a long pole, was placed before the north gate. This time the prisoners were spared, and sent as slaves to the royal domains.

The cité Juliana was now shut in on all sides and reduced to its walls, which were able long to defy the attacks of the Franks. But Clodoald's death thoroughly disheartened the besiegers, and the Burgundian king was not energetic enough to replace his skilful lieutenant. On the evening of this unfortunate day, he assembled the chiefs of the defending forces to deliberate on the measures to be adopted. Accustomed to the bold enterprises of Clodoald, they thought themselves sufficiently numerous to attempt a sortie at two points—the southern *place d'armes* and the eastern gate; they believed that the cité would be destitute of provisions in a few weeks, since they could get no more supplies from without, and they considered that this extremity and the disgraceful surrender that must follow should not be waited for. The sortie from the southern *place d'armes* was to be supported by a body issuing through the south west gate.

Thus they could drive back the Franks as far as the wall which they had just passed. The sortie from the eastern gate would occupy them during this time, on the left side of the plateau.

But while they were engaged in these deliberations, Secondinus understood well how to avail himself of the advantage so dearly bought. During the night he had an intrenchment made at some distance from the gate of the *place d'armes*, caused the road to be intercepted and the slopes of the cité covered with abatis of trees, and thereupon commenced without delay a mining tunnel under the descent from the castle to this *place d'armes* to destroy the fortified wall.

In the morning, therefore, when the Burgundians were preparing to pass the north gate from the great *place d'armes*, they saw before them a well-guarded intrenchment, bristling with pointed stakes and intertwined branches of trees. Reckoning, however, on the attack to be made by the body that was to issue by the south-west gate, they advanced resolutely against the intrenchment, whose defenders might thus be taken in the rear. But this contingency had been foreseen by Secondinus; another intrenchment at right angles was already raised before this gate, and the road cut off; the approaches being furnished with barricades. After losing a hundred men, therefore, the two bodies re-entered without having been able to execute their design. Originating power and promptness in execution were henceforth wanting to these brave people, who were, however, determined not to capitulate.

Three days afterwards the descent to the *place d'armes* was undermined, and part of it fell. The defenders of the post and of the *tête de pont* were surprised, and had only time to retire in haste by the road ascending to the eastern gate: and some of them fell into the hands of the Franks.

The cité was then completely surrounded within bow-shot distance. No sortie could be of any serious use to the besieged; for Secondinus had established posts supported by intrenchments around the ramparts. Seeing the success of his last efforts, the Frank chiefs began to place more confidence in the Latin engineer, and were obedient to his orders.

Then Secondinus resumed his attack on the north front, and began four mining galleries, making use of that which he had been forced to abandon. Three were led under the square tower of the north-west corner[1] (Fig. 33). The besieged soon heard the strokes of the miners' pickaxes, and attempted a countermine, starting from the tower itself, at A; but Clodoald was no longer there to direct the workmen, who, wishing to repeat the manœuvre previously adopted, dug too deep, crossed the enemy's galleries underneath them, and had no clear perception what direction their sapping should take.

The sounds they heard were diffused, and seemed to issue from several points; and, in fact, the Franks were working in more than one direction, and, as Secondinus ordered, immediately under the foundation; sometimes they were digging in the sand, and all noise ceased; sometimes they would meet with rock, and then the blows of the pioneers again became audible.

The countermine gallery, therefore, was winding about, and only weakened the basis on which the tower rested; and four days after the commencement of the work, it was supported only by dry props, greased and smeared with

[1] See B, Fig. 16.

pitch. These being set on fire, the tower fell in, bringing down with it a large piece of the north wall. Anticipating this result, King Gondomar, who, after Clodoald's death, took the command in the cité, had ordered an interior retrenchment to be raised, with a strong wooden tower in

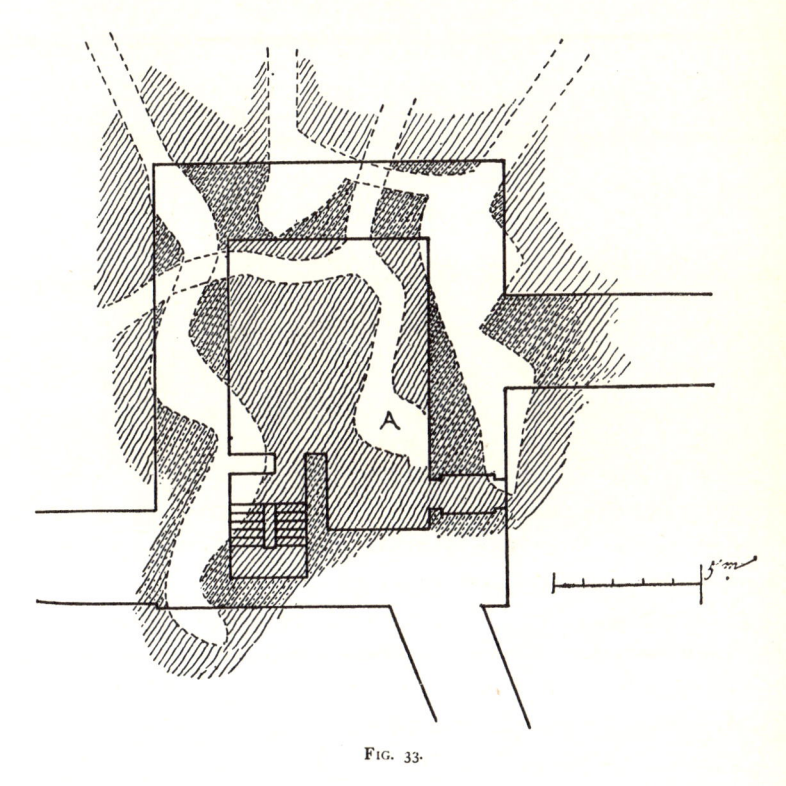

FIG. 33.

the middle of the curve, projectile engines being placed behind. He had sufficient time to complete these works after the fall of the tower; for the breach was scarcely practicable, and was stoutly defended. The Franks were two days in getting possession of it and occupying the corner of the cité in front of the retrenchment, not without having lost two or three hundred men.

Secondinus interdicted the advance of the troops, who were eager to storm the retrenchment and take it by main force; and this time he was listened to. He had timber and mantelets brought, and gave orders for the erection, on the very ruins of the angle, of a tower of green wood, which he took care to protect with woollen blankets and fresh hides. The engines of the defenders did not cease to discharge large stones at the workmen, which greatly hindered them and killed many; but the Franks had acquired confidence, and worked incessantly night and day with enthusiastic ardour.

Twice the defenders of the cité endeavoured to sally forth from their retrenchments to drive off the assailants and destroy their works; they met with a warm reception, especially as the Franks could avail themselves of the ruins as a rampart.

On their side projectile engines were hurling stones and darts on the rampart walks of the extremities of the curtains that remained standing, and made it impossible for the defenders to remain there. As soon as anyone showed himself, showers of arrows were aimed at him. These rampart walks were repeatedly furnished with mantelets, which were soon thrown down by the stones from the engines. The wooden tower of the besiegers was rising rapidly, and at the end of the second day overtopped that of the retrenchment. An engine was planted at the top, which incessantly discharged heavy stones on the works of the Burgundians. The latter kept the old countermine gallery on the north front; but they had not been able to extend it, because blocks of stone had been thrown by the besiegers into the connecting opening, and were replaced by others when the besieged ventured to remove them. The enemy's miners were no longer heard on this side. The reason was that Secondinus, having become better acquainted with the nature of the soil, had perceived that by digging deeper he found a stratum of sand easy to work in and carry away. From the old abortive gallery, however, which the besieged could not speedily enter, he had conducted two oblique tunnels, in an inverse direction and at a deep level, descending into the sand, under the foundations of the curtain; one of them, A, gradually rose again obliquely as far as the inner side of the ramparts (Fig. 34). He expected in this way to make an entrance into the cité in any case.

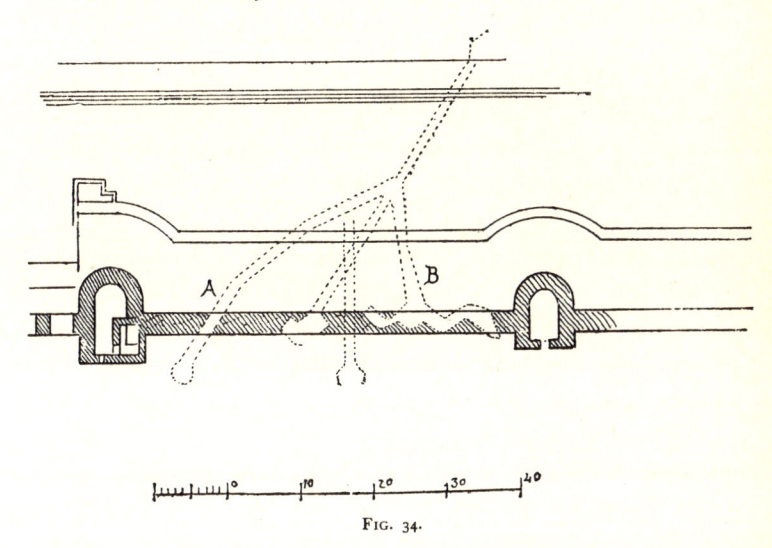

FIG. 34.

But a thick bed of limestone prevented the ceiling from being speedily penetrated. The gallery was far enough from that marked B, intended to undermine the curtain wall, not to be destroyed by its fall, and he reckoned on making use of it on occasion.

Five days had been spent in these labours, and on the fifth day—that is to say, the next day after the fall of the square tower of the corner—the curtain near the north

gate was undermined for a length of thirty paces. The
stays and props were set on fire during the night, and
in the morning the curtain sank down into the fosse, separating into two masses. The Franks immediately threw
a quantity of fascines into the fosse, brought ladders, and
rushed in great numbers on the ruined wall, which still
rose about six feet above the interior level of the cité.
The Burgundians, taken by surprise, could scarcely offer
any resistance to this escalade, and their efforts were at
most confined to hindering the assailants from crossing the
breach. The position of the defenders was one of the
most unfavourable that can be imagined, especially as
they had raised no retrenchment at this point. They
barricaded themselves, however—making use of the houses,
and hurling a quantity of projectiles from the top of the
neighbouring tower upon the assailants; and the struggle
was prolonged. Then it was that Secondinus sent workmen to destroy the ceiling of the mine gallery, A, which
terminated on the inside of the wall. In four hours this
was effected, and the besieged saw a large hole on their
left. In a few seconds this gaping orifice poured forth a
stream of enemies, who spread themselves along the wall,
outflanked the defenders, and hurried towards the gate to
burst it open.

The guard that defended this gate were massacred, and
the doors being smashed with axes and battering-rams,
fresh troops were enabled to get into the city. The town
was taken, but the conflict was being kept up in the streets
and houses. Night came on, and the defenders of the
retrenchment, perceiving that the enemy had got round
them, had retired in haste towards the interior of the cité.

The Franks no longer gave ear to the orders of their
chief, but rushed in small bands into every opening that
presented itself, burning, killing, and pillaging; many of

them fell in with numerous bodies of the besieged and met their death.

The women, mad with fury, threw tiles, furniture, logs of wood, and stones upon the Franks dispersed in the streets. As most of the houses were of timber, the fire, fanned by a wind from the west, spread rapidly in every direction. Besiegers and besieged fought till they were surrounded with flames. It was a series of isolated struggles, in which the voices of the chiefs on either side were unable to make themselves heard.

Gondomar, with about a thousand men, had taken refuge in the castle; and from the summit of its towers the Burgundian king could see his faithful cité burning, and hear the shouts of the victors and the vanquished approaching nearer and nearer the walls of this last retreat. He had been unwilling to close the gates, that he might gather in the unfortunate defenders; and towards the end of the night these, driven into the southern extremity of the cité by the enemy and the fire, began then to arrive in crowds, many being wounded, and among them women and children. The castle was being filled, and the enemy was approaching; so the bridge was thrown into the fosse and the gates were shut.

Engrossed with pillage, the Franks allowed the day which succeeded this disastrous night to pass by without attempting anything against the castle; and not before evening could the Frank king restore any degree of order in the burning cité.

There were not enough provisions in the castle to feed its numerous occupants for forty hours. This was just what Secondinus anticipated; accordingly he had no difficulty in persuading the Frank king to rest content with investing the stronghold. Gondomar, overwhelmed with grief, and seeing his helplessness, sought death by throwing himself from the top of one of the towers. The fugitives were forced to surrender at discretion, and most of them were carried away into slavery.

The Frank kings destroyed the most important of the defensive works, so as to render the cité Juliana incapable of sustaining a siege. But those Roman works were massive; and two centuries afterwards the remains of the towers and ramparts still presented an imposing mass of ruins. The plateau was then a waste, and the ruins were overgrown with a luxuriant vegetation; only a few shepherds' huts were to be seen in this desolated region. On the western declivity, between the river and the ancient ramparts, extended a poor little town, whose population did not amount to more than twelve or fifteen hundred souls.

CHAPTER IX.

THE FEUDAL CASTLE.

IN the year 1180, the valley had again become a fertile and prosperous district. Several villages had arisen along the course of the river; and a town of some importance covered, as in former times, the western slopes of the old cité Juliana, and extended on the opposite shore. This town was then called Saint Julien. How was it that the cité founded by the Emperor Julian the Apostate had changed its appellation of Juliana for that of Saint Julien? We shall not attempt to explain the fact. It will suffice to say, that about the eighth century a legend arose respecting a companion of Lucian, Bishop of Beauvais, named Julian, a native of the Val d'Abonia, who had been martyred with Maximian a short time before his holy bishop. His body, transferred to the place of his birth, had there wrought numerous miracles, and was then resting in the crypt of the church placed under his invocation, and which was the appanage of a rich abbey, situated at the northern extremity of the plateau. On the site in question, therefore, was to be found the city and abbey of Saint Julien, and the castle of Roche-Pont, occupied by the lords of Roche-Pont. As for the valley, it had preserved pretty nearly its old name; it was the Val d'Abonia. Ever since the ninth century the lords of Roche-Pont had been possessors of the vale, the town, the lands contiguous, and the forests stretching northwards on the plateaux; they claimed descent by the female side from the ancient kings of Burgundy, and were rich and powerful. One of their ancestors engaged in a war against King Robert, in the year 1005, and had contributed greatly to the failure of that prince's expedition into Burgundy. On the submission of this province at a later date to the king, the lord of Roche-Pont had made conditions that had notably improved his domain. This lord was the founder of the Clunisian abbey which stood on the north of the plateau; he had endowed it with the uncultivated lands of the rivulet valley. The monks soon made a capital domain of this valley, by taking advantage of the little water-course, which never failed. With the aid of dams they secured very productive pools; waterfalls turned mills, worked forges, and irrigated fair meadows for flocks and herds, and, on the slope of southern aspect, vineyards renowned for their fine produce.

There were occasional misunderstandings between the abbots of Saint Julien and the lords of Roche-Pont. According to their foundation charter, they claimed to be perfectly independent of the lordship of Roche-Pont— indeed, of all superiority but that of Rome—and to have complete suzerainty over the lands they possessed; they refused to render feudal dues to the castle, and on several occasions disputes resulted in acts of violence. Then the abbots appealed to the Duke of Burgundy; men of war interfered in the contest; and, as a matter of course, the vassals had to pay the costs.

One of the abbots, a restless and ambitious man, had presumed to commence fortifying the abbey, and had persisted in doing so in spite of the opposition of the lord of Roche-Pont. The lord had consequently laid waste the abbey domain. The fraternity then appealed to the king of France, who had intervened in the dispute. After much litigation and cost to both sides, it had been decided that the abbey might be surrounded by a wall without towers, and that in the event of a war in which the interests of the suzerain were concerned, the lord of Roche-Pont should garrison the abbey at the expense of the latter.

The retainers of the abbey and those of the lord continued, nevertheless, in a permanent state of antagonism; and not a year passed in which there were not differences to be settled on this score at the court of the duke.

The castle of the lords of Roche-Pont was built on the remains of the *castellum* of the cité Juliana, and about the year 1182 it was very old and dilapidated.

Anseric de la Roche-Pont was at that time its owner. He was a young man of ardent temperament and ambitious disposition, married to a niece of the Count of Nevers, deceased in 1176—an alliance which had increased his possessions. He bore with impatience his subjection to the Duke of Burgundy, and in endeavouring to shake it off, his first step was to rebuild his old castle, and put it in a condition to defy every attack. Anseric de la Roche-Pont was encouraged in these ideas of independence by one of his uncles, an old seigneur, who, having spent fifteen years of fighting in Syria, had returned, worn out and impoverished, to Burgundy. Anseric had given him an asylum in his declining years, and he soon acquired an influence over the mind of his nephew, and even of his niece. During the long winter evenings, the recital of adventures beyond seas, to which the Baron Guy knew how to give a life-like interest, would inflame the breast of the young lord. Often on such occasions the latter would rise and pace the hall, with sparkling eyes and clenched hands, stung with shame at his own inactivity,

and consumed by the desire of some nobler occupation
than killing boars, and disputing with monks concerning
mill or fishery rights. At such moments the old baron,
far from seeking to calm his nephew's ardour, would seek
to direct it to a more attainable end than the conquest
of towns in Syria. The Baron Guy was a personage of
remarkable idiosyncrasy—physically an elderly man, tall
and angular, and somewhat bent by the weight of arms:
his head, still covered with rough grey locks, square in the
crown, exhibiting projecting cheek-bones, and—beneath
shaggy eyebrows—eyes of sombre green, deeply sunk in
their orbits. His wide mouth with its thin lips showed,
when he laughed—which rarely happened—rows of sharp
white teeth. When he was relating long stories, seated, his
hands on his knees and his head bent down, the light of
the wax tapers fell only on his bushy hair, his high cheek-
bones, and nose. Sometimes, at exciting passages in the
recital, his head would slowly rise and, still in shade, his
eyes would send forth flashes which reminded one of
distant lightning.

Morally, the Baron Guy is not so easily described. He
hated monks—but that is neither here nor there—and
adored children; which is proof of a happily constituted
disposition. But the baron had seen so much of men and
things that it is not to be wondered at that there existed
in his mind a shade of scepticism, if such a term can be
applied to the *désenchantement* of a noble at the end of
the twelfth century. The baron had, we say, acquired a
marked influence over the mind of his nephew; but to
Anseric's two children their great-uncle was as indulgent
as possible. He was no less complaisant to his niece; she
alone could succeed in lighting up that stern visage with a
ray of cheerfulness.

The very high and noble dame Jeanne Eleanor de la

Roche-Pont was a woman of middle height. When animated, her somewhat oval face reflected a lively intelligence; her eyes of light azure then assumed the hue of the *lapis-lazuli*, and her complexion, habitually pale, was suffused with a rosy flush. She had a bewitching smile, though her mouth was slightly drooping; her swan-like neck, and the exquisite contour of her figure, lent to all her movements a perfect grace, rendered still more charming by an address and vivacity which was the delight of the old baron.

The baron, therefore, would pass whole hours with his eyes fixed on his niece, as if he wished to study the least gestures of the Lady de la Roche-Pont, and discover the marvellous mechanism in which their grace and beauty originated. High-spirited on occasions, Eleanor was capable of the greatest devotion and absolute self-sacrifice for those dear to her. Her vassals loved her, and used to call her *la Gentil-Dame*.

It has seemed necessary to describe at some length persons who will play an important part in the course of this narrative. Events were, in fact, more ruled by the individual in feudal times than during any other period. The personal character of a noble exercised a preponderating influence around him for good or evil.

The Baron Guy, worn out, impoverished, and childless, was essentially one of those sensitive spirits, bruised by contact with men and events, which, having lost all elasticity where their own interests are concerned, direct their entire energy and their need of something to which to attach themselves, towards an object apparently distant or fragile. The baron had certainly an affection for his nephew; but as far as he alone was concerned, he would have contented himself with leaving him to hunt peacefully on his domains, and helping him at need; but for his niece and her two children—handsome boys of five and eight years old respectively—he had a love amounting to adoration, and which formed the chief interest of his life. To him it seemed that for beings so dear in his eyes the castle de la Roche-Pont and its domain were a very pitiful heritage; and we may question whether even the duchy of Burgundy would have appeared to him worthy of their acceptance.

Ambitions of this *indirect* character, as they may be called, are the most insatiable and tenacious; they are of the kind stimulating to the most daring enterprises, because they are disinterested and irresponsible.

When the Baron Guy spoke of the fortresses built by the Franks in Palestine and Syria, he never failed to enumerate their towers, to describe their lofty walls, their fair and strong defences; and, invariably instituting a comparison between the wonderful fortresses of Margat, Krak, Antarseus, Laodicea, Antioch, Ascalon, Giblet, and many others, and the castle de la Roche-Pont, he exhibited the latter as a mere hovel fit only for serfs to hide their heads in.

When the baron's discourse took this turn—and it frequently did—Anseric's face clouded over. Eleanor looked down, blushed, and went to look for the children.

One evening, as the baron had been complaisantly expatiating on the advantageous site and solid construction of the castle of Krak, which he had seen commenced shortly before his departure from Syria, and which was to exceed in extent and strength the other Christian fortresses, Anseric suddenly interrupted the recital. "Uncle," said he, "the position of the castle de la Roche-Pont appears to me as good as that of the knights beyond sea; and if it is only a question of making more solid towers and higher walls than ours are, the thing is easy:—what do you say to it?" The baron did not raise his head. "Yes," he replied, "but you must resolve upon it."

"Well, if I did resolve upon it?" "Perhaps you might, my good nephew; but he who builds a strong castle must expect to see it attacked." "Well, what then?" "Why, you will have to defend it, my good nephew." "And have we not men and ourselves?" "Yes, we shall indeed want men—men accustomed to fighting; and we shall want arms and mangonels; moreover, the work must be done quickly if you would avoid an attack before it is finished; and remember the duke's court is not far off, and he will perhaps be curious to come and see for himself what the Sire de la Roche-Pont is about." "The duke! the duke! what business has the duke to inquire whether I am rebuilding my castle? It is my affair, not his!" "The monks of the abbey, too, they will go and complain to my lord duke (though he shows no great deference for these white, black, or grey habits), and will persuade him that in building a stronger castle your object is to lay hands more readily on the wealth of the Church; whereas the duke prefers to keep the convent treasures for himself." "As to the monks," said Eleanor, "you need be under no anxiety about them; leave the matter in my hands, and I engage that they shall give you no trouble." "Eh! what what will you do, *belle amie?*" replied Anseric. "Will you let me act as I think best?" "By all means; as you please, *belle amie.*"

It must be observed that Eleanor—as a wife and a lady of high descent—entered into the baron's views, though without letting it appear that she did so; and her most cherished desire was to leave to her firstborn the finest domain in the province. As allied to the house of Nevers, she had no liking for the duke; and the feudal bonds which connected her domain with the duchy of Burgundy were perhaps a greater annoyance to her than to her husband.

Next day Eleanor sent for the abbot, under the pretext

of having something of importance to communicate to him. The abbot was a little man of pale complexion, with sharp black eyes, and always elegantly attired, as far as was permitted by the order of Cluny, which in point of costume was then very tolerant. He came to the castle on a handsome mule, richly caparisoned, followed by two monks, also mounted. Wine and sweetmeats were offered them on their arrival, and when the abbot was in Eleanor's presence, she spoke thus to him: "Sir abbot, you are aware in what veneration I hold your sacred abbey, and how much I desire to add something to its splendour; if my lord and myself have not done so hitherto, it is because we have been waiting for a favourable opportunity. My lord and myself are happy that such an opportunity presents itself while you are ruling the abbey, because we have a particular and profound esteem for you personally. While, then, what we propose to do has for its object the securing to ourselves the more especial protection of the holy apostles, Peter and Paul, it is also prompted by consideration for your own virtues and wise administration.

"Our castle is very old and ruinous; my lord is intending to have it repaired; and to draw down upon its walls the benediction of heaven, he thinks of building within its inclosure a handsome chapel, which will be served by your fraternity as you shall direct, and which will consequently be dependent on the abbey. An annual revenue of a hundred livres will be devoted to the maintenance of the chapel, to be raised from our estate of Try. Moreover, your dependency of Vieil-Bois is unsightly and dilapidated; my lord wishes to have it rebuilt, and to assign for its support, which is at present insufficient, twenty-five days' labour in such vineyards of our domain as are near that dependency."

At each of these announcements the abbot bent his head in courteous submission. "Lady," replied he, "the abbey of Saint Julien, founded by one of my lord's ancestors, will be delighted by the new donations you graciously promise. Though it has witnessed with sorrow the differences that have sometimes arisen between the lords of Roche-Pont and its abbots, it has never ceased to address prayers to God, to the Blessed Virgin, and the holy apostles Peter and Paul, for the illustrious house of its founders; and in the words that have proceeded to-day from your gracious mouth, what it will appreciate beyond the announcement of your intended gifts, is the assurance that its privileges and its independence will receive fresh guarantees of that protection which was accorded to it in the past."

"Assuredly," replied Eleanor; "we shall take care that no harm is done you or your vassals; and, the charter we shall give you will expressly mention our desire to respect the immunities of the abbey, and if need be, to enforce that respect on others. Moreover, sir abbot, you are not ignorant that in these unhappy times the property of the Church is not always respected, even by those who ought to defend them. You know the trials the abbey of Vezelay has experienced: it is our intention to shelter the cloister of Saint Julien from these insults; and there is no surer means of protecting your abbey than putting the castle in a state of defence."

On his way back, the abbot asked himself what could be the cause of this new turn in affairs. He re-entered the monastery, however, none the less gratified; and after vespers a *Te Deum* was sung.

"To-morrow, my dear lord," said Eleanor to her husband, when all met at supper, "you may set about rebuilding your castle; the abbot of Saint Julien will not feel himself aggrieved." "A good fairy has intervened, no doubt," said the Baron Guy; "we are bound to proceed." "By the bodies of the saints!" said Anseric, when he learned the conditions by which the abbot's acquiescence was to be secured, "you propose to build so much for the Church, *belle amie*, that there will remain nothing for the castle!" "In good sooth," replied the baron, "I am not so very well pleased that these monks should get a footing among us." "Pshaw! we will put the chapel in the bailey;[1] and if we have to defend the castle, the monks will remain outside." "But why, sir uncle, are you always so severe upon the good monks?" "Ah! gentle fairy, if you had seen them, as I have, in lands beyond the sea, you would agree with me that it is the worst breed——" "Come, do not blaspheme, sir uncle; here we are in a Christian land—not among the Saracens."

A few days afterwards, in fact, Anseric set the labourers to work. The burgh and the villages of the domain had to furnish their contingent in men, and in draught cattle and carts; materials were not wanting in the vicinity. Kilns were erected for burning lime, and the forest supplied timber in abundance. Baron Guy, in virtue of his military knowledge, undertook the office of director. He sent secretly for a master of the works—a native of Troyes, whom he had known in Palestine. This person was kindly received at the castle, was well provided for and newly clothed, but carefully watched, lest he should take it into his head to run away. The plans of the new castle were devised by himself and the baron. Use was made of a part of the Roman fortifications which still existed. But the reader must know the position of the buildings then occupying the plateau (Fig. 35) to understand what is to follow.

[1] Outer court.

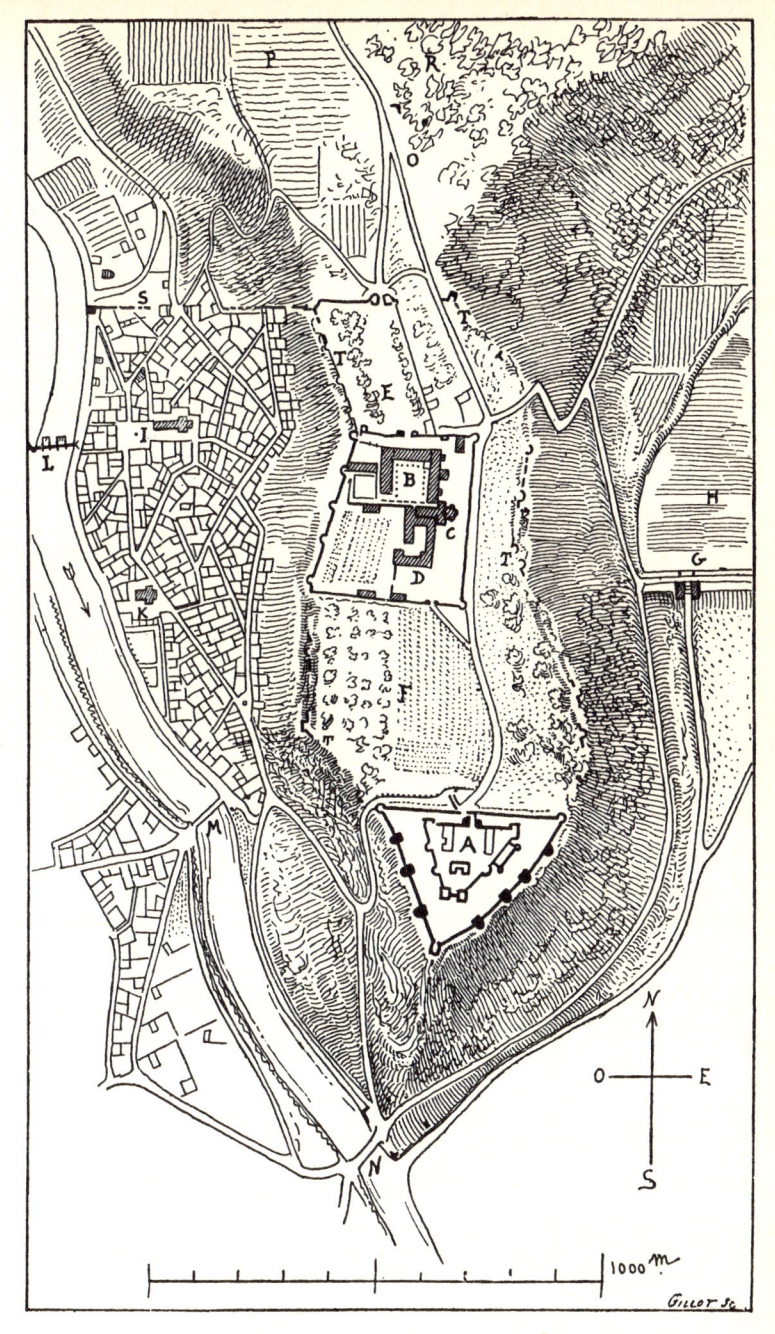

FIG. 35.—THE OLD CASTLE DE LA ROCHE-PONT.

At A was the castle of la Roche-Pont, erected on the Roman remains, and composed of irregular buildings out of repair; at B the cloister of the abbey; and at C its church: at D the abbot's building.

The monastery was bounded on the west by the ruins of the ancient Roman enclosure, and on the other three sides by battlemented walls, with a few turrets.

At E was the pleasance of the abbey; at F that of the castle.[1] Two fine mills, dependencies of the castle, stood at G; and at H was the pond, filled by the pent water of the stream.

The upper town, built on the western incline of the plateau, contained two parish churches, I and K. A wooden bridge, with mills belonging to the castle, existed at L, another wooden bridge at M, and the Roman stone bridge at N.

On the right bank were several houses with gardens. At O the road along the plateau branched into two—one leading to the entrance of the abbey, the other to that of the castle. At P was a breadth of cultivated land, and at R the forest, which extended in a northerly direction more than two thousand paces. Of the ancient ramping wall of the Romans, S, and of the enclosure, T, there existed only heaps of *débris*. These remains, overgrown with vegetation, formed, nevertheless, an elevation which it was possible to defend.

This sketch of the general topography premised, we proceed to explain the dispositions adopted in the building of the new castle (Fig. 36).[2] At O existed a fosse,

---

[1] "The pleasance" was a garden, planted with fruit trees and groves, which served for a place of promenade, and for divers outdoor pastimes.

[2] In this figure the black tint indicates the Roman substructions preserved and surmounted by new works; the outline the Roman buildings entirely razed; the grey tint the defences added by the lord of La Roche-Pont; and the vertical hatching the domestic buildings rebuilt or repaired.

FIG. 36.

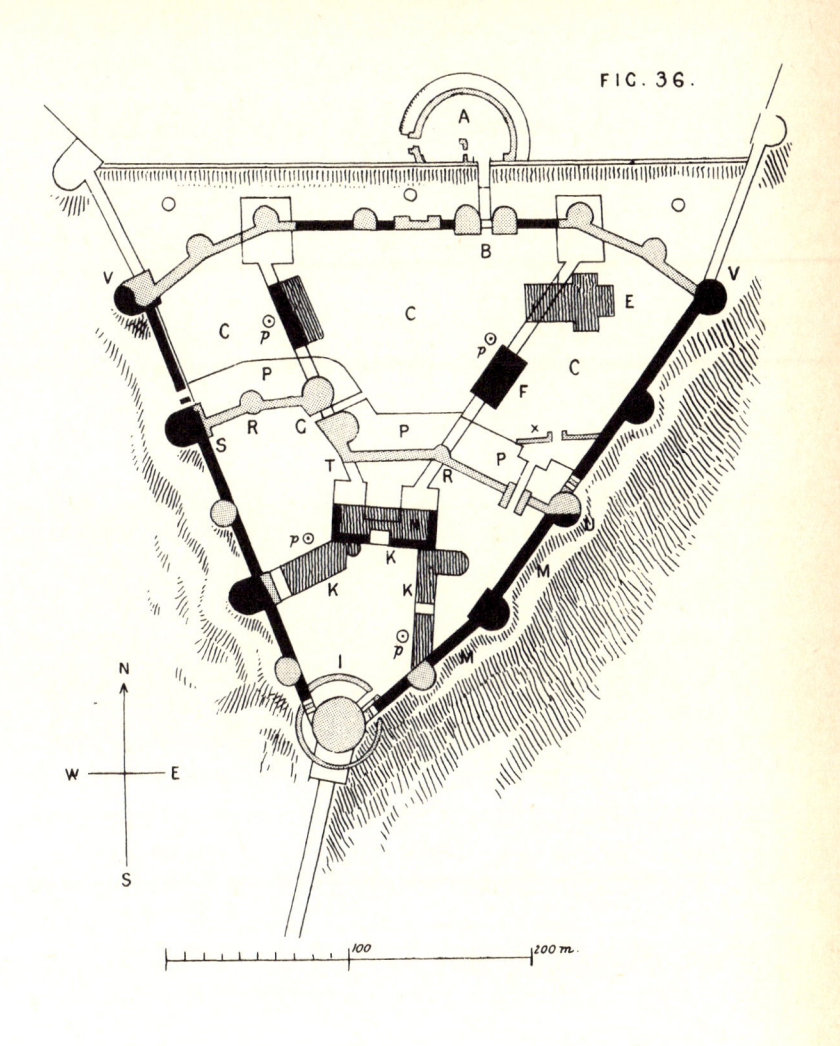

THE CASTLE OF LA ROCHE-PONT, 12TH CENTURY.

which was re-excavated. A barbican stood at A, entered on the left side.

The main entrance of the castle, with its drawbridge, was necessarily placed at B. This gate had to be protected by two towers. Upon a part of the ancient Roman north front, five towers were planned, whose curtains were to join the two ancient towers, Y, which were repaired and re-crowned. A wide space, C, therefore necessarily remained behind this foremost defence. It was the *bailey*, a fore-court or outer-court, in which were laid out the chapel, E, promised to the abbot; stables, D; and outbuildings, F, upon a Roman ruin. At P was sunk a second fosse for the protection of the castle, whose gateway was disposed at G. A postern gave egress at H. The ancient Roman wall, M, received a new crowning, and three new towers were to add to its strength.

At I were laid the foundations of the donjon—partly on ancient masonry—a donjon defended by a chemise and ditch. The buildings designed for habitation were situated at K, with a chapel at I. At the extremities of the ditch, P, cuttings were contrived in the two Roman curtains, to intercept, if necessary, all communication between the defences of the bailey and those of the castle. This contrivance was also adopted for the two curtains abutting on the donjon.

The baron spent his whole time, ever since the decision come to by his nephew, with the master of the works, Alain of Troyes; while the workmen first called in cleared the ground and levelled the Roman ruins, and quantities of stone, sand, gravel, and timber were brought in, and the ditches and trenches for the foundations were excavated by the forced labour of the tenants.

The baron designed to erect opposite the plateau (the point of attack) a great front, slightly convex, to screen the projections, W'. He wished to have a wide barbican in the middle of this front, in which to collect the troops intended for sorties, and to shelter them in case of retreat. He had observed that in all the good defences erected by the Christians in Syria the entrances were so disposed that the assailant was obliged to present his right flank to the defender—with good reason, since the left is protected by the shield or buckler. The position of the gate, C, of the castle had been the subject of considerable study and discussion on the part of the baron and his master of works. The latter wanted to place it parallel with the front, but the baron insisted on its forming a decided angle with the entrance of the bailey. The master of the works urged that the left-hand tower of this gate, G, would then form a projection insufficiently defended, and open to attack; but the baron maintained that if the besiegers endeavoured to attack or mine this tower, they would be commanded obliquely by the tower, R; that by giving sinuosities to this front of the castle all points of the bailey would be commanded; that the principal gate was thus well masked; that nothing more would be needed than to give a considerable thickness to the walls and a greater diameter to the entrance towers; and lastly, if the enemy succeeded in reducing the projecting tower on the right hand, a barricade might still be raised from S to T, and the defence prolonged, with the favourable consideration that if this tower of the salient were thrown down, the other would remain intact and would command the breach.

The postern, H, was also the subject of lengthened consideration on both sides. This postern was necessary to secure the provisioning of the castle without encumbering the main entrance. Placed near the angle tower, U, which the enemy could not attack because of the steep escarpment of the plateau, the postern was well protected by that tower; moreover it was to be surmounted by a quadrangular work with double portcullis and double doors; lastly, a *braie*.[1] X, defended its approach. It was agreed, moreover, that the great central habitable part of the castle, erected on the remains of the square Roman towers, should be crenelated, and should command the curtain, and consequently the two entrances. Wells existed or were sunk at *p*.

Every part having been thus carefully determined, the works were vigorously prosecuted. The baron was always at hand, and persisted in seeing everything for himself. The north front of the bailey, and the chapel, E, were first begun. This exterior work did not greatly alter the appearance of things; but the donjon was next commenced. And when this tower, whose diameter was ninety feet, had reached an elevation of thirty, its aspect had become formidable. The townspeople viewed from a distance this huge mass rising on the point of the plateau, and began to wonder what their lord was intending to do with such an enormous tower. The abbot was somewhat disquieted; but he was so handsomely entertained at the castle that he gave no sign of dissatisfaction, especially as the great chapel of the bailey promised to be very beautiful.

Fortunately for Anseric, the Duke of Burgundy had at that time some rather important matters in hand—a misunderstanding with the King of France. Philip Augustus gave him considerable uneasiness, and at such a time he did not wish to alienate his nobility. More than two years thus passed without anything of serious consequence occurring to the lord of the castle. By that time the building was very nearly finished. We give a bird's-eye view of it (Fig. 37), taken from the north-east angle.

[1] An outer wall of no great height.

FIG. 37.—BIRD'S-EYE VIEW OF THE CASTLE OF LA ROCHE-PONT.

Nothing was talked of throughout the province but the beauty and strength of the new castle of Roche-Pont, and there were men of family in the neighbourhood, envious of the wealth and connections of Anseric, who did their best to represent him to the duke as an ambitious person, impatient of the feudal ties which bound him to his suzerain. It was even insinuated that the Sieur de la Roche-Pont, on the strength of his descent, aimed at nothing less than supplanting the duke; and that he had already begun to intrigue for that object with the king of France and with Pierre de Courtenai, who had married Agnes, sister of the last Count of Nevers and aunt of Eleanor; that his tenants were crushed under the burden of forced labours; and that the duke ought not to allow one of his vassals to oppress the poor people thus, in order to erect a castle surpassed in strength by none in Burgundy.

As only too frequently happens, malevolence was thus suggesting to Anseric the course he should pursue to fulfil his ambitious designs.

The Duke of Burgundy (Hugh III.) was anything but a protector of ecclesiastical property. The abbot of Saint Julien knew this; so that, although he was troubled in mind by the defensive preparations of the lord of Roche-Pont, and augured no good to the abbey from the vicinity of so strong a castle, he did not dare to manifest his fears, or endeavour to communicate them to the ducal court; for he was perhaps more afraid of the duke's intervention than of the power of his immediate neighbour.

At length Hugh was moved, and lent an ear to all that was reported concerning the character and intentions of his vassal. An opportunity soon offered of revealing his real intentions. While Anseric had enemies and enviers at the ducal court, he had also some friends; and they did not fail to inform him of the sinister impressions produced in the duke's mind respecting him, and which he took no trouble to conceal. He had been heard to say that he would soon go and try whether the fortress of La Roche-Pont was as strong as was asserted. Prudence was not the duke's forte, any more than reticence. He had sent a body of his men-at-arms to examine matters closely. Now, the duke's men-at-arms had acquired the habits of their master; they were great robbers and plunderers. Whether they acquitted themselves of their mission I cannot say; but certain it is that they plundered some hamlets and set fire to several granges belonging to the abbey of Saint Julien.

The monks were greatly disquieted, and did not fail to complain to the lord of Roche-Pont.

The fief of Roche-Pont lay under the obligation to send every year to the Duke of Burgundy, as its feudal dues, six war horses caparisoned. It was the custom of the lord of Roche-Pont on this occasion to present himself at the ducal court after Easter. The current year was 1185. Anseric did not appear at court, and did not send the six horses. Hugh demanded them; Anseric replied that the duke's men, plunderers and brigands as they were, had themselves taken off the horses that were destined for him; and that it was their place to give them up to their master; that as for himself and the abbot of Saint Julien, they claimed compensation for damages, and demanded that the plunderers should be hanged on the public gallows. Moreover, that he, Anseric, was aware that the Duke of Burgundy lent an ear to the malevolent insinuations of the enemies of Roche-Pont, and he would choose his own time for giving them the lie.

At this haughty answer Hugh's anger was roused, and he swore that he would take no rest till the castle of

Roche-Pont was razed to the ground, should it cost him a fourth of his dukedom.

Baron Guy had observed the storm increasing not without a secret joy; but though he liked fighting, and cherished an unbounded ambition, he was a prudent man, and one who—like all who had long sojourned in the East—knew how to intrigue and to secure the favour of circumstances. Most of those old knights of Syria joined the character of the diplomatist to that of soldier, in consequence of their relations with the court of Constantinople and the Saracens.

After Anseric's reply, there was no alternative but to prepare for war, and war *à outrance*. But, however strong the place might be, Baron Guy knew well that every besieged fortress must, in the end, fall into the besieger's hands, if it is not relieved. Anseric had no army to bring into the open field against the duke's; he could assemble two hundred and fifty men-at-arms—which would imply a total of about twelve hundred fighting men, as each man-at-arms was accompanied by three or four fighting men. Adding to this body the men in the town who owed service to the lord, a garrison of fifteen to eighteen hundred men might be reckoned upon.

Baron Guy had therefore a long conference with Eleanor and Anseric the evening after the answer had been sent to the duke; when it was resolved that the Lady de la Roche-Pont, with a sufficient retinue, should repair to the court of the king of France, promising him liege-homage for the lordship of Roche-Pont; and asking help from him against the Duke of Burgundy, who was devastating the lands of his vassal, and plundering the estates of the abbey of Saint Julien without cause or reason. Baron Guy had some motives for believing that these overtures would be favourably received; but he refrained from saying all he knew about the matter. He advised his niece to take the abbot in her train, if possible, or, at any rate, some of the fraternity, authorised by him.

Dame Eleanor undertook the commission without making the least objection, and, with apparent calmness, though her heart was ready to burst under her slender corset.

She employed the night with her women in making preparations for her journey, and early in the morning sent for the abbot. The abbot, who foresaw but too clearly—whatever might happen—the devastation of the abbey domains, gave vent to repeated sighs, protested, and denounced the barbarity of the times, but came to no resolution. "Sir abbot," said Eleanor to him, at length, "with or without you or your monks I am going to set out this morning; would you rather plead your cause yourself, or have it pleaded by a woman?" "Ah! most gracious lady," replied the abbot, "can I quit my flock when the wolf is preparing to devour it?" "Well, then, give me three of your monks." "Yes, you are right—it must be—it must be." "Let them be here on horseback in an hour." "Yes, noble lady, they shall be here, under the protection of God and the Holy Virgin!" "But, before all things, sir abbot, not a word about this journey, and do not let the brotherhood know where I am taking them." "Yes, certainly; the fraternity are to understand that they are sent to some dependency or some neighbouring abbey." "Very good, but make haste!" Dame Eleanor, weeping, embraced her children, her husband and uncle; but, drying her tears as she mounted her palfrey, she presented herself to her small retinue with a calm countenance. "Fair niece," said Baron Guy to her, just as she was waiting on the horse-block, "the duke will certainly do his utmost to be here as quickly as he can. He might possibly arrive before your return. If it should be so, proceed with caution, conceal yourself and your train at the vavasor's,—Pierre Landry's—two leagues hence, in the valley; he will be informed of your intention, look out for your return, and give me news of you. Then we shall see what can be done."

The Lady de la Roche-Pont's train consisted of a dozen trusty men, retainers of the castle, commanded by a veteran knight of prudence and experience, with two women and the three monks. The party was supposed by the servants at the castle, to be making a visit to the Lady de Courtenai, Eleanor's aunt.

CHAPTER X.

THE FOURTH SIEGE.

THE Duke of Burgundy was making all speed to reduce his vassal. In the space of a fortnight he had gathered six or seven thousand men, and was beginning his march. Anseric and Baron Guy had not failed to make the most of this respite. They provisioned the castle for three months at least. They fabricated four large trebuchets and half-a-dozen catapults. Timber in sufficient quantity had been cut in the forest for making hoardings, palisades, and wooden defences. Thirty stone-cutters were constantly at work making projectiles of sixty and a hundred pounds weight for the mangonels. Each workman could produce ten in a day, and at the end of a fortnight they had amassed a store of four thousand five hundred. In the town, crossbows and quarrels were being made ; for the townsmen who had to render service were bound to come armed, equipped, and provided with missiles in sufficient quantity. There were archers also, for whom arrows of ashwood, bows of yew, and cords of long-fibred hemp were being made.

Although the lord of Roche-Pont could not, as stated above, assemble more than eighteen hundred men, and therefore could not contemplate defending the whole plateau—that is to say, the castle and the abbey—Baron Guy, who had reasons for it, urged him not to allow the enemy to occupy the monastery without defending it, even were it feebly. "You ought to defend the monastery," he would say to his nephew, "whenever the interests of the suzerain are involved; and since henceforth you are going to do homage for your fief to the king of France, he is your suzerain; his interests, therefore, are involved, and it is your duty to defend the abbey."

To this specious reasoning Anseric could find nothing to answer. The northern wall of the abbey was therefore put in a state of defence; they connected its northeast angle with the *débris* of the Roman wall still existing on the edge of the plateau by a strong palisade and ditch, and barricaded the western brow above the town, between the abbey and the bailey of the castle.

The abbot had made a show of opposing these works, asserting with reason that the abbey was not at war with the Duke of Burgundy, and did not refuse its customary homage. But Baron Guy, as an old crusader, was a casuist of the first order, and, relying on the letter of the charter, maintained that the lord of Roche-Pont was fighting for the cause of his suzerain, and that consequently he must be faithful to the stipulations respecting the abbey. These debates did not stop the workmen; and although the abbot had sent for his vassals with a view to guard the monastery, they were in no hurry to obey his summons, believing that they were not in a condition to resist Anseric's vassals, and preferring to await the result of what was being done before taking any side.

The baron also had a trench dug from the south-east angle of the abbey wall to the eastern ridge of the plateau; then he had the trench covered with timbers and faggots, and the turf replaced above it, so as to leave no external sign of its existence. Outside the barbican of the castle and the ditch was raised a strong palisade which protected its circumference, leaving between it and the wall a space of twenty paces, and which gave lists thirty paces wide in front of the counterscarp of the ditch.

The twenty-second day after Anseric's answer (the 5th of May), the duke's troops appeared on the plateau before the abbey. The first comers spread themselves in the town, and were beginning to plunder it, when the duke interposed, and, contrary to his wont, gave orders that the inhabitants and their property should be respected. Listening to wise counsels for once, he was intending to separate the interests of Anseric's vassals from those of their lord, to isolate the latter, and thus subdue him more easily. So that very evening he issued a proclamation by sound of trumpet through the whole town, to the effect that he was attacking the lord of Roche-Pont only, who had been declared a felon for having broken his fealty to the Duke of Burgundy; that the inhabitants of the town and of the valley would be respected as long as they did not take part with the lord of Roche-Pont; that from this day forwards they were free of all dues and services towards the said lord; but that those who should be convicted of taking part with him should be hanged as traitors to their lawful lord, the Duke of Burgundy. A herald presented himself before the walls of the abbey, and in a loud voice uttered the same proclamation.[1] But the baron had foreseen this contingency, and all the townsmen who had come in arms at Anseric's summons were shut up in the castle. He had appointed for the defence of the abbey, only men on whom he could rely—men who were directly dependent on Anseric, and attached to his fortunes —with some of those adventurers whose services were enlisted in any wars that might arise, and who, having no ties of family or country, used to fight for those who paid them best.

[1] See Fig. 35.

These defenders of the abbey were scarcely more than one hundred resolute men. They received the herald's proclamation with derisive shouts, answering that they knew no other lord but the king of France; and that if it came to hanging, they could play at that game quite as well as the duke's people. During the night two mangonels were mounted opposite the north wall of the monastery, and had soon dismantled the defences; but Anseric's men had retrenched themselves in the building behind that wall; and when the Burgundians advanced with ladders to scale the wall, they received them with a shower of darts, which killed some of the assailants.

Nevertheless, the besiegers mounted the wall and descended into the long narrow court enclosed by the building. There they were exposed to the stones and *débris* of timber which the defenders threw at them out of the windows. The east court was barricaded, and Anseric, with about twenty men, was guarding the barricades. He defended it bravely for a good hour, and the Burgundians, fighting in a narrow space, sustained some losses. They succeeded, however, in breaking open a door of the building, and rushed into the cloister. There they were still exposed to the darts and stones hurled at them by some of the defenders posted on the north side of the church.

A body of Burgundians began to attack the south-east barricade, outside the enclosure, to take the abbey in the rear. It was there that the baron was posted, with about fifty men. The combat was severe and sanguinary, and before withdrawing, seeing that the defenders were gradually abandoning the abbey, he had the faggots in the trench behind set on fire.

Already Anseric and his men were on the road to the

château, and were sheltered by the defences of the barbican. Guy rejoined them, pursued by a large body of Burgundians. But a thick smoke soon began to issue from the trench, and the assailants who were coming up, seeing the ground undermined beneath them, dared not advance. On this Guy and Anseric fell upon those who had ventured within bowshot of the barbican, and killed a good number of them. Excited by the struggle, and exasperated by the resistance they met with, the duke's men entered the various buildings of the abbey, killing the wounded, and plundering. Fire, kindled by the defenders or the Burgundians, soon reached the cloister and the roof of the church.

The poor monks, assembled in the choir during the struggle, were soon forced to quit this retreat; for burning brands were falling on the pavement through the holes in the vaulted ceiling. It was already night, and many were massacred by the drunken soldiery. Most of them had cowered down trembling in a vaulted chamber on the ground floor. It was there that the duke found them when he entered the burning abbey. The abbot threw himself on his knees; but the irritated duke repulsed him harshly, saying: "Sir abbot, it ill becomes ecclesiastics to fight against their lord; and if I do not have you and your monks hanged, you may thank your habit. Begone, and tell your brethren of your *forfeitures!*" Vainly did the abbot protest his innocence, and asseverate that if the abbey had been defended, it was against his will; and the duke, whose anger seemed to gather warmth at every word the father spoke, ended by ordering his men to drive out all the monks.

The unhappy fraternity, perishing of hunger, betook themselves to the town, where some kindly-disposed persons took them in; but the duke would not allow this, and proclaimed next day that every inhabitant who should give shelter to a monk should be hanged. Collecting some provisions, therefore, they started for Cluny on foot.

The duke had given orders to extinguish the flames, for he was intending to reside in the abbey during the siege of the castle; but there remained no part of it fit for habitation except the abbot's dwelling, situated north of the church.[1]

Retired within the castle, after having lost a fourth of their men who had been engaged in the struggle, Anseric and the baron were making their final arrangements. The troops who had re-entered with them were in high spirits, for they had inflicted sensible losses on the enemy; and thought of nothing but defending themselves to the uttermost. Guy was delighted, and his sombre visage was lighted up with an air of gaiety.

"We are getting on bravely," said he to his nephew, when they were alone, "bravely, I say: now that the abbey is burned we are sure to be aided by the king of France; we have made a capital commencement." "But these poor monks; what has become of them? Ah! my worthy uncle, it would have been better to leave them alone; we should now have some thirty brave fellows more here, and should not have to reproach ourselves with having caused the convent to be burned and the monks massacred, perhaps." "Stay, stay, my good nephew; monks always get out of their difficulties, and they are sure to be able to restore their abbey. Besides, it is the duke's men who have burned it! Besides, was it not our duty to defend it? Say no more about it. Jean Otte will get out to-night by the donjon postern. He is a rough sort of fellow, but a cunning blade; in five days

[1] See Fig. 35.

he will be with our gentle Eleanor, and tell how that the noble duke has sacked the abbey, and burned all the monkery! It's capital! capital!"

On either side about a dozen prisoners had been taken. The next morning, May 7th, the people of the castle saw three of these unhappy men hanging up, by the duke's orders, on the trees of the pleasance. Immediately three

FIG. 38.

Burgundian prisoners were hanged on the battlements of the barbican.

None of the bridges had been destroyed by the besieged. They were occupied by the duke's men, and defended each by a good *bretèche* (Fig. 38), to hinder any communication from one bank to the other. The south wall of the abbey was strengthened by palisades joining the two ridges west and east of the plateau. A guard was posted in the two mills belonging to the monastery,[1] and a wooden tower built by the side of the rivulet, below the south-east part of the castle.

These first measures adopted, the duke had a ditch dug, with a mound crossing the pleasance of the castle within bowshot, and connecting the two ridges. This intrenchment of contravallation was strengthened by two wooden towers, one at each end, with an outlet near each of them, and one in the middle (Fig. 39). The castle was thus completely invested (May 15th).

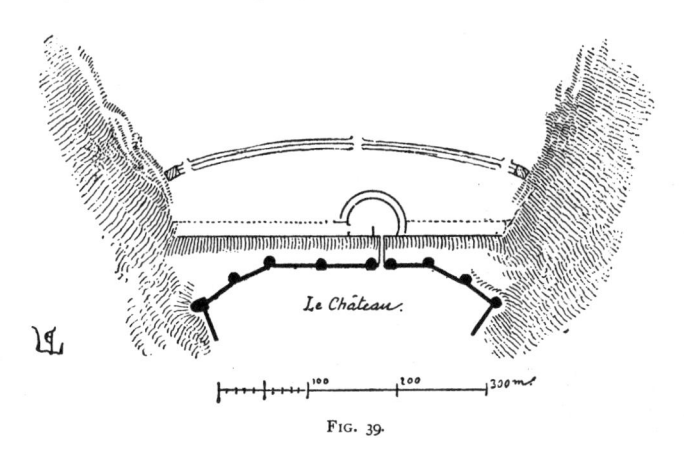

FIG. 39.

While these works were being executed, there were trifling skirmishes every day between the defenders and the besiegers. They were trying each other's strength, but nothing serious was attempted. The duke bent his whole strength towards preventing the lord of Roche-Pont and his men from escaping: he was taking his time. Baron Guy was often closeted with a certain individual whom he called his chaplain, and who had accompanied him from Palestine. In the castle, this so-called chaplain never went

[1] See G, Fig. 35.

by any other name than the *Saracen*. He was a tall, thin personage, with dark brown skin, black eyes and hair, always dressed in a coarse grey surtout. He spoke little, and drank nothing but water; but never failed to be present at mass in the chapel of the castle, and would remain long hours in prayer. The baron asserted that he was a monk of the order of Bethlehem. Whatever he was, he had charge of the sick, and possessed remedies for wounds of all kinds. He was gentle in manner, never looked a woman in the face, was a scholar, and would read aloud so as to charm the most delicate ears. His official name was Brother Jerome. Now, during the leisure which the enemy left the besieged (who were not sufficiently numerous to offer any hindrance to the siege works of the Burgundians, and could do nothing but keep a careful look-out), it was remarked at the castle that the baron and Brother Jerome passed whole hours together, in the lower apartment of one of the towers, of which they alone had the key. Their clothes were often observed to be blackened when they came out.

It was the eighth day of the investment, which appeared now to be complete (May 22nd). The baron had a secret conference with his nephew and Brother Jerome in the evening, and about six o'clock, orders were given to prepare one of the largest trebuchets, whose framing had been transported thither during the preceding night, at the western end of the lists, outside the ditch.

About two o'clock in the morning, the engine was mounted, the night being still completely dark, as it would be at that season. They then tried its range against the right-hand tower of the besiegers' contravallation, with stones; and when the proper range had been secured—a point ascertained by the noise of the projectiles that fell on the woodwork—Brother Jerome placed in the lowered

FIG. 40.—NIGHT SORTIE OF THE GARRISON OF THE CASTLE.

pouch of the stone-propeller a barrel provided with a match, and giving orders to let go the beam of the engine, set fire to the match with a brand taken from a brasier kindled for the purpose.

With a whizzing sound, the end of the beam traced a bow of fire, and the barrel was shot forth, leaving a long and luminous trail behind it; it struck the wooden tower, and in bursting spread a sheaf of white flames which seemed to cling to the woodwork. The engine, lowered anew, sent a second barrel and a third. The wooden tower then resembled a furnace (Fig. 40).

Great was the agitation among the guard of the besiegers, and the defenders could hear their shouts from the ramparts. Taking advantage of their confusion, Anseric had the barrier of the lists opened, and followed by two hundred men, went at full speed to the contravallation, passed through the central gate, which was but slightly guarded, and turned to the left, passing along the interior of the enemy's earthwork.

The Burgundians had betaken themselves to the tower to try to extinguish the flames. The besieged rushed upon the disorderly mass, most of them being unarmed. The baron had also gone out with a second body to protect his nephew's retreat. The duke heard the shouting from the abbey, saw the fire, and immediately gave orders to march forward. But during the last hours of night, men are not very active. Before help arrived, Anseric had had time to kill or put to flight all who were guarding the contravallation. He could therefore re-enter the lists at his leisure, and without having lost a single man; some few being wounded. Daylight revealed to the duke the smoking remains of one of his towers.

This sally raised the courage of the besieged; none of them, except those who had been in the wars of the

Crusaders, knew the effects of the Greek fire. They deemed themselves, thenceforth, invincible. This was the baron's object in planning this attack, whose result was otherwise of little value to the besieged.

In place of the wooden tower that had been burned, the duke had a platform raised, consisting of wicker-work and turf, on which was placed a substantial floor of beams to receive a *trebuchet* which swept the lists, and almost reached the barbican. Then he raised a second platform, in the very centre of the front of the contravallation, with a mangonel, whose projectiles fell right into the barbican. To these engines the besieged opposed the first trebuchet, and another mounted in the barbican. But on neither side was any great damage effected by them during a whole day's working, for as soon as the soldiers saw the beam of the enemy's engine lowered, they got out of the way. The besiegers enlarged the central platform, and were then able to mount the mangonels upon it, which succeeded in utterly destroying the trebuchet set up in the barbican, and the palisades in front, and in dismantling the battlements. The garrison of the castle were obliged to cower down against the walls, if they would avoid abandoning the works. When the besiegers deemed the palisades indefensible, and the battlements sufficiently broken down, the signal was given for the assault (May 25th).

In the first place, protected by mantelets or by their bucklers, the archers and crossbowmen advanced to about sixty paces from the barbican, forming an arc of a circle around it—the archers in the front rank, the crossbowmen behind. Immediately one of the defenders showed himself on the rampart, he was hit. The garrison, sheltered as far as possible by the remains of the merlons, and by their bucklers, replied as best they could, but ineffectually, for their situation was a very trying one. Not wishing to risk his men's lives uselessly, Anseric made them lie flat on their faces on the rampart, so as to be ready at the moment of assault.

Two bodies of Burgundians then advanced, provided with ladders having hooks, and with planks, which they threw over the little ditch of the palisade. Some resolute men defended the palisade, but it was so broken by the projectiles that these defenders had to abandon it. Then about thirty ladders were set up against the barbican, and strings of men climbed their rounds; but the garrison succeeded in unhooking the ladders and throwing down the assailants; others, making use of the *débris* of the merlons, crushed them. Those of the assailants who reached the summit were received with blows of bills, boarspears, and crowbars.

The foot of the barbican was already covered with dead and wounded, with the *débris* of ladders, and stones. From the towers of the bailey gate skilful crossbowmen, well protected, hit most of those assailants who succeeded in mounting on the remains of the parapet. The assault, three times renewed, was as often repelled, with considerable loss to the Burgundians. The assailants had burst in the gate of the barbican; but the baron, seeing that the lists could not be defended, had caused the gate to be barricaded, leaving only a narrow egress to allow the last defenders of the palisades to re-enter. As soon as these had got in, beams and barrels were heaped up against this gate. On this side the assailants were exposed to the projectiles hurled from the towers and curtains of the bailey. They succeeded, however, in setting up mantelets to protect them, and throwing sulphur and resin on these remains of the gate, set it on fire. The flames were communicated to the barricade, but the defenders incessantly brought up fresh pieces of wood, and night came without the enemy having been able to occupy the work. He nevertheless maintained his position around the barbican, sheltered behind fascines and mantelets, and piling against its walls trunks of trees, clods of turf, and mattresses taken from the scattered houses; while a trebuchet was incessantly discharging stones on the area of the defence. The besieged had abandoned it since midnight, and had thrown down the bridge giving entrance to the bailey.

At sunrise, therefore (May 26th), the Burgundians were able to get within the walls of the barbican without opposition, but they found themselves directly exposed to the projectiles thrown from the defences of the bailey, which were provided with hoarding. It was not without loss that the besiegers got a lodgment within the barbican, a considerable length of whose wall they threw down. Then, having cleared the breach, they set to work to bring forward a *cat* which had been framed together beforehand out of range, at some distance from the contravallation, while two terraces were being raised outside the walls of the barbican, and abutting against them (Fig. 41).

The Burgundians could not undertake a new attack before these works were completed. Baron Guy determined to avail himself of this respite. Behind the left-hand curtain of the bailey gate, he set up the two remaining trebuchets on a wooden platform, and then connected the corner of the chapel and the corner of the building D, belonging to the stables, by a good palisading with a ditch.[1] The trebuchets were mounted within this palisading, forming an interior retrenchment. The timbers of the hoarding were thoroughly wetted and smeared with mud—as far as the enemy's attacks permitted. This

[1] See Fig. 36.

FIG. 41.—THE BESIEGERS GET POSSESSION OF THE BARBICAN.

precaution was not useless, for the Burgundians soon discharged on these hoardings, with their catapults, darts furnished with tow dipped in pitch and lighted. The besieged, armed with poles to which were fastened pieces of wet blanket, extinguished these missiles without much trouble; for the flame had not the intensity of the Greek fire, and did not cling to the wood. In fact the tow would sometimes be extinguished in its passage.

In twelve hours the trebuchets of the besieged were mounted, and began to hurl stones of sixty and a hundred pounds weight on the barbican occupied by the enemy, and even beyond, which annoyed them excessively; for not seeing the engines, they were unable to aim in return —except by guess—with the mangonels they had set up on the terraces; and all the projectiles passed over the heads of the defenders. During three days no change occurred in the situation on either side. The Burgundians, however, had succeeded in filling up the fosse on the right of the bailey gate; and they had thrown so many stones with their mangonels against the hoarding of the neighbouring towers, that these timber defences fell to pieces; but the stone battlement behind remained intact, and the defenders were still perfectly sheltered behind their merlons, whence they sent showers of quarrels and arrows.

The fosse having been filled up (May 30th), the *cat* advanced, rolling on planks between the two terraces, through the breach of the barbican. Then as the filling in of the fosse had an inclination towards the curtain, the *cat* of itself went striking its iron muzzle against the wall (Fig. 42). Thereupon the besieged threw down on its double-sloped roof huge stones, beams, and small barrels of Greek fire. But the roof was solidly plated with iron; its slopes greatly inclined, and covered with earth and

FIG. 42.—THE CAT.

wetted mattresses, allowed the stones, beams, and barrels to slip off right and left. Men placed within the *cat* thrust away the inflammable projectiles with long forks, so that they might not set fire to the sides of the gallery. This latter was preserved, therefore, despite the efforts of the besieged, and the miners, protected by its roof, set to work at the base of the wall.

The following night Baron Guy determined to make a last effort to set the *cat* on fire. The working of the miners could be heard. Beneath the gate B[1] of the bailey, there was a drain which discharged the rain-water of the court into the ditch. This mouth had been in great part walled up when the enemy presented themselves before the place. The floor of the bridge, in falling, had moreover hidden it from the besiegers. The baron had the walling removed noiselessly with crowbars, and when the opening was large enough to allow a man to pass, he chose three determined fellows who, with Brother Jerome, slid down into the ditch. Crawling up the mound which supported the *cat*, they slipped beneath its gallery two small barrels of Greek fire. Lighting the match with the aid of a preparation which the brother brought in a box, they went back as they had come, and the mouth of the drain was again walled up.

From the summit of the neighbouring towers the besieged had then the pleasure of seeing the barrels spread streams of white flames, which, clinging to the timbers of the gallery, set it on fire.

The more water the besiegers threw on the flames the more intense they became, so they began to try turf and mould. The defenders then recommenced throwing beams and stones on the roof of the *cat*; then more barrels of Greek fire, bundles of straw, and faggots.

[1] See Fig. 36.

In spite of the efforts of the Burgundians, the gallery being quite filled with suffocating smoke, was no longer tenable. They were forced to abandon it; and it was with great difficulty that they were able to preserve from the fire about eighteen feet by cutting it away with axes. The besieged on their side had not been able to prevent part of the remains of the hoardings above the *cat* from catching fire; but these hoardings were already past service, and their efforts were confined to preventing the fire from extending right and left. The entire head of the *cat* against the wall and twenty feet of its length was burned. The operations of the miners were not much advanced, still they had already removed enough material to give shelter to two men from the projectiles falling from the ramparts. Under favour of night, therefore, some pioneers returned to the mine-hole by creeping under the *débris* of the *cat*. The darkness was great and the defenders did not observe them. But Brother Jerome was on the watch for suspicious sounds, and soon came to inform the baron that they were mining again. "Well," said the latter, "let us repeat yesterday's manœuvre; send men out through the mouth of the drain which these Burgundians are so stupid as not to have looked for; and let some good thrusts of the knife relieve us of these burrowers; but let there be no noise!" The mouth of the drain was once more unwalled, and Brother Jerome with his three companions in the previous exploit, armed with long knives and gliding along the wall, reached the hole of the mine. Three pioneers, intent on their work, were noiselessly killed; a fourth, who was outside hidden in the *débris* of the *cat* to watch, slept, heard nothing, and remained there unperceived by Brother Jerome and his companions. Waking up soon afterwards he called in a low voice to his comrades . . . there was no answer; he felt with his hand, touched a dead body—then a second, then a third. Terrified and not daring to return to the Burgundians from fear (a very reasonable one) of being hanged, he followed the wall, came to the *débris* of the bridge, and found himself in front of the mouth of the drain, which was being silently walled up for the third time. Only a dark lantern threw its faint light on the workmen who were visible through the small opening which remained to be closed. The Burgundian comprehended, and immediately determined what to do. "A deserter!" said he in a low voice at the orifice. "Thy hand!" replied Brother Jerome. The hand appeared at the entrance of the hole, and the whole body was forcibly dragged through, not without excoriations, by the friar and one of his companions. The new comer was disarmed and conducted before Anseric and the baron as soon as the mouth of the drain had been securely closed. The poor wretch remained trembling before the two Seigneurs and naïvely recounted what had happened to him. He was a young man from Semur, in Auxois, who, like most of his countrymen, was not wanting in intelligence. He gave all the information demanded of him concerning the duke's army: "Listen attentively to what I say," said the baron: "if the castle is taken, thou wilt be hanged by us before the first Burgundian enters. If the duke's men take the castle, thou wilt be hanged by them, to a certainty. If thou servest us faithfully and the duke's troops are obliged to raise the siege, the Lord of Roche-Pont will take thee into his service: what is thy calling?" "A harness-maker." "Well then! thou shalt be attached to his stables—shall he not, my worthy nephew?" "Certainly; and if he aids us efficiently, and if events show us that he speaks the truth, he shall have two pounds of silver on the raising of the siege."

FIG. 43.—THE BOSSON.

These last words completely loosened the harness-maker's tongue; and he told all that he knew as to the number of the engines, the arrangements of the besiegers, the posts they guarded, and the towers of the contravallation; after which he was sent to the servants' hall, where he soon made friends with Anseric's dependants. Friar Jerome, however, was ordered not to lose sight of him.

It was not before the time when the miners were to be relieved (by another set) that the Burgundians discovered what had happened. The vanished harness-maker was strongly suspected of having assassinated his comrades while at work; they sought for him—to no purpose, of course.

Before sunrise the baron commenced a countermine at the point indicated by the deserter, inside the bailey wall. "If thou mistakest by so much as a yard," said the baron to the harness-maker, "thou shalt be hanged."

The work was carried on by both parties, and towards the close of the day the miners and counterminers met and attacked each other in their close quarters with crow-bars and pickaxes. The Burgundians and the Lord of Roche-Pont each sent men to seize the mines. A barrel of Greek fire dislodged the duke's men; but the masonry of the wall, whose mortar had not thoroughly set, cracked above the mine. Seeing this, the Burgundians next night, making use of the rescued portion of the *cat*, set up a kind of front-work, formed of pieces of timber; and in the morning brought a *bosson*, or battering-ram on wheels (Fig. 43), with which they set to work to batter the base of the wall. At each blow the masonry was shaken, and stones fell down within and without.

The besieged tried to break the *bosson*, by letting fall great pieces of timber on its head, and to set fire to the timber; but these had been wetted, covered with mud, and filled round with manure at the bottom: the parapet was so well swept by the duke's mangonels and by the cross-bow men that it was scarcely possible to retain a footing on it. Besides the men upon this wall, shaken as it was and vibrating at every blow of the ram, lost their self-possession and did not do their best; while the *bosson* held out, especially as the assailants had put large pieces of timber in an inclined position against the wall, which caused the beams thrown by the besieged to slide off.

At the end of three hours of continued effort, the wall gave way, and a piece about twelve feet long fell on the bosson. The Burgundians immediately bringing up planks and ladders rushed to the assault through the narrow breach. The struggle was severe, and the garrison themselves, mounted on the ruins of the wall, fought bravely and maintained their front unbroken.

From the parts of curtains that remained intact and from the towers the defenders showered darts and stones on the assaulting column. The trebuchets within the rampart continued to send stones which, passing over the heads of the defenders and assailants on the breach, struck those who were gathered around the remains of the *cat*, and made wide lanes among them. By the evening, the Burgundians were masters of the breach; but seeing the interior rampart before them they did not venture to descend, but took up a position on the breach, protected by mantelets and fascines.

The same evening they set miners to work between the tower of the north-west angle and its neighbour; reckoning on thus getting round the retrenchment by passing through a second breach.[1] They likewise took

[1] See Fig. 36.

possession of the two rampart walks of the curtain in which the breach had been made; but the tower of the gate and that on the left were still holding out at eight o'clock in the evening.

An hour later, the assailants being masters of the rampart walk in that quarter, set fire to the roofs of these

FIG. 44.

towers (Fig. 44), which the defenders were forced to abandon.

In the morning, therefore, the gate was in the power of the enemy. The defenders still held the rampart walk to the east and west of the towers that had been burned, had raised barricades, and were determined to contest the position inch by inch.

The assailants as well as the defenders needed rest. Notwithstanding their progress, the Burgundians were suffering considerable losses, while of the force in the castle there were only a hundred killed and wounded. By a kind of tacit agreement the day following the assault passed without fighting. The duke, alarmed at the losses he had already sustained, determined not to continue the attack without taking every precaution; for his men were complaining that they were always made to fight unprotected against soldiers carefully shielded, and asserting that even if they got as far as the donjon, there would not be a man left in the duke's army to enter it.

That day was spent by the Burgundians in thoroughly protecting their quarters on the breach, in placing a catapult, then in crenelating the back walls of the towers, of which they had got possession, and in constructing a kind of wooden tower provided with a second catapult at the interior opening of the gateway. The defenders, on the other hand, made a second retrenchment from the angle of the building D of the stabling to the western curtain, and a strong barricade from the angle of the chapel choir E, to the neighbouring tower. Next, in front of the main gateway of the castle, a *bretèche*, or outwork with palisading to protect the men in case of retreat. It was evident that next day, the 6th of June, a decisive action would render the Burgundians masters of the bailey, even if they did not exert themselves to the utmost; but the defenders were resolved that they should pay dearly for their success. Anseric, firmly resolved to resist to the last extremity, and to perish under the ruins of his donjon, congratulated himself on Eleanor's absence, and regretted that his children were not with her. The noble lady was, however, not far off. The evening of the day that had been entirely employed in preparations for attacking and defending the bailey, she and her escort had arrived at the dwelling of the vavassor, Pierre Landry, who had immediately despatched a trusty messenger to the castle.

At the base of the donjon was pierced a slanting aperture one foot six inches square, which, opening into the lower hall, ended in the rampart walk left between the great tower and its outer inclosure. From this rampart walk a subterranean passage made along the foundations of the Roman wall, descended the slope of the plateau for a length of sixty feet, and opened out in an old quarry overgrown with brambles. Two strong iron gratings closed this tunnel. Watchmen were posted night and day in this passage; they were let down and hoisted up through the inclined shaft of the donjon by means of a carriage worked by a windlass.

By this passage Anseric had often sent out and brought in spies, who at night made their way furtively among the Burgundian posts. Now in the dead of night, Pierre Landry's messenger presented himself at the entrance of the subterranean passage, gave the signal agreed upon, and handed to the watchman a little box, saying that he was awaiting the answer hidden in the quarry. The box was immediately transmitted to Anseric. Eleanor informed him of her return, and said that she would contrive to re-enter the castle with her train the following night by the donjon postern. Anseric hardly knew whether to rejoice or grieve at this return. But the baron called his attention to a flower which Eleanor had attached to the end of the vellum on which the letter was written, and which was a token of good news.

On the morning of the 6th of June the Burgundians

were in no hurry to attack; they contented themselves with sending darts inside the retrenchment, with their catapults and quarrels and arrows in great numbers from the top of the abandoned towers; they were replied to from the top of the church, the stabling, and the great towers of the castle gateway. About three o'clock in the afternoon, the miners engaged (as above mentioned) at the north-west curtain, threw down a part of it. The duke had thus three openings into the bailey; this last breach, the one effected two days before, and the gateway. Baron Guy advised that time and men should not be lost in defending this second breach, since they were intrenched behind; but, thanks to the corner tower, he was able to resist the immediate capture of the rampart of the curtains on that side. The defenders occupying the tower Y[1] were thus cut off. Anseric sent them a note by means of an arrow, urging them to hold out as long as possible. Fortunately this tower had no doors opening on the bailey, and no perceptible communication except with the ramparts. Now those adjacent to this tower still remained in the power of the occupants of the castle; as the Burgundians only possessed the defences of the middle part of the front. About five o'clock the signal for the assault was given. Three columns entered in good order by the two breaches and the gateway, and rushed, protected by their shields and bucklers, against the palisading, resolutely throwing themselves into the little ditch, in spite of the missiles which the defenders, who still possessed the tower Y and its curtains, hurled upon them from behind.

An egress had been left in the strong barricade which connected the angle of the chapel choir with the adjacent tower.

[1] See Fig. 36.

Anseric and a party of his best men issued by this outlet and fell upon the flank of the attack, which fell back in disorder.

Then other egresses well masked were opened on the front of the retrenchment, and the defenders resumed the offensive. They very nearly regained possession of these breaches and of the gateway; but the duke, on seeing his force in disorder, brought up his reserves, and the three bodies of assailants, four times more numerous than the defenders, obliged the latter to retire again behind their retrenchments. Then about seven o'clock in the evening—for the combat was prolonged without decisive success on either side, and the days are long at this period of the year—the two catapults discharged a quantity of darts furnished with burning tow on the roof of the stabling and of the chapel. The men of the castle exclusively occupied with the defence of the retrenchment, had no time to think of extinguishing the fire, more especially as the crossbowmen stationed on the defences of the bailey, now in the hands of the Burgundians, struck every defender showing himself on these buildings. The fire, therefore, soon gained the roofs. During the attack on the retrenchment, the duke resolved to get rid of the defenders remaining in his rear in the tower Y, and who annoyed the assailants. He called to them by a herald, that they could no longer hope for relief, that if they did not instantly surrender they should all be put to the sword. These brave men sent, as their only reply to the herald, a crossbow bolt, which wounded him. Then the duke, much irritated, ordered straw and faggots to be collected within the bailey and in the outside ditch, and all the wood they might have at hand, and set fire to, in order to smoke out the rebels. Very soon, in fact, the tower was licked by curls of flame, and communicated the fire to the hoarding and roof. Not one man cried "quarter!" for all seeing the fire gaining them, and blinded by the smoke, had retreated by a subterranean passage which from this tower communicated with the gateway of the castle—it was a Roman work preserved beneath the ancient curtain.[1] In withdrawing, they had stopped up the outlet of this passage, which, moreover, was soon filled up by the smoking *débris* of the tower floors. The duke was persuaded that they had perished in the flames rather than surrender, and that set him gravely thinking.

To the last glimmering of daylight succeeded, for the combatants, the illumination of these three fires.

It seemed as if the heavens were bent on adding to the horror of the scene. The day had been fiercely hot; a storm soon arose accompanied by gusts of wind from the south-west, which blew down the smoke and strewed burning brands over the combatants.

At one time Anseric began to resume the offensive with his best soldiers by the barricade of the chapel; then transporting himself to the opposite palisade, he debouched along the western rampart upon the assailants, who on this side tried to get round the stable building. The direction of the wind was most unfavourable to the Burgundians; they received full in their faces both the smoke and the sparks from the western building. The attack languished, despite the efforts of the duke to obtain a decided advantage, and to bring his united force to bear on one point. A pouring rain and fatigue stopped the combatants about nine o'clock in the evening.

They almost touched one another, being only separated by the retrenchment. The rain fell so heavily that, in every direction, assailants and defenders sought shelter,

[1] See Fig. 36.

until there remained none but the watchmen within and without the palisading.

At nightfall, Eleanor and her escort, habited as Burgundian soldiers, departed on horseback from the house of the vavassor, Pierre Landry, and under his guidance. They ascended the valley in silence, and saw before them the outline of the castle in dark relief before the sky, lit up by the fires. With hearts full of anxiety, none dared to express their fears . . . . What was burning? Was the enemy already within the bailey? Had he succeeded in setting fire to the northern defences of the castle? Having got to within two bow-shots of the wooden tower, erected by the duke, at the junction of the river with the stream, they kept along the latter, forded it below the mill, left their horses there under the care of the vavassor's men, and ascended a-foot the slope of the plateau in the direction of the quarry. But at some distance from the opening, Pierre Landry, who was walking in front, perceived through the rain some men occupying the point of the plateau beneath the outer wall of the donjon. The duke had in fact sent some parties to watch the environs of the castle during the combat, and especially the base of the donjon, supposing, with reason, that this defence possessed a postern, as was usual, and fearing, that if the assault turned in his favour, the garrison, in despair of maintaining the defence any longer, after the taking of the bailey, might attempt to escape by some secret outlets.

Pierre Landry turned back towards Eleanor's escort and communicated to it this disagreeable discovery. To enter the quarry was not to be thought of. What was to be done? . . . .

The vavassor concealed Eleanor, her two women, the three monks, and the twelve men-at-arms, as well as their captain, in the best way he could, and made his way along the escarpment by creeping through the underwood. Flashes of distant lightning enabled him from time to time to make out the eastern walls of the castle. No troop appeared on that side; he advanced therefore gradually as far as the foot of the rampart.

After the combat, Anseric, full of anxiety, and without stopping to change his martial accoutrements, covered with mud and blood, had hastened towards the postern of the donjon. There he had learned from his watchmen that the environs of the outer wall were occupied by the Burgundians about bow-shot distant, that they were numerous, well shielded, and communicated with another post established beneath the western rampart, and with a third on the eastern side.

Anseric felt a cold sweat cover his face; but he said to himself that the vavassor was cautious, and certainly would not come and throw himself blindly into the snare. He thought for the moment of sallying with his bravest men by the postern to fall on the troop; but to what purpose? The latter would quickly be supported, the post of the wooden tower would take to their arms, and all chance of getting Eleanor and her party in would be compromised. It would be better to send away his wife and to await events . . . . But how communicate with her? It was impossible to send her a message. He then remounted the steps of the postern in anxious thought. The baron came that way, and Anseric related everything to him.

"Nothing is lost, dear nephew; we will get Eleanor in, for it is necessary that we should know from herself the result of her mission; that must influence, one way or the other, the sequel of our defence. . . . . Leave me to act. . . . . Brother Jerome is an intelligent fellow; we will consult together. . . . .

"In the meanwhile, go and watch without from the top of the eastern ramparts; for, whether Pierre Landry comes alone or with our party, it can only be by that side, since he cannot cross the river whose bridges are guarded. He must have crossed the rivulet in order to get to the outlet of the postern. Go, look and listen attentively!" . . . . Anseric, ascending the eastern defences, enjoined on his men the greatest silence, and put his ear to the listening places—first in one tower then in the next; but he only heard the dripping of the rain on the roofs, and the sighing of the wind. In a little while the baron and brother Jerome, provided with a long rope, came to seek him. "Make yourself easy, dear nephew; Brother Jerome is first going to reconnoitre. . . . . But call four men to help us."

A board was fastened transversely to one end of the cord; this end was thrown over the outside through one of the embrasures, while the cord was held by the four men. Brother Jerome, with his grey dress tucked up, a large knife at his belt, put his feet on the board, grasped the cord with both hands, and he was gently let down. When the rope was slack, the brother was at the foot of the rampart, and they waited.

At the end of half-an-hour, which seemed an age to Anseric, a slight movement given to the cord intimated that brother Jerome was returning. The cord tightened, and the four men had soon hoisted the brother up to the merlons. "Well?" said Anseric. "The vavassor is there; I was very nearly killing him, taking him for a Burgundian, for he has the dress of one; it was he who recognised me and called me by my name." "Well! well! Eleanor?"—"All are there concealed, for the Burgundians are not far off; in this diabolical weather they are earthed like rabbits; no time must be lost. Let down a *barquette* at the end of the cord ; we will hoist up the Lady Eleanor, and the others afterwards, if the Burgundians let us."

The *barquette* was quickly brought, and firmly attached to the cord, then let down ; a shake of the rope intimated that Pierre Landry was below ; soon after, a second shake intimated that the *barquette* was loaded. They hoisted, and dame Eleanor very soon showed her face at the battlement ; all hands lifted her to the arms of her husband. The two women, the captain, the eleven men-at-arms, and the three monks were thus hoisted, without mishap, but were wetted to the skin.

In spite of the loss of the bailey, and the death of a good number on their side, Anseric's men were full of joy when at dawn the defenders were told that an army of the King of France was coming to their relief, and that it was only a question of continuing the defence a few days longer.

Eleanor's mission had perfectly succeeded. The king, Philip Augustus, who appeared to hesitate at first, had quickly determined when the messenger Jean Otté came to tell Eleanor of the burning of the abbey. The king had desired to see this messenger, and the latter, who knew whom he had to deal with, had recounted how the duke's men, without warning, without any provocation, had taken possession of the monastery, had set it on fire, had massacred some of the monks, and driven out those who remained. Soon after, a letter from the abbot of Cluny came to confirm the fact, imploring the justice of the king.

Eleanor, as a woman who knew what she was about, had not failed to make known to the suzerain that the dearest wish of her husband and herself for a long while had been to put the fief of La Roche-Pont into the hands of the king: that they should not, however, have declined the homage rendered to the duke for the fief, if that noble had not, by his violence and the plundering of his men, provoked this decision on their part; that far from being the protector of his vassals, the said duke was bent upon ruining them: and that if he (the king of France) presented himself on the domain of Roche-Pont, he would be received there as the sole and puissant justiciary, alone worthy to govern.

The opportunity was too tempting for Philip Augustus not to be eager to avail himself of it. To lessen the power of a great vassal under so plausible a pretext, and with the rights of the case in his favour, accorded too completely with his general policy to allow him to display less than the full measure of that vigour and firmness for which he was so distinguished. Eleanor quitted the court with the assurance that, a few days after her return to Roche-Pont, the royal army would confront the forces of the Duke of Burgundy.

The grand point, therefore, was to sustain the enemy's attacks with firmness. The defenders numbered no more than a thousand men capable of offering an effective resistance; but the perimeter of the defence was sensibly diminished, for it was impossible to recover the inclosure of the bailey. They must limit themselves to the castle walls, arresting the progress of the Burgundians as far as possible. The baron made no great account of the retrenchment raised between the stables and the chapel; but he considered it of the greatest importance to preserve the west part of the bailey as long as possible, for the north flank of the castle gate evidently presented a weak point, although it was defended by three towers. The baron, convinced that the duke was not sparing of the lives of his men, had no doubt that by sacrificing a

P

thousand soldiers, this front might be broken into in forty-eight hours; the works designed to bear upon this point must therefore be interrupted at all risks. The building, D,[1] of the stabling had been burned; but fortunately the lateral wall of the building looking eastward was part of the Roman curtain, of thick and solid construction. Between this building and the castle ditch the enemy could not pass. He could only attack by the breach made on the side of the tower, Y, or by the interval left between this tower and the building, D, that had been burned. The tower, V, of the western angle had remained in the hands of the defenders. It was wide and solidly built, resting on the Roman substruction, and covered by a platform on vaulting. Towards daybreak the baron had caused two trebuchets remaining within the palisade to be dismounted with all speed. Their timbers were carried into the court of the castle, for, as he foresaw that the palisaded retrenchment would not hold out long, he did not wish these engines to be taken possession of by the Burgundians. A strong catapult had been reserved in the western corner tower V. The baron had it mounted on the platform by daylight, not without difficulty.[2] But that a clear idea may be formed of what follows, we must give a plan indicating the position of the enemy, and the state of the defences (Fig. 45).[3]

[1] See Fig. 36.
[2] See the general bird's-eye view, Fig. 37.
[3] The parts of the castle marked in grey tint are those taken by the Burgundians; those marked black are still retained by the defenders. At *a* is marked the breach in the barbican; at *b* the filling up of the fosse and the first breach made in the curtain; at *c* the second breach. At *oo* are seen the Burgundian posts established on the night of the 6th and 7th of June; at *x* the outline of the subterranean passage of the refuge postern of the donjon; at *z* the quarry; at P the route traversed by Pierre Landry and Eleanor's escort; at R their place of concealment, and at s the point where they were got into the castle by means of a rope.

FIG. 45.

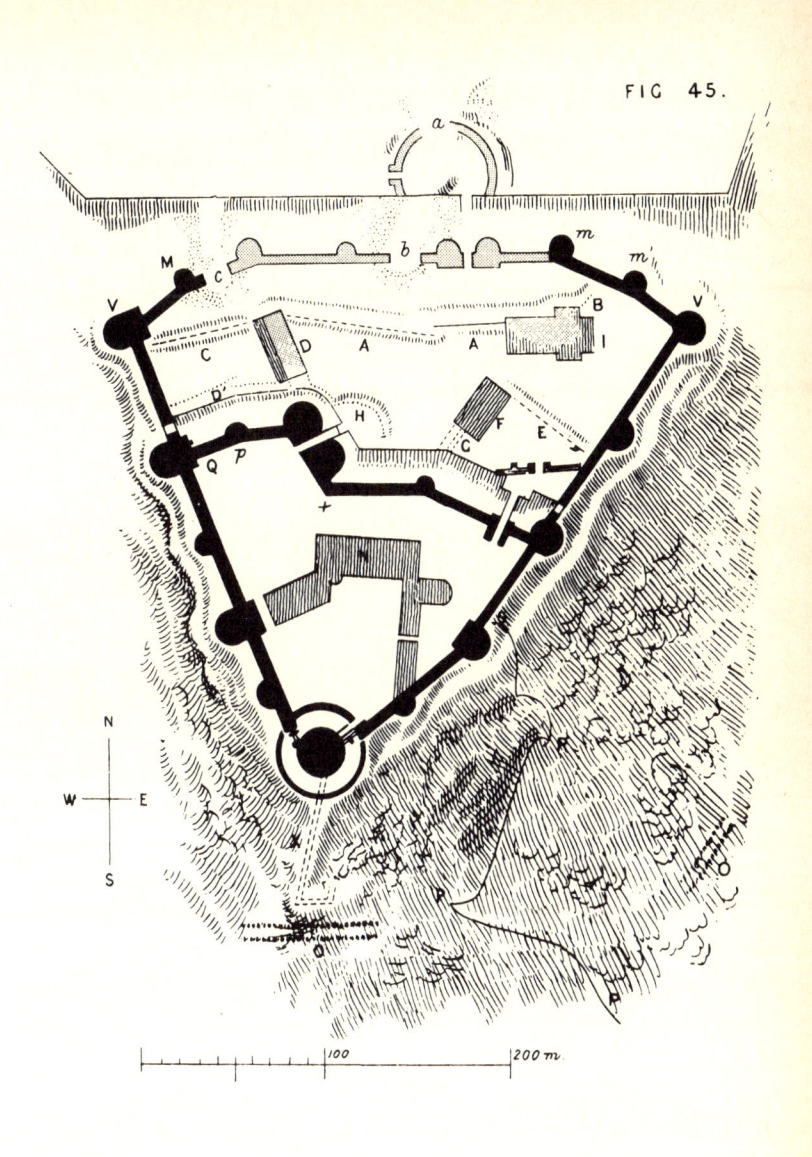

THE TAKING OF THE BAILEY.

On the morning of the 7th of June the defenders were still in possession of the retrenchment C, of that marked A A, and of the barricade B ; at H a strong palisade, with a *bretèche*, had been erected before the entrance at the very commencement of the siege. At D' another palisade arose in front of the ditch ; at E was a second retrenchment, before the postern entrance ; and at G a strong barricade. The building, F, part of the old Roman construction, crenelated at the top, might hold out for some time. The towers, V, M, *m*, *m'*, and V' were still in the hands of the defenders, and could take the assailants in the rear, should they attempt to enter the chapel, I, and the stables, D, that had been burned.

Anseric and his uncle came to the determination to abandon the retrenchment, A A. To defend it was only to lose men, since the enemy could not venture into the return formed by the two towers of the gate and the building F. It was preferable to direct all their efforts to C, for this was evidently the point of attack.

About five o'clock in the morning, therefore, the retrenchment, A A, was abandoned ; and in fact the Burgundians contented themselves with making gaps in it without advancing further. In the early morning the duke had directed a quantity of burning darts on the roof of the tower, M ; but the catapult planted by the defenders on that of the angle, V, greatly annoyed the assailants grouped outside, who were preparing to make a vigorous attack through the breach C.

It was about noon that the duke gave orders for a simultaneous attack on two points ; the roof of the tower, M, was already on fire. The first attack was vigorously directed to the retrenchment C. The second made a gap in the crenelated walls of the chapel, the intention being to get possession of the palisade E. At the same time, two

P 2

catapults planted outside were showering burning darts upon the roofs of the towers *m, n′* and V, while a trebuchet was destroying the hoarding and battlements with volleys of stones.

The defenders posted on the summit of the tower, V, by discharging stones and quarrels on the flanks of the assailants, who were impetuously assaulting the retrenchment, C, did them much damage, their bucklers not availing to protect them in front and flank; and from the narrow front of the castle, skilful archers discharged arrows in abundance over the heads of their own party on the assailants who presented themselves at the breach, C; for they were within bowshot.

Fig. 46.

Seeing they could make no impression, the duke withdrew his men, and had mantelets brought forward and placed perpendicularly to the wall, and fronting the tower in the angle, and then a small bosson on wheels—its head strongly armed with a solid iron point. The wheels of this bosson were screened (Fig. 46), to shelter those engaged in working it. Twenty men under shelter, with heavy crowbars, were awaiting the effect of the bosson. The fourth time it encountered the palisade a dozen stakes were greatly shaken, and the cross-rails broken. Then the pioneers, armed with crowbars, set about bringing down the shaken stakes, or at least turning them aside. The assaulting column threw itself upon the openings. There was a hand-to-hand fight, and so densely were they pressed together, that the men posted in the tower at the corner dared not shoot for fear of wounding their comrades.

On the opposite side the Burgundians had succeeded in making a wide gap in the wall south of the chapel; and screened by its ruins, they attacked the angle of the retrenchment E.[1] From the east curtain, however, the garrison discharged stones and arrows on their rear; and this assault was but feeble, as the duke was entirely occupied with directing the others.

Anseric defended this point by the desire of the baron, who had urged him to resume the offensive, supported by the building F, however difficult the undertaking might be.

One of the men posted at the defences of the gate hurried down, and, passing the postern, came and told him that the retrenchment, C, was forced and his people in great danger at this point. Anseric, therefore, taking two hundred and fifty men whom he had with him, issued from the retrenchment by its eastern extremity, rushed furiously on the assailants, threw them into disorder, and leaving forty brave soldiers to defend the gap in the chapel, and the barricade, B, that had remained almost intact, traversed the area of the bailey in an oblique direction, crossed the retrenchment, A, which was partly destroyed, and fell on the left flank of the assailants, uttering the war-cry: "Roche-Pont! Roche-Pont!" ... The Burgundians, surprised by this unforeseen attack, and not

[1] See Fig. 45.

knowing whence these soldiers came, abandoned the retrenchment, the bosson, and even the breach, C.

The baron's troops, seeing this, plucked up courage, and killing all that had remained within the bailey, occupied the breach, *c*, once more, while Anseric was occupying the barricade, C. The bosson was destroyed with hatchets, and the mantelets left by the enemy were put in readiness for repairing the broken-down palisades.

The duke was furious, and had broken his sword on the backs of the runaways. But no further attempt could be made that day, and the advantages he had gained with so much trouble were jeopardized. The defenders were seen barricading the breaches, and he could hear the cries of the unfortunate men who had remained in the bailey, and were being pitilessly massacred.

The Burgundians had lost more than two thousand men since the commencement of the siege; and on the 7th of June the duke's army amounted to no more than four thousand five hundred or five thousand men at most. The besieged were reduced to about a thousand; but they were full of hope, and assured of success, while the besiegers were losing confidence. Their advantages had been gained only by enormous sacrifices, and this last affair threatened altogether to "demoralize" them.

The duke had reckoned on taking the place in a month at most; and now at the end of thirty-two days he found that he had lost the third of his army without being much more advanced than the second day after his arrival. Order and method had been wanting in the various phases of the siege; this he could see when it was rather too late. If, instead of pursuing their advantages in the centre of the front of the bailey, the besiegers had contented themselves with taking the barbican, so as to hinder any sortie from that side, and if with good earthworks they had advanced under cover against the western end of this front towards the tower, M,[1] directing all their efforts to this point and raising a movable tower, they would be in possession of the western court, would destroy in succession the works on their right, would be able to protect themselves against offensive re-action on their left, and would attack the castle on its weak side; that is, between the gate towers and that marked Q. Thus they might take in the rear all the eastern defences, moving along the western curtain by successive breaches.

The duke, it is true, was not acquainted with the place, and believed that in making a wide breach in its centre he was striking at its heart.

These reflections occurred to him too late; he could not draw back, and it was necessary to act with decision. Assembling his chief captains, therefore, in the evening, he announced that a decisive effort must be made; representing it as evident—in spite of the check just experienced—that if they could gain a permanent footing in the western court of the bailey, they could soon break into the castle on the flank of the gateway defence, and this flank once seized the castle would be theirs. The soldiers, rather ashamed of the panic that had lost them the advantages they had acquired, cast the blame of the failure upon each other; and those who had been the first to run away were bent upon vindicating their bravery. So that when, on the morning of the 8th of June, the order was given for attacking the lost breach, *c*, and every preparation had been made for protecting their position within the bailey, the Burgundians were eager to advance.

A vigorous return to the charge was expected by the garrison, and the baron concluded that the breach, *c*, would be attacked. Part of the night, therefore, had been

[1] See Fig. 45.

occupied in strongly barricading this breach. Two Burgundian catapults and a trebuchet covered the breach with darts and stones, so that the defenders had to shelter themselves to the right and left behind the remains of the curtains; and about ten o'clock the barricade was destroyed and only a heap of rubbish remained. The palisade of the retrenchment in the rear was also damaged, and the projectiles that were showered upon this point precluded the defenders from repairing it. Then the first attacking column advanced, passed through the breach, and reached the palisades. Anseric, posted behind the building, D (belonging to the stables), was on the point of taking this column in flank, as on the previous day, but a second troop rushed through the breach, and the Lord of Roche-Pont was all but taken. With great difficulty he and his men retreated to the outwork of the gate, and brought aid to the defenders of the western court. The surging host of the Burgundians was continually increasing, the palisade was taken, and the second palisade, D', was the scene of a desperate struggle between assailants and defenders. The garrison could not bring their forces to bear on this point, and Anseric feared they might be cut off, and not be able to retire into the outwork of the gate, H; he therefore ordered a retreat in the evening, while from the three towers and the curtain of the castle, quarrels and arrows were showered on the assailants confined in the court.

The tower, V, which still remained in the hands of the besieged, took the Burgundians in the rear; and the latter employed all the rest of the day in securing themselves in front and in flank, while the duke had the tower, M, undermined.

The door of the tower, V, opening into the bailey, had been broken in; but the stairs were so well barricaded with stones and *débris* that it was impossible to clear it; and even should this be done the assailants would be easily overpowered by the defenders.

A wooden bridge connected the curtain of the bailey on this side with the corner tower of the castle. By means of a catapult the Burgundians succeeded in throwing combustibles on it, which obliged the defenders to abandon the tower, V, in haste. They were seen re-entering the castle just when the flames were beginning to consume the bridge. The roof of the tower, Q, was all but set on fire; and the defenders had great difficulty in arresting the progress of the flames.

If Anseric had had five hundred more men he might from the central court have resumed the offensive at the moment when the Burgundians were trying to gain a lodgment in the western court. But he had lost a hundred men in the last engagement, and had no more soldiers than were absolutely necessary for the defence of the castle. In the evening the central part of the bailey was occupied by the Burgundians, who took up their quarters there, and intrenched themselves securely this time.

Next morning, the 9th of June, the tower, M, being undermined, fell, and the breach, *c*, was proportionately widened. The ditch was filled up, and the tower, V, occupied by the Burgundians. The defenders, before they abandoned it, had set fire to the catapult mounted on the platform.

The crown of the tower, Q, in the corner of the castle, rose more than twenty feet above the curtain, and thus hindered the Burgundians from moving at will on the rampart-walk of this curtain, which was not furnished with covered hoarding.

The whole of the 10th of June was employed by the Burgundians in completing their works in the western court of the bailey, clearing the breach, *c*, and working at a wooden movable tower, designed to attack and command the rampart between the gate and the corner tower, Q, of the castle; for this rampart, raised on the rock, could not be undermined. The duke, aware by this time of the strength of the place, and supposing the defenders to be more numerous than they really were, was unwilling henceforth to run any hazards. As far as was possible he manned the tops of the ramparts of that part of the bailey which was in his possession, succeeded in setting fire to the roofs and floors of the towers *m* and *m'*, and commenced a mining attack on the tower *v'*. It was no longer the interest of the defenders to guard these works, which weakened them to no purpose. They therefore evacuated them, threw down the bridge uniting the eastern rampart of the bailey with the corner tower, and retired permanently within the castle. Meantime the Burgundians were working at their movable tower outside the old palisade, C, that had been destroyed, and covered the outside with fresh hides to preserve it from the Greek fire. They filled up the ditch in front of the tower *p*,[1] not without difficulty protecting themselves with fascines and mantelets.

On the 20th of June the tower was completed, and the road for it constructed of strong planks firmly fastened as far as the filling up of the ditch. For the few last days the enemy had been incessantly working the catapults and two trebuchets against the crest of the defences of the castle between the gate and the tower, Q, and had tried to set fire to the hoarding and roofs; but these ramparts were higher than those of the bailey, and the baron had covered all the timbers with hides and blankets always kept wet, so that the flaming darts of the Bur-

[1] See Fig. 45.

gundians were ineffectual against them. The roofs, too, were carefully watched. The hoarding, however, was almost entirely destroyed by the projectiles, and its *débris* had been removed by the garrison, as only embarrassing the defence. The whole of the crown of the tower, P, was greatly damaged, especially as it did not rise above the crest of the curtain. Seeing the enemy's preparations, the baron mounted a strong mantelet of thick wood and a catapult on the platform of this tower, P, which had no roof. Then, to meet every contingency, he had a strong retrenchment made from the angle, t, to the opposite tower, behind the tower, Q.

In the evening of this day, the 20th of June, the wooden tower began to be moved, borne along on huge rollers. As soon as it was about thirty yards from the rampart, the baron had the catapult directed upon it, and sent against it cases of Greek fire fixed near the iron points of the darts. The fresh hides protected it well, and the points did not stick in the wood; so the fire fell on the ground, and the Burgundians, under cover of the base-work of the tower, flung off the flaming cases by means of forks. This gave them plenty to do, and the tower advanced but slowly, while the further it proceeded the greater was the chance of its taking fire. The baron, who had but a small quantity of Greek fire remaining, was afraid to waste it. Already five cases had been thrown without effect; so he resolved to wait till the tower was close to the ramparts.

At this time of the year (June 21) the nights are not completely dark, and day breaks early. At two o'clock in the morning the wooden tower was on the counterscarp of the ditch. The mound that filled it presented a slope towards the ramparts, and was covered with planks. At a signal, the tower, urged on from behind by means of twenty powerful levers, rolled quickly along its inclined plane and came into collision with the summit of the tower P, above which it rose ten feet. The shock made the walls tremble, and a shower of stones and darts was poured upon the defenders from the top of the wooden tower. Then a bridge fell noisily on the head of the tower above-mentioned, shattered the mantelets and the catapult; and the assailants, uttering formidable shouts, leaped on the platform.

Anseric was at the top of the tower, Q, and Baron Guy was posted on the battlements of the gate. Both of them, rushing towards the curtains, attacked in their turn the assaulting column on this narrow rampart; many on both sides fell within the court, and were killed or had their limbs broken.

Numbers conferred no advantage, since it was impossible to deploy; so that the crowd of assailants that continued to pour forth from the wooden tower had to fight on the right and the left in a space six feet wide. The staircase of the tower, P, having been blocked up, the enemy could not get down through it; so that, driven into a corner on the platform of the tower, they had to make their way along one curtain or the other. Anseric, at the head of his troop, was cutting an ensanguined road before him with a long-handled axe. At his side, his men, armed with pikes and hooks, stabbed or grappled with and threw down the wall those who attempted to approach their lord. These unfortunate men fell from a height of twenty-five feet on the *débris* of hoarding which the garrison had thrown down within, to clear the rampart walk.

The crossbowmen, posted at the top of the wooden tower, discharged quarrels on the two bands; but the men were well protected with armour, and the quarrels rebounded from their helmets or were arrested by their hauberks. Friar Jerome, armed with an enormous mace, mounted on a merlon, felled all who came within his reach.

The duke, remaining at the bottom of the wooden tower, and supposing the rampart taken, was urging on his men-at-arms that they might follow up with overwhelming numbers those who had first reached the rampart. Thanks to Anseric's efforts and those of the baron, there was some amount of delay at the top of the tower, and the exit from the bridge could not be readily effected. The assailants who were coming up behind the front of the assault were pressing upon those before them, and this pressure only increased the confusion.

By dint of numbers, however, the Burgundians succeeded in gaining a footing on the tower; and the two bands of defenders were not sufficiently numerous to thrust them back. Seeing that they were going to be absolutely overwhelmed, the baron called Father Jerome, who, leaping from merlon to merlon, succeeded in reaching him.

A word spoken in the friar's ear made him run towards the neighbouring tower belonging to the gate. A moment afterwards and a strong crossbow mounted on the upper story of the work, behind the hoarding, shot quarrels, to which cases of Greek fire were fastened, against the sides of the wooden tower, which was not so well protected by skins as its front. The friar took a cool aim at the exposed part of the timbers, chiefly about seven or eight feet above the base of the tower. He had ten of these cases left, and all were aimed with a sure hand, being attached to strong quarrels, whose points were well sharpened. Four of the quarrels failed to stick, but the six others were fixed firmly in the timber, and the cases they bore spread a tenacious and burning lava over the wood.

At the first moment the Burgundians, absorbed in the

attack, did not perceive the danger. Those who had reached the top of the tower could not be aware of it.

The duke was one of the first to see the thick smoke issuing from the kindled wood. Immediately he gave orders for the extinction in all haste of the fire with the aid of small hand-ladders; but as soon as anyone mounted one of these ladders, a dozen archers and crossbowmen posted in the gate tower made him their mark. Four or five men had been killed or wounded before the level of the flame was reached. Inside, the soldiers who, like a rising flood, were ascending to the top of the tower, soon found themselves surrounded by the suffocating smoke produced by the Greek fire. Some were the more eager to mount, others hesitated and were for going down. "Now! to the rescue! Arde le beffroi!" cried Friar Jerome, coming to rejoin the baron's troop, which was almost driven into a corner close to the tower; and with his long mace he took the lead, breaking heads and arms. "Arde le beffroi!" he shouted at every blow. "Roche-Pont! Roche-Pont! Arde le beffroi!" shouted, in its turn, the baron's small troop (Fig. 47). Anseric's men, who were crowded up in the corner tower, re-echoed this cry.

The Burgundians, however, did not retreat; in fact, if they had wished to do so, they could not. They tried to place ladders to get down into the court, but they were too short. "Burgundy! Burgundy!" shouted the assailants, in their turn. "Place prise! Place prise!"

The grey light of dawn faintly illumined this scene of carnage, and its pale, cold gleams mingled with the ruddy glow of the fire. The smoke, driven by a breeze from the north-east, beat down upon the combatants, and sometimes hindered them from seeing each other; but the struggle raged on. Heaps of the dead and wounded—the latter being speedily dispatched by menials posted in the court

FIG. 47.—THE MOVABLE TOWER.

to resist any who should try to get down into it—lay at the interior base of the curtains.

Although Anseric and the baron had ordered those who remained in the two neighbouring towers (that of the angle and that of the gate) not to quit their post under any pretext, and not to unbar the gates till the two troops were absolutely driven back upon those defences, these brave men, seeing so fine an opportunity of routing the Burgundians, and observing the weakness of the two bands of the defenders compared with the host of assailants, opened the gates and sallied forth to help their comrades.

Eleanor and her waiting-women, with some of the wounded, perceiving the critical state of affairs (for the combat took place in front of the western inhabited part of the castle), had proceeded along the western curtain and had reached the corner tower, Q,[1] behind the troop commanded by Anseric. The lady of the castle was the first to encourage the men on guard there to go out, saying that she knew well enough how to bar the doors. As to the wounded who were with her, they posted themselves as best they could at the hoarding, to shoot at the enemy outside and the compact mass of Burgundians engaged on the platform of the tower. These two reinforcements arrived very opportunely. The new comers, fresh and vigorous, made their way, some on the tops of the merlons, others on the *débris* of the hoarding, and relieved their comrades exhausted by the struggle.

The fire was catching the framework of the tower, and the Burgundians soon found their retreat cut off. Those who had gained the rampart, however, sold their lives dearly, and the struggle did not cease till the flames of the burning tower curled round the platform and the rampart walk.

[1] See Fig. 45.

Nearly five hundred Burgundians were killed, wounded, taken prisoners, or burned. The sparks of fire, driven by the wind, were borne down upon the roof and the hoarding of the tower at the angle, and it caught fire about six o'clock in the morning.

The day was a fortunate one for the defenders, but they had lost nearly two hundred in killed and wounded. Anseric had been struck by several quarrels that pierced his hauberk, and was covered with blood. The baron, that he might be more at his ease in fighting, feeling himself oppressed by his helmet, had taken it off during the struggle, and had a large wound in his head. They hastened to throw over the battlements the bodies of the slain Burgundians upon the last blazing timbers of the tower, and to bury in the court the dead that had fallen there. All in the castle were exhausted with fatigue. Eleanor and her attendants were engaged in dressing wounds and in bringing food and drink to the various posts. The lady of the castle preserved her tranquil countenance and gentle look amid these sanguinary scenes, and during the whole day and through the following night she did not cease to render aid to all who needed it. "Fair niece," said the baron to her, while she was dressing his wound, "if the king's army does not make haste it will find no more defenders to deliver; but we have given the duke some trouble, and if he goes on he, too, may have to return to his court alone."

The 22nd of June passed without fighting. The duke had a *cat* constructed with a view to sapping the rampart at its base—which seemed the more feasible, since the destruction of its hoarding and the burning of the tower in the angle deprived the defenders of the means of opposing the sapping effectually. The garrison could see the enemy engaged in this work in the bailey behind the mantelets, and they accumulated within the rampart all the materials they could procure, with a view to blocking up the mouth of the mine at the moment it reached the court

On the morning of the 25th of June, the watch posted on the gateway tower were much surprised at seeing not a single Burgundian in the bailey. They went immediately to inform Anseric and the baron. "It is either a ruse, or the king's army is coming," said the latter; "let there be a sharp look-out in every quarter." They ascended the donjon. The posts on the south were abandoned. The *cat* and the mantelets remained in the bailey as well as the trebuchets. About noon the baron sent out ten men with the deserter, who was to conduct them to the various points occupied by the Burgundian captains. In three hours' time they returned, saying that they had met only some laggards, who had fled at their approach, and some wounded; that the encampment was utterly deserted, but there were some waggons and military engines left.

The duke having been informed of the advance of the king's army, which was only a day's march from the castle, had decamped in the night, abandoning his material of war.

Great was the joy at La Roche-Pont. The inhabitants of the town soon came and confirmed the news. The last of the Burgundians had departed about noon, not without leaving many of their men on the field; for, in spite of the injunctions of the duke, the inhabitants of the lower town of Saint-Julien had been considerably plundered and had driven out the last of the soldiers with stones and pike thrusts.

Soon afterwards the Sieur de la Roche-Pont did homage for his fief to King Philip Augustus; and the monks re-entered their abbey, for the repair of which the king gave five hundred livres.

CHAPTER XI.

THE FIRST DEFENCES AGAINST FIRE ARTILLERY.

KING JOHN had possessed himself of the duchy of Burgundy and united it with the crown; he resigned it in favour of his son Philip, who, as is well known, had distinguished himself on the fatal day of Poictiers. From that epoch till the time of Charles the Bold, the duchy had remained in the hands of the descendants of King John; and although the dukes of Burgundy were very warlike, and had formed a league with the English against the crown of France, in consequence of the quarrel that arose in 1400 between Philip and the Duke Louis d'Orleans, brother of Charles VI., the duchy was relatively at peace, while the north of France, as far as the Loire, was in the power of foreigners.

After the death of Charles the Bold before Nancy, King Louis XI. lost no time in despatching to the province of Burgundy La Trémoille, baron of Craon, who, acting in concert with the Prince of Orange, soon reduced the whole province into subjection to the king of France · this was in 1477.

The town of La Roche-Pont (at that time the abbey alone preserved the name of Saint-Julien, and the town had adopted that of the castle) had been deemed by Charles the Bold worthy of special attention. Recognising the advantageous site of the place and the importance of its strategic position, this prince had adapted the ancient defences to the new mode of attack. The old castle of La Roche-Pont, several times repaired, still showed some of its defences dating from the end of the twelfth century, the donjon being particularly well preserved; but the abbey and the entire plateau had been surrounded by a new wall by Philip, about 1380, and the town had been rebuilt within this enclosure, the right bank of the larger stream being completely abandoned. At the end of the fourteenth century there existed only a suburb on the slopes of the plateau along the left bank, and this suburb had no other defence than a wall of inconsiderable strength on the north. The great-grandson of Anseric, Sieur de la Roche-Pont, having died without male heirs, the fief of La Roche-Pont had reverted to the Duke Philip, who, as well as his successors, appointed the governors of the town and castle, henceforth a ducal domain.

The enclosure of the town had been rebuilt in great part on the Roman foundations. It consisted of a substantial wall rising about twenty-four feet above the outside ground level, without machicoulis, strengthened with cylindrical towers thirty-six feet in height surrounded by machicoulis and covered with conical roofs. Machicoulis formed also the upper defence of the curtains and towers of the castle, whose plan had not been changed.

This place had not suffered any attack since the date of these new works, and it was intact under Charles the Bold. During his struggle in the north with the people of Ghent and Hainault, and as a precaution against the intrigues of Louis XI., he had thought it needful to put the town of La Roche-Pont in a good state of defence. Now, limited though its efficiency was, the artillery of the king of France already played a sufficiently important part in sieges to render it necessary to provide against its effects.

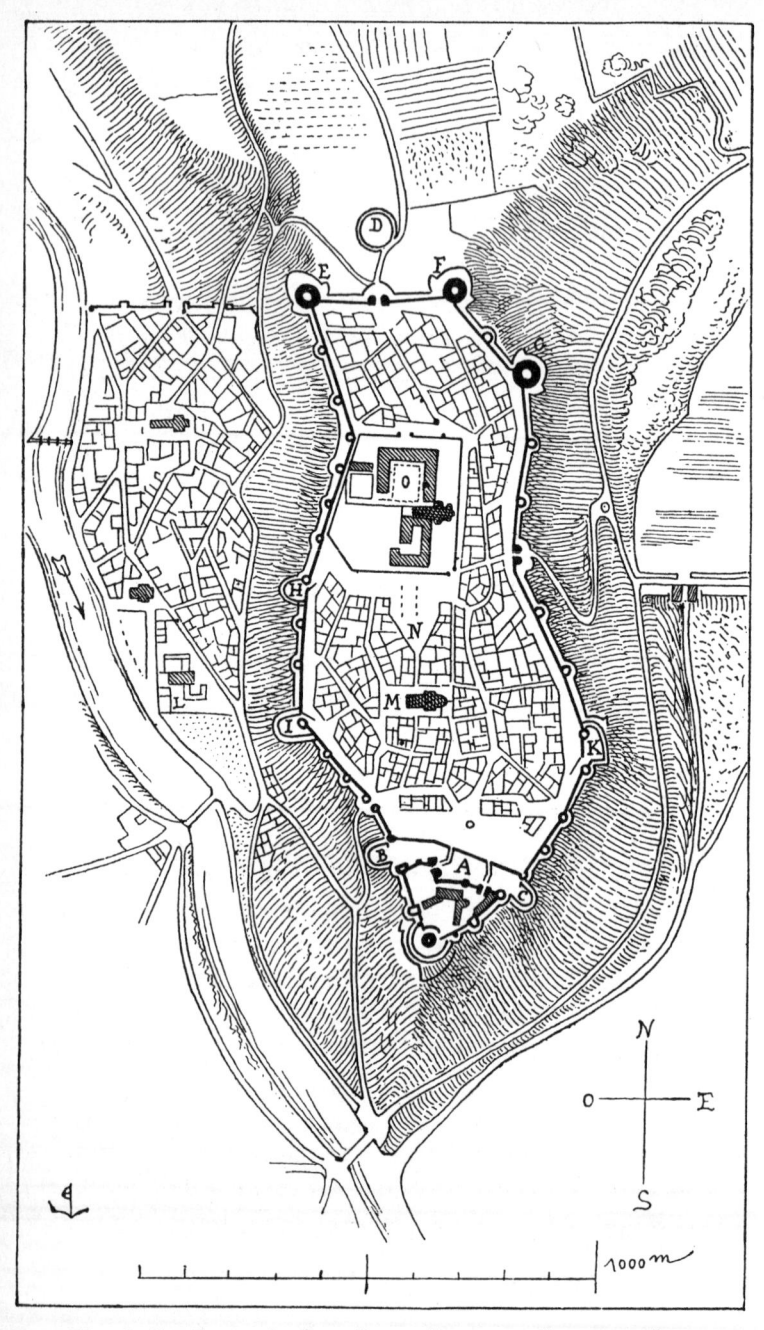

FIG. 48.—THE TOWN OF LA ROCHE-PONT IS FORTIFIED BY CHARLES THE BOLD.

The duke therefore raised several boulevards to replace the walls and receive artillery. (Fig. 48.)

As shown in our plan, the bailey of the castle no longer existed. It was replaced by a wide ditch, A, of little depth; its bottom was on a level with the two boulevards, B and C. A third boulevard surrounded the base of the donjon externally, in the place of the ancient *chemise*. This boulevard commanded the stone bridge rebuilt in the fourteenth century on the Roman piers. Before the north front was raised an isolated boulevard of earth, D, of slight elevation, but commanding the road of the plateau. At the angles of the north front two large towers, E, F, adapted to receive cannon, flanked the angles and were in a position to sweep the boulevard, D. Set back on the eastern side, a similar tower, G, commanded the valley of the rivulet. Two boulevards, H and I, forming projections beneath the defences of the fourteenth century, commanded the course of the river, and could cross their fire with the boulevard B, and the tower E. A boulevard was also raised on the eastern salient at K.

The faubourg had preserved its two parish churches, and a convent of Jacobins had been built at L, on lands bought by Saint Louis while the fief of La Roche-Pont was still directly dependent on the crown of France.

The abbey of Saint-Julien, O, had diminished its enclosure, and yielded a part of its estates. Houses arose in its ancient pleasance, whose perimeter had been somewhat altered. These habitations were within its liberties and belonged to the abbey, which granted them on lease.

At M, a parish church under the invocation of Our Lady had been built towards the end of the thirteenth century, when the lord of La Roche-Pont, wanting money, sold some lands—formerly belonging to the castle—for building. At N was the market-place. Three gates gave admission to the *cité:* one on the north, called Saint-Julien's gate; one on the east, Mill-gate; and the third on the south-west, called Castle-gate.

We must enter into some details respecting the new defences raised under Charles the Bold. Figure 49 presents a bird's-eye view of the northern boulevard, D, with the *cité* front in the background, its gate of the fourteenth century, and the two great corner towers.

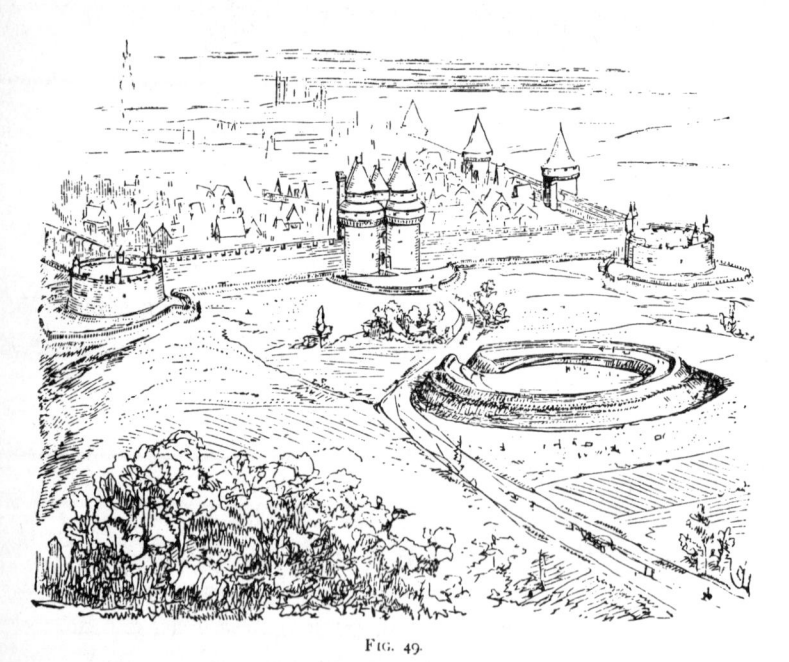

Fig. 49.

Fig. 50 A gives the plan of one of these towers at the level of the lower battery, and B its section through *a, b*.

These towers were forty yards in diameter on the outside, and consisted of a low battery, whose floor was six feet beneath the upper level of the plateau. The descent to this low battery was by a slope ending in an octagonal hall whose vaults rested on four great cylindrical pillars.

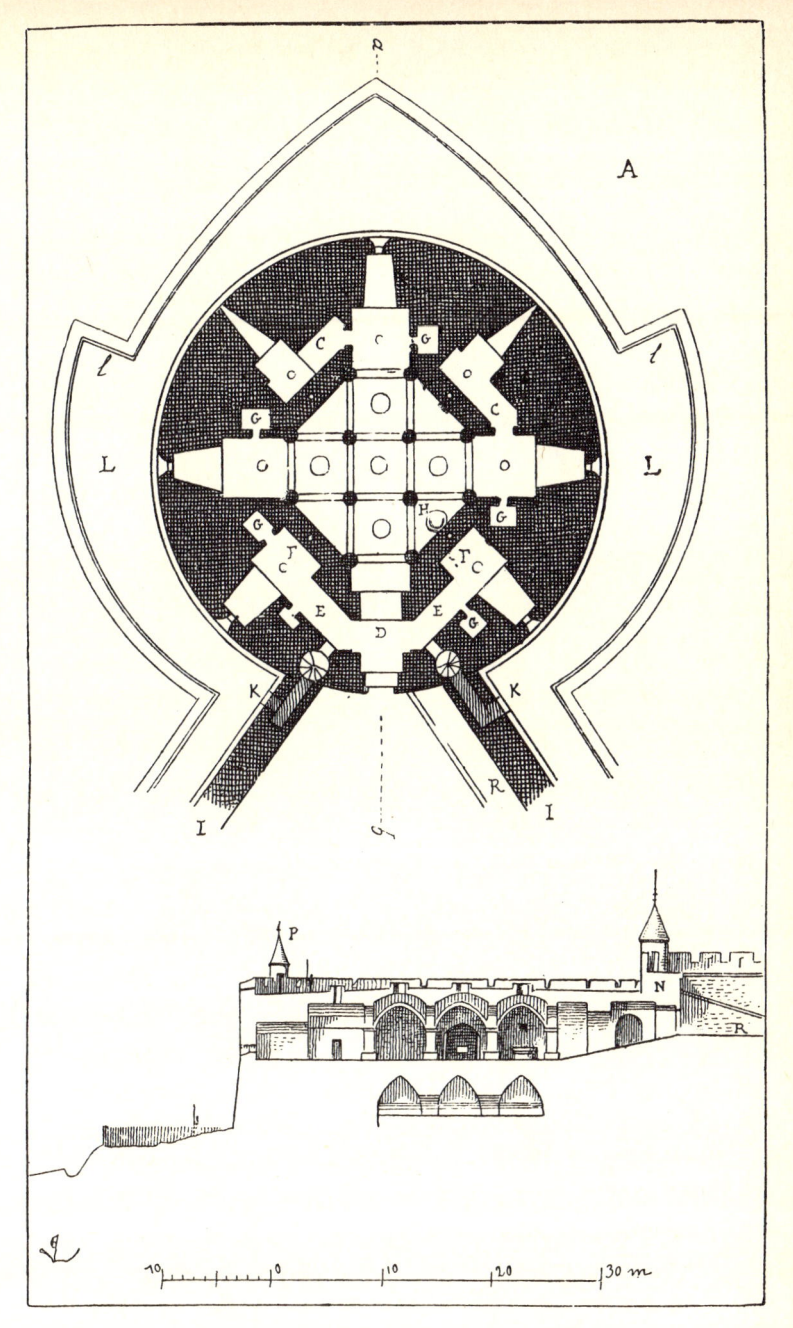

FIG. 50.—MASONRY TOWER FOR ARTILLERY.

Three chambers with embrasures for three large cannons opened into this hall. By the galleries, C, there was a communication between two of these chambers and two other smaller ones pierced with embrasures for culverins. From the descent D, two passages, E, gave access to two chambers, F, likewise arranged with embrasures to receive two large guns.

The barrel vaults of these rooms had openings to allow the smoke to escape. Small powder magazines, G, opened near each of the chambers, and five large lunettes pierced in the vaults of the central hall gave air and light to the interior. At H, a well was connected with a cistern constructed under the central hall, as indicated in section B. This cistern was supplied by rain-water falling on the platform and discharged by four pipes passing down through the inner walls. Two winding staircases connected the lower battery with the platform and the curtains of the fourteenth century, I I, and allowed of a descent through two posterns, K, into the braie, L, defended by an epaulement, a palisade, and narrow ditch. Flanks, *l*, raked the salient of this braie. The curtain, whose rampart walk rose six feet above the level of the platform, closed the gorge of the tower, as shown in section B at N. Two watch-towers, P, were built in the thickness of the parapet, pierced with nineteen embrasures for small pieces. This parapet was not too high for arbalisters to shoot over its slope. A wide incline, R, facilitated the getting up of guns and the ascent of men to the platform.

Fig. 51 presents a bird's-eye view of boulevard I,[1] with the ramparts of the fourteenth century. These boulevards were earthworks, and their interior surface was four yards below the level of the plateau. The boulevards, B and C, raised at the western angles of the castle, had their

[1] See the general plan, Fig. 48.

platforms on a level with the bottom of the ditch, as mentioned above. Having thus described the general plan and the details, we proceed to narrate the events of which the town of La Roche-Pont was the theatre in 1477 and 1478.

With a view to securing the aid of the Prince of Orange, after the death of Duke Charles, Louis XI. had been most

FIG. 51.

liberal to him in promises, one of which was that he would place in his hands all the strong towns of Burgundy that belonged to the estate of the Prince of Orange, his grandfather, and which Duke Charles had forestalled.

But when the Seigneur de Craon had taken possession of these places he would not give them up, notwithstanding the demands made upon him by the Prince, and the apparent orders of King Louis XI.

The marriage between the daughter of Charles the Bold, sole heiress of his domains, and Maximilian, Duke of Austria, took place in the meantime. The latter proceeded to recover possession of the duchy of Burgundy, and had a conference with the Prince of Orange, exasperated at the non-fulfilment of the promises made him; while the province was soon to a large extent roused against the French, whom the Seigneur de Craon, eager for gain, and by no means faithful in accomplishing his engagements, rendered detestable.

The Seigneur de Craon had left in the town of La Roche-Pont only a somewhat feeble garrison. At the instigation of the agents of Maximilian, who was filling the country with emissaries, the inhabitants barricaded themselves one evening in the streets, and attacked the French posts. The latter, small in number, and indifferently commanded, took refuge in the castle after having lost some soldiers. The castle was ill supplied with provisions and munitions. Surrounded by the townspeople, the garrison could not hold their position long; so that one night it escaped on the south side, passing right through the Burgundian posts to join the Seigneur de Craon's army near Dijon. The inhabitants immediately hoisted the Cross of Burgundy on the keep, and hastened to Maximilian to inform him of the success of the rising, and to ask assistance against a return of the king's armies; for they were scarcely in a condition to defend themselves. Maximilian sent them a body of twelve hundred Germans, Swiss, and Brabançons, with cannon, munitions, and engineers. The first thing these troops did on arriving was to commit some depredations in the environs and the western faubourg, after which they set about the defence of the place.

The Sire de Montcler had been invested with the command of the foreign troops and of those he was able to collect together in the town and neighbourhood. He was an active, enterprising, and rather shrewd man, of noble bearing and handsome countenance, in the prime of life, capable of enforcing obedience, and trusting to himself alone in getting his orders executed. He had soon decided on his plans.

The able-bodied population of the town amounted to about two thousand men, half of whom were in a condition to render effective service, and were accustomed to war. Some days after the arrival of the foreign troops, some Burgundian lords who favoured the young duchess, and were much incensed against the Seigneur de Craon—who, for no other reason than to get money, had plundered their estates and taken away their most valuable property—assembled at La Roche-Pont. They brought with them two hundred lances and some convoys of provisions. The effective garrison might therefore be said to amount to three thousand fighting men, of whom five hundred were horse—each lance being followed by an esquire.

The place was not in a good state of defence; the braies were much dilapidated, the earthen boulevards crumbling away, while the ditches wanted clearing out. No piece was mounted. There were neither gabions nor fascines nor stakes for palisades. The Sire de Montcler made the following arrangement:—All, whether captains, soldiers, pioneers, inhabitants of the town, men or women, were to go every morning before daybreak to the posts assigned them beforehand, on pain of death. And with a view to impressing this order on all, gallows were set up in the various wards, which bore the following names: Tower ward (on the North); Saint-Julien's ward (including the abbey and the eastern part of the *cité* opposite the monastery); Saint-Louis's ward (situated between the abbey and the castle, on the west); the Mill ward, looking towards the east. The tenants of the abbey had claimed exemption from the service, but the Sire de Montcler had paid no attention to their claims any more than to those of the abbot, whose gardens and buildings served as a central arsenal. Two or three obstinate burgesses had been hanged, and since then none had failed in his duty. At noon all went to dinner, and returned at two o'clock to work till nightfall. The women and the children from eleven to sixteen years of age carried earth in baskets and traies; and the soldiers, pioneers, and townsmen, under the direction of the engineers, began to restore the parapets of the boulevards, cleared out the ditches and restored the braies again. A sawing machine was established at the mill and cut wood to make palisades. In a few days the inhabitants, who had at first thought this very hard work and regretted having driven away the French garrison, had become habituated to this life of fatigue, and endured it quite cheerfully. Singing and laughing were heard in every quarter while the work was going on. It might have been supposed that they were engaged in a *fête*.

The governor had not overlooked the supply of provisions. It was the end of the summer. All the harvest produce of the neighbourhood had been ordered to be brought into the town. A pair of millstones, which were still available after the establishment of the saw-mill, was at work night and day. All the provisions stored in the houses were to be deposited in the abbey or the castle, on pain of death, and the inhabitants received their several rations like the soldiers. A large store of grain and vegetables laid up in the abbey considerably increased the supplies of provisions. The Sire de Montcler had of course laid hands on these provisions.

The old men and young children were occupied in making gabions and cutting turf for the taluses of the boulevards. Behind the north front the governor had a good

FIG. 2.

trench dug, demolishing some houses, with retrenchment and good gabionades on the flanks for artillery. The north wall of the abbey was terraced and united to the east curtain by a retrenchment with a ditch.

The Sire de Montcler was a good-humoured man, familiar with all, present everywhere and talking to everybody; and, thanks to his jocular and pleasant ways, the good people saw their houses demolished and the soil of their gardens taken away to make ditches and epaulements without being greatly distressed.

When everything was well prepared for the defence, however, the governor sent away all useless mouths. Women, children, and old men had to seek an asylum in the environs. After this, the western faubourg was burned to prevent its being occupied by the troops of Louis XI.

A *tête du pont* had been formed on the right bank outside the drawbridge (Fig. 52), with a large cavalier on the left bank; the two other bridges were destroyed. On the plateau towards the north arose, in front of the boulevard D,[1] an intrenchment of earth, with barricades of trees and large gabions screening two culverins. The boulevards and towers on the north were armed with bombards.

Every night the governor took care to reconnoitre the environs.

[1] See Fig. 48.

CHAPTER XII.

THE FIFTH SIEGE.

THE 4th of September, 1478, the army of King Louis XI. was reported by a company of horsemen to be half a day's march from the town. This army, consisting of five hundred lances and infantry, forming a total of about six thousand men, was commanded by Messire Charles d'Amboise, lord of Chaumont, a sage and moderate man, no plunderer as his predecessor had been, and as valiant a man of war as he was a clever politician.

Messire Charles d'Amboise was expecting a reinforcement of twelve hundred Swiss; for he had been able to push his interests so ably with some of the gentry of the Cantons by offering them attractive advantages, that they had resolved to furnish him with troops.

Besides the four florins and a half a month which he gave to each man, Messire Charles d'Amboise paid for this service twenty thousand francs to the cities of Berne, Lucerne, Zurich, Solerne, and twenty thousand to the private individuals who undertook the recruiting. For which consideration, a body of Swiss troops for the service of the king was to be raised, amounting to six thousand infantry.

The king's army took with it a good and powerful artillery, consisting of twelve large bombards, twenty-four spiroles, veuglaires and ribeaudequins, without reckoning fire-arms and the munitions for this ordnance. Thus accompanied it marched slowly and in good order, well guarded on its flanks.

Some of the Burgundian lords, with about forty lances, having wished to try the strength of the French previous to their arrival before the city, suffered for their adventurous spirit; for they left half their number on the field. The governor, therefore, commanded that no one should go out without his orders. The first troops of Messire Charles d'Amboise showed themselves at nightfall on the northern side of the plateau, just beyond the range of boulevard D[1], and began to install themselves, setting up between them and the town, mantelets brought on carts, and fixed with the help of stakes driven in the ground. When it became quite dark, the Sire de Montcler tried to attack them; but perceiving that this vanguard was efficiently sustained by a large body posted in the rear, he retired after a slight skirmish.

Next day, the 5th of September, Messire Charles d'Amboise sent some scouts into the lower town, and on the eastern side towards the mills, which he took without striking a blow, for they were not guarded. Immediately, some bombs were discharged at these mills, and the besiegers were obliged to abandon them for the moment, for at the second discharge one of the roofs fell in. The Sire de Montcler organized his troops as follows:—

In each of the four wards mentioned above, 200 armed men from the town were intrusted with the guard and defence of the ramparts . . .	800
There remained 500 Burgundian foot soldiers, among whom there were bombardiers and culvrineers	150
Skilled javelin men, archers, and arbalisters	250
Pioneers	100
The Germans who were not on friendly terms with the inhabitants were posted in reserve in the abbey, amounting to	800
And in the castle, amounting to	400
The men-at-arms, partly in the abbey	200
Partly in the castle	200
Partly in the neighbourhood of the gates	50
Total of force	2,950

---

[1] See Fig. 48.

It was evident that the garrison was not numerous enough to attempt sorties; it had already enough to do to guard its defences in presence of a besieging army amounting to nearly six thousand men; an army moreover which might receive reinforcements. The governor was clearly awake to the facts, and felt that he must economise his strength.

He resolved, therefore, to limit himself at least for the moment to an energetic defence; but this did not prevent him from sending messengers to Maximilian before the complete investment, to ask him to intervene and send a corps of relief, if he did not wish to see the place fall into the hands of the king of France, which would certainly happen if it were left to itself. But he added it would resist to the last, and he could answer for the disposition of the garrison.

On his side, Messire Charles d'Amboise seemed not to wish to precipitate matters; he hanged several soldiers who had been guilty of acts of pillage in the neighbourhood, and ordered that the dwellers in the suburbs should be considerately treated. By the evening of the 8th of September the town was completely invested. A body, consisting of three thousand two hundred men, remained encamped on the northern plateau, acting in conjunction with five hundred men posted among the ruins of the lower town, and three hundred men behind the walls on the lower slopes of the hills on the east.[1] Most of the cavalry occupied the right shore of the larger stream and the valley on the south. A body of about five hundred men blockaded the *tête du pont*, and had orders to seize it when a favourable occasion offered. That night some pieces of artillery were brought into position on the lower slopes of the eastern hills to command all the eastern declivity of the *cité*.

[1] See the topographical map, Fig. 1.

Some were assigned to the body of troops blockading the *tête du pont*.

The besiegers' artillery was thus disposed:—

	Bombards.	Veuglaires, Spiroles.
Attack on the northern boulevard	4	2
Battery on the slopes of the eastern hills	2	4
Before the *tête du pont*	...	4
On the western slopes of the plateau commanding the lower town	...	2
Park of reserve	6	12
Total	12	24

The artillery of the besieged consisted of:—

	Bombards.	Culverins.
On the platforms of the three great northern towers	3	3
In the casemated batteries of these towers	—	6
On the earthwork in front of the northern boulevard	—	2
On the northern boulevard	1	2
On the boulevards B, C, H, I, K	5	5
On the cavalier commanding the bridge	1	2
Reserve in the abbey and the castle	4	8
Totals	14	28

On the 10th of September the besiegers began a cavalier in form of a horseshoe, three hundred paces from the boulevard, E, towards the north-east, to rake its gorge at A (Fig. 53). This cavalier was armed with two bombards and a spirole. Northwards, on the side of the road, a second cavalier, B, was also provided with two bombards. Next was commenced an earthwork, running obliquely with traverses, to reach from this cavalier in a south-west direction as far as the edge of the plateau near the defenders' intrenchment C, D. The great boulevard, E, of the defence was armed with a bombard and two culverins, and two other culverins flanked the intrenchment C, D. On the morning of the 17th of September, the four bombards of the besiegers sent into the boulevard stone balls two hundred pounds weight, which very much damaged the gorge, and about noon dismounted the bombard and one of the culverins. The besieged had answered their fire as well as they could, both from the boulevard and the two great towers G, H. But it was only the balls of the

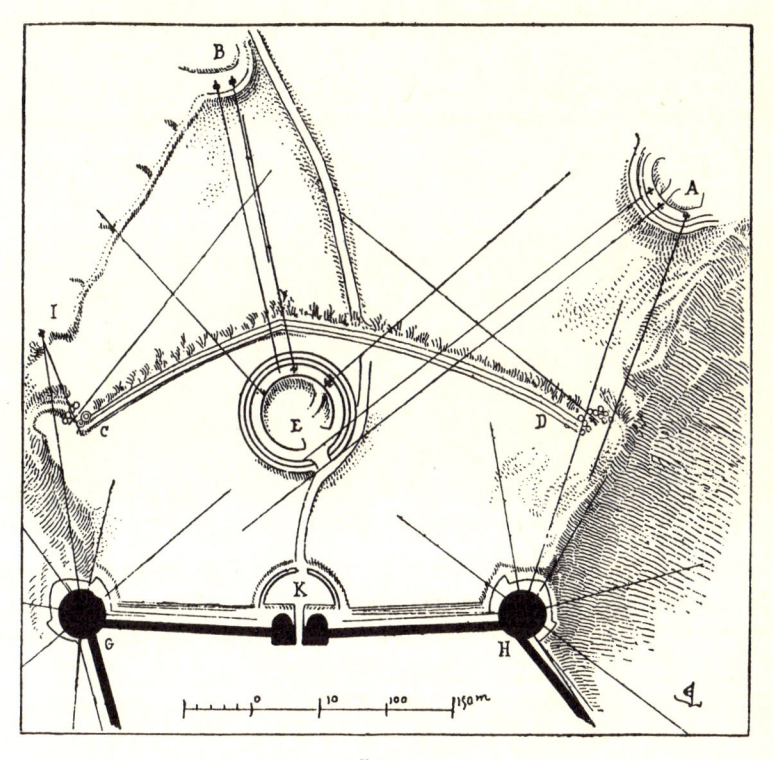

FIG. 53.

bombard mounted on the platform of the tower H, that reached the cavalier A. Those of the tower G only rolled as far as the slope of the cavalier B. The governor might have mounted other bombards on the boulevard E; but he was afraid of losing the pieces, and preferred reserving them for the defence at close quarters. On the 18th the besieger had terminated his earthwork as far as the point I, and there he brought up a veuglaire to dismount the flank culverin C. At this point some men were lost on both sides; for the besiegers sent among those engaged in the works large balls of stone and leaden bullets, fired from the bombards of the tower G, and from small cannon.

On the 18th of September, at daybreak, the bombards of the cavaliers, A and B, redoubled their fire on the boulevard; then Messire Charles d'Amboise, having massed a body of four hundred men at the point, I, sheltered by gabions and fascines put up during the night; at the word of command this body fell upon the flank, C, which was vigorously defended for an hour. After this the Sire de Montcler, observing that the besiegers were continually sending reinforcements to this point, withdrew his troops into the barbican, K, and the boulevard, E, which enabled the artillerymen posted in the tower, G, to keep up a brisk fire from their bombard and their small cannon upon the assailants.

From the boulevard, E, the besieged, in spite of the projectiles they received in their rear, sheltering themselves as best they could, discharged volleys of stones with their culverins on the point occupied by the enemy. The latter sought to avoid them by descending a short distance below the ridge of the plateau; but they were none the less exposed there to the fire from the tower, G. They brought up gabions and fascines, and endeavoured to gain a footing on this flank, not without some loss, when about three o'clock in the afternoon another attack was contrived against the flank, D. Passing round the end of the intrenchment, and hastening with all speed along the slopes, the enemy attempted to take the defenders in the rear. This attack was unsuccessful. Those who served the bombards and culverins of the tower, H, seized the right moment for discharging volleys against this column of assailants, which made deep lanes in the battalions. These, moreover, who were retired within the barbican, precipitated down the slopes those of the enemy who had already passed beyond the intrenchment; and the struggle ceased towards evening, the besieger occupying the point C alone, without being able to advance. He was endeavouring to find shelter there, both against the projectiles and against any attack in retaliation. The citizens had lost only a few men and a culverin. The enemy reckoned one hundred and fifty dead, and a large number of wounded.

During the night the Sire de Montcler brought up fascines, casks, and timber *débris* with which he raised a barricade connecting the barbican with the boulevard along the road, and a second connecting the eastern extremity of the intrenchment, D, with the fausse-braie of the tower, H, along the ridge of the plateau. He brought up one of the reserve culverins, and mounted it in the centre of the first barricade, then, with gabions, he strengthened the shelters and parados of the boulevard. The bombard was remounted as well as it could be, and directed against the point, C, of the intrenchment. And a second bombard was brought from the abbey to the platform of the tower G.

On his side, Messire Charles d'Amboise had not remained inactive. At the point, I, an earthwork was raised with gabionades, and two bombards were brought thither. The point captured was strengthened by great gabions, all covered with fascines, and well furnished with small cannon. These works were scarcely terminated when the day broke (September 19th). It was the besieged who began to direct the fire of their bombard from the boulevard, E, against the point C.

Immediately one of the bombards from the platform, I,

replied, while the other discharged balls on the tower G, whose pieces were not slow in responding. Then the bombards of the cavaliers A and B joined in as on the previous day. The fire of these five pieces, converging at once on the boulevard, soon threw down the gabionades, killed most of the artillerymen, and dismounted the bombard a second time. This defence was no longer tenable. However, the governor would not yet abandon the advanced work: protecting his men as best he could along the interior slopes, he sent for five hundred Germans held in reserve in the abbey, and when duly marshalled, at a signal agreed upon, all the pieces of the tower G, the culverins of the barricade, and another culverin that had remained in battery on the boulevard, fired at once on the point C; and immediately putting himself at the head of the Germans and one hundred volunteers, among whom were most of the Burgundian men-at-arms, crossed the barricade and charged the enemy's position, who, surprised by this bold attack, defended themselves but feebly, and were partly driven on the slopes of the plateau. Messire Charles d'Amboise, who was on the platform I, seeing this rebuff, threw two large battalions, held in reserve behind the earthwork, against the intrenchment between the point C and the boulevard.

His men crossed the obstacle quickly enough, in spite of the barricade and the defenders posted at this point, and attacked the troop of the besieged in flank and in rear. In the midst of this *mêlée*, the artillerymen on both sides were prevented from firing; it was a combat with sharp weapons only. The Sire de Montcler found himself much jeopardised when, from the barbican and the boulevard, those who were on the field, although they had orders not to quit their posts, fell in their turn on the troop of besiegers. Immediately dividing his forces into two bodies, the governor was able with one to hold his ground against the assailants thrown on the slopes, and with the other to make head against the French, in their turn attacked on both sides.

The conflict was sanguinary. The besiegers, driven back against the intrenchment, could neither deploy nor manœuvre. Messire Charles d'Amboise sent a reinforcement, but the bombardiers of the tower G, at the risk of killing some of their own party, discharged stone balls and leaden bullets over the intrenchment at the fresh troops. Some well-aimed shots threw this battalion into confusion, as the soldiers could not see what was taking place in the interior, and were besides exposed to projectiles thrown by defenders mounted on the salient of the intrenchment. In fact the utmost these last comers could do was to facilitate the retreat of their comrades, which had become a very perilous one. The outwork was therefore recovered by the besieged—were they able to keep it?

Messire Charles d'Amboise saw that it was not prudent to hurry on an attack, and that in the face of a resolute garrison he must determine to proceed methodically. As the last rays of daylight faded the besiegers had all repassed the intrenchment conquered the day before, and were leaving on the field more than a hundred dead, wounded, and prisoners.

They had been obliged to abandon the culverin they had seized. The wounded were transported to the abbey and consigned to the care of the monks, who attended to them as well as to the wounded among the besieged. The prisoners were shut up in the castle, where they were well treated. Some Swiss were among them.

It was painful to the Sire de Montcler to abandon the outwork after this success; but it was evident that the besiegers would make new efforts to seize it, since the place was accessible only on that side, and many men must be sacrificed in retaining it. Now the garrison had suffered in the last struggle losses at least equivalent to those of the enemy; and these losses could not be repaired, while the troops of the king of France would be reinforced, if necessary. The Swiss prisoners, when questioned, had not concealed the fact that the enemy might reckon upon a fresh body of their own countrymen, five hundred in number, before long.

At nightfall therefore the governor assembled the captains of the various posts and the Burgundian lords, and spoke to them as follows:—" Gentlemen, our troops have displayed courage and intelligence in this day's struggle; and this assures us success, with the help of God. Though inferior to the enemy in numbers, we have defended and recovered the outwork; it would therefore be possible to keep it. Yet we cannot do so without directing all our means of resistance to this point, and imposing a severe task on the garrison. We should be rapidly exhausting our strength, while the enemy, which is much more numerous than we, can employ fresh troops every day. It would seem wise, then; to abandon this outwork, exposed to the batteries of the enemy, and to retire behind the ramparts; but besides the disinclination which men of honour must feel for retreating, after a success has been gained, and not trying to avail themselves of the advantages they have secured, there is the consideration that if we abandon the boulevard this defence will be turned against us by the besieger, and will support him in attacking our front. I have, therefore, resolved to unite this boulevard with the extremities of the curtains by two intrenchments, which will be flanked by the towers. This very night we must begin; and if we have not finished the works to-morrow morning we must defend our present intrenchment, that we may secure time to finish the new one. Be so good, therefore, as to assemble the townspeople in their various quarters within an hour, and let them be in readiness on the ground to work at the said intrenchments."

Fig. 54

The orders of the governor were peremptory, and about nine o'clock four hundred workmen, and even women, issued by the north gate to raise the earthworks marked out on the ground by the engineer (Fig. 54). This intrenchment consisted of a small ditch with an earthwork surmounted by stakes, rubbish from the demolition of houses in the town, fascines, and barrels filled with earth. On the western side it started from the boulevard at N, and joined the fosse of the curtain at L, leaving a passage of twenty-four feet between its extremity and the ditch. On the eastern side it reached the entrance of the boulevard O, and followed the line O M, with a similar passage at M. At R and P two culverins were mounted, protected by strong gabionades. On the enemy's side an embankment, with platform and gabions, had been raised at S, and the two bombards of the cavalier, B, were mounted on this platform. At T, Messire Charles d'Amboise had placed a culverin, protected by a gabionade.

The bombards of the cavalier B were replaced by three veuglaires to crush the battery S, if the besieged, taking the offensive, endeavoured to seize it.

On the morning of the 20th of September the works of the besieged were almost completed, or at any rate were high enough to present an obstacle to the assailant. The boulevard, E, had been well furnished with fascines and gabions that very night. The bombard, remounted, swept the point C, and the two culverins the exterior. The intrenchment, C D, was strongly occupied by the defenders at the break of day with small cannon and powerful catapults. The barricades on the flanks, V and X, were strengthened. The Sire de Montcler sent two hundred men to the boulevard, E, with orders to keep under cover as far as possible, and to use their weapons only in case of the intrenchment being forced. The attack commenced about six o'clock. The two bombards, S, discharged stone balls on the salient of the intrenchment and on the boulevard; at the same time the two pieces, I and T, directed their fire on the epaulement, C, and the interval, S T, was occupied by arbalisters and men who served the small cannon under cover of mantelets. From the cavalier, A, the bombards continued to discharge balls broadcast on the boulevard E, as on the previous days. From the platform of this cavalier A, Messire Charles d'Amboise had observed the intrenchment which the besieged had raised during the night; he therefore resolved to bring all his efforts to bear on the salient and the boulevard. With this view, about eight o'clock, he brought up two culverins at Y, which, protected by gabions, were also made to do duty. The besieged replied only with their small cannon and the two culverins of the epaulements, C and D, and their arbalisters. They were husbanding their fire for the moment of assault. At noon, the salient of the intrenchment was broken down, and the escarpment of the boulevard was greatly damaged. The defenders were driven from their position at Z; their culverin, C, was dismounted, and the western epaule rendered untenable. They dispersed or took refuge along the intrenchment from Z to D, which was less exposed. The Sire de Montcler gave orders to return within the second intrenchment. They brought away the culverin D, which was mounted at the extremity L; but they were obliged to leave the piece C after having spiked it. As soon as Charles d'Amboise saw the besieged abandon his intrenchment he ceased firing, and, having marshalled an assaulting column furnished with ladders, poles, and cutlasses, ordered it to cross the ruined salient and assault the boulevard without giving the enemy breathing time. This was the moment for which the commandant was waiting. As soon as he saw this column begin to move and pass the intrenchment, he directed upon it a simultaneous fire from the pieces of the two towers G and H, the two culverins mounted on the boulevard, and all the small cannon. The assaulting column, thus taken obliquely and in front, hesitated and fell back; when it was greeted by a shower of crossbow bolts from the ramparts of the boulevard. It rallied, however, behind the battery S, which discharged a volley upon the boulevard, and, turning slightly on its right so as at least to shelter itself from the fire of the tower H, it passed the intrenchment once more and threw its scaling ladders on the escarpment of the boulevard. The defenders sustained the assault resolutely. The tower, G, then began to fire on the assailants as well as the culverins brought up at L and P.

The besiegers suffered severe losses. On two occasions some of their number reached the parapet, but could not hold their ground. They did not fall back, however; and most of them heated by the fight, not obeying or not hearing the voice of their captains, advanced along the new intrenchment N L, hoping to force it, for it was but weak. In fact, in a few moments this defence was passed, and the assailants then endeavoured to take the boulevard by the gorge. The defenders posted between C and M seeing themselves taken in rear, took refuge, some in the boulevard and others in barbican K. A hand to hand fight began in this triangle. In this *mêlée* the garrison dared not shoot from the curtain. The Sire de Montcler, who was in the barbican, then put himself at the head of his men and encouraged them by saying that the enemy was taken in a snare from which he could not escape; he sallied forth in good order, driving the scattered assailants before him as far as the gorge of the boulevard, which was crowded by the defenders, crying "Burgundy! Burgundy!" (Fig. 55). The works of this boulevard were commanded by a cool-headed captain, who was able to prevent his men from being disturbed by the struggle going on behind them; and who maintained

FIG. 55.—ASSAULT ON THE BOULEVARD.

his ground against the assault—now diminishing in vigour—issued from the gorge, and rallying all the panic-stricken soldiers who were massed together at this point, rushed on the enemy. The French were then obliged to retreat as best they could, not without leaving many of their men on the field. But it was evident that the boulevard P could hold out no longer. Surrounded by the enemy's fire, and the outer intrenchment taken, a fresh assault would place it in the power of the enemy. Its parapets were ruined, and its three pieces disabled. All night the besiegers occupied both sides of the intrenchments N, L, O, M and kept up an incessant fire to hinder the besieged from reinforcing this defence. The Sire de Montcler determined, though with regret, and only to avoid a useless sacrifice of life, to give the orders required for bringing back into the town such pieces of ordnance as were still serviceable. He was obliged to abandon the bombard, of which indeed the besiegers could make no use. Two of the five culverins were placed on the platforms of the great towers, and the three others on terraces raised behind the curtain, together with three pieces taken from the reserve.

On the morning of the 21st of September, the besiegers found the outwork abandoned; but in occupying it themselves they were exposed to the fire of the two great bombards of the towers and of ten culverins, which did not cease to fire on the boulevard and the intrenchment.

Towards evening, however, they had succeeded in opening a wide breach in the boulevard, opposite the gorge, and inclosing the latter. They were occupied all night in restoring its slopes and parapets in front of the town, and raising platforms and mounting three bombards on the boulevard.

At the two epaulements of the intrenchment C, D they

raised two gabioned cavaliers, and placed a bombard and two veuglaires on each of them.

On the 21st of September, these works having been terminated by noon in spite of the fire of the besieged, one of the bombards of the boulevard discharged its stone balls at the gate, the two others at the two towers. At the same time the veuglaires of the cavaliers fired on these towers with iron balls and the bombards with their stone balls. These projectiles left only feeble traces on the masonry, but often threw down the gabionades and the parapets, and dismounted the pieces (Fig. 56).[1]

This artillery fight lasted till evening; on both sides pieces had been dismounted or were silenced; and the whole of the night was employed both by besieger and besieged in replacing the cannon on their repaired carriages or in bringing up new pieces.

Messire Charles d'Amboise was irritated; the affair was advancing but slowly. He had already received pressing letters from the king; for Louis XI. was afraid that a prolonged resistance would determine the other parts of Burgundy which had remained faithful to the court of France, to declare for the young duchess. He knew that emissaries of Maximilian were going through the province and endeavouring to persuade the authorities of the great towns that the king's army was feeble and disheartened; seeing that, in spite of formidable artillery, twenty days had not enabled it to make any impression on the little city of Roche-Pont.

Although the besiegers concentrated their fire, the number of pieces mounted by them was inferior to that of the cannon of the besieged. The stone balls of the bombards did no great damage to the defences. Messire Charles

[1] In this figure the lines at the top indicate the works occupied by the besieger and the direction of his fire.

FIG 57.

FIG. 56.

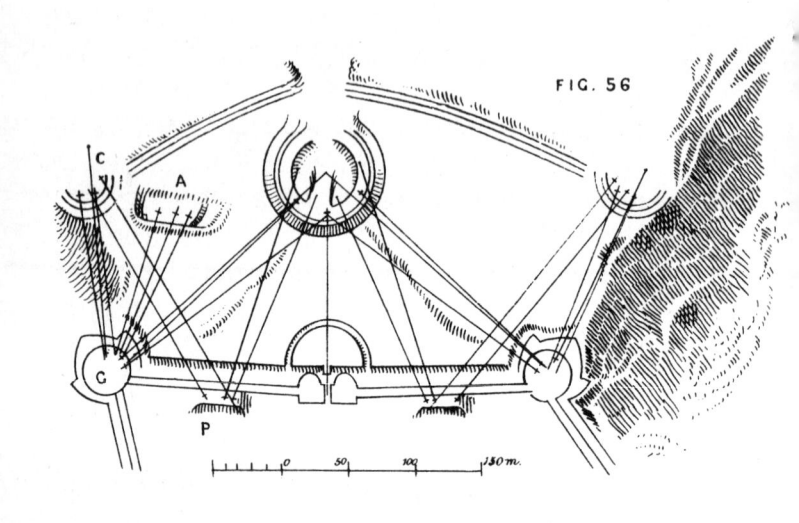

ATTACK ON THE OLD FRONT.

d'Amboise, therefore, during the night intervening between the 22nd and 23rd, raised a cavalier at A, strongly gabioned and terraced, and armed it with three large culverins. On the morning of the 23rd of September the corner tower, G, received the fire of five pieces loaded with iron ball and of a bombard discharging stone balls. After two hours' fire all the defences of the platform were knocked down and the three pieces dismounted, the embrasures of the tower battery shattered, and the defenders killed or wounded. Then orders were given that the tower should be fired upon only by two pieces from the cavalier C; and the fire of the three culverins of the cavalier A, and the three bombards of the boulevard, concentrated their fire on the gate and its barbican. Towards the end of the day this fine gate presented the appearance shown in Fig. 57. In the evening the besieger's pieces that had not been dismounted—that is to say, two culverins of the battery A, a veuglaire of the cavalier, and one of the bombards of the boulevard—concentrated their fire on the terrace P, of the besieged.[1] By evening the wall was dismantled, the gabionades tumbled down, and only one of the three culverins was available. However there was no breach, and an assault could not be attempted.

The Sire de Montcler decided that he must at all risks retard the besieger's progress if he could do nothing more. He reckoned that in two days the enemy would be able to effect a breach, either by his cannon or by mining, and that then the *cité* must be taken; for the garrison could not long hold out behind the interior retrenchments. In the cannonade of the preceding days the Sire de Montcler had lost but few men, and his reserve force had not been drawn upon. He therefore got them under arms about

[1] See Fig. 56.

nine o'clock, summoned a troop of one hundred well-
mounted horsemen, and gave the following orders:—The
hundred horsemen, accompanied by a hundred *coutilliers*
on foot, were to sally forth by the eastern gate against the
post established at the mills, attack the small encampment
installed in the meadows below, fall back by the road skirting the plateau on the east side, skirmish on the outskirts
of the French camp, or cut down the posts they came upon
on their way, and then return at full speed to the east gate.
A second body of a hundred foot soldiers was to be at
the cross road above the mills to protect their retreat.
During these attacks, designed to attract the enemy's
attention to the left, a troop of five hundred men on
foot would issue from a masked postern giving egress
below the front of the abbey on the west, and filing off
along the ramparts, vigorously attack the cavalier C, and
the battery A, spike the pieces, and do all possible damage.
It was to retire by the same way, protected by the western
ramparts.

Messire Charles d'Amboise was too experienced a warrior to fail in pushing his advantage. He knew that
success, especially in sieges, ultimately accrues to him
who leaves the enemy no repose, and does not fall asleep
when his first advantage has been gained. The north
front of the place was rendered powerless; but an energetic governor of a town may, in a single night, accu-
mulate many obstacles, devise a hundred stratagems, and
very greatly hinder the efficiency of an attack. Charles
d'Amboise had therefore resolved to have fascines conveyed to the ditch by a body of a thousand men, some
yards from the great tower of the corner G, and to
attempt an escalade, while the ordnance, firing on this
tower at discretion, hindered the defenders from fortifying
the platform again. He had observed the embrasure on

the flank of this tower raking the ditch, and had summoned a body of twenty men, furnished with mattresses, and pieces of wood to mask it. As regarded the *faussebraie*, that was ruined, and could not present any serious obstacle.

The Sire de Montcler had some reason to expect a night attack; but he intended to be beforehand with it, and crush it in the bud. "Whatever happens," he said to the troops ordered for the sorties, "act according to your instructions: do not allow yourselves to be diverted by any attempt at an assault; on the contrary, execute the orders given you to the letter. We are still numerous enough to sustain an attack."

At a quarter past ten the two detachments were in the act of issuing forth by the eastern gate and by the abbey postern. The governor then mounted the *débris* of the defences of the tower at the corner C, and attentively examined the attitude of the enemy. The fires they had lighted were no longer to be seen; but, on listening, he heard indistinct sounds along the works of the besieger. The sky was overcast, and drops of rain were in falling. The Sire de Montcler descended to the lower battery; all the embrasures fronting the exterior were in ruins, and all the pieces of ordnance covered with rubbish. The embrasure of the flank was intact, and the small piece with which it was furnished was in good condition. He had it loaded in his presence with nails and old iron, and gave orders to those serving it not to fire till they saw the enemy a few paces off; behind this piece he had a second placed similarly loaded, so that two volleys might be discharged one after the other. Then he went up again to the rampart walk of the curtain, and himself drew up his men, who were armed with long bills and good daggers and axes. He next visited the ruined gate.

It presented such a pile of rubbish that the enemy would not have been able to pass it in the night; nevertheless, in every corner he posted troops, with orders not to use their weapons till they found themselves face to face with the enemy, to observe absolute silence, and not to shout during the fight. This done, he placed a reserve of two hundred men behind the interior retrenchment, and fifty men, furnished with tarred bundles of straw, on the ridge of this retrenchment, with orders to kindle them when they heard the cry "Burgundy!"

About three-quarters past ten the Sire de Montcler again ascended the platform of the corner tower, and recognised the presence of the enemy some yards from the ditch. Notwithstanding the darkness, he could see a black mass deploying in silence; then he heard the fascines rolling into the fosse and the wood cracking under the men's feet. In a few minutes, about fifty ladders were set up against the curtain, and each of them was covered by the enemy. These ladders were provided with hooks at the top and stays along the sides, so that the defenders could not throw them down: two, however, fell, dragging the assailants with them.

At this moment the small pieces of ordnance on the flank of the tower fired, and the cries of the wounded resounded from the ditch, while three more ladders were broken and fell. The hosts of assailants surged over on the rampart walk, and at the cry of "Burgundy!" the fires having been kindled, the encounter with keen weapons in this narrow space presented the strangest spectacle.

The artillery of the besieged was then directed to the flank of the curtain and the exterior, from the platform of the corner tower; while shouts arose from this battery, and the five hundred Burgundians who were ordered to the sortie on the west began an attack, and the troops that were preparing to reinforce the assault turned their backs to the town to fall on this attacking body.

The Sire de Montcler heard shouting in the distance on the north-east side, and saw a bright gleam through the darkness. He then went down to bring his reserves to the curtain. The French, however, succeeded in getting to the top of the rampart, and reached the corner tower. The few men who were on the summit of the dismantled platform struggled bravely until the moment when the reserve sent by the governor, ascending the incline on which the artillery was posted, fell on the French, and drove them back to the rampart walk of the curtain. The assailants then forming in a column on the rampart walk, directed a vigorous attack against the tower. From the interior retrenchment, showers of bolts, arrows, and small-shot were discharged upon them in flank; and although they had bucklers, the French lost a great many. As the rampart walk was narrow, the head of the column could present only three men abreast, and was met by a compact mass of defenders. It was not advancing; the soldiers in the rear, who were exposed to darts in flank, were pressing on those before them in order to force the platform and fight. In this press many fell mutilated within the town. One of the culverineers of the tower, aided by a dozen men, had succeeded during the struggle in getting a culverin out of the rubbish and carrying it without its carriage, loaded, into the midst of the group of Burgundians defending the passage. Thrusting the mouth of the piece between their legs, he fired it: the ball, and the stones with which the bore of the culverin had been filled, made a frightful lane in the compact body of the French: some leaped down into the town, others ran towards the towers of the gateway, and several climbed the parapet to regain their ladders. The Burgundians made another rush along the rampart, killing all who resisted.

But at that juncture a large body of the French issued forth through the gate of the lower battery. By aid of pickaxes and crowbars they had succeeded, after filling up the ditch with fascines, in enlarging the openings of two of the embrasures, already broken down by the cannon; then, throwing into these openings lighted bundles of straw and tar mixed with gunpowder so as to drive away the defenders, they had made their way into the interior at the risk of being themselves suffocated by the smoke, and rushing towards the gate, killing the few that had remained in the battery, they had forced the doors and made an entrance for their comrades by the same road. Issuing forth into the town they ascended the incline at full speed.[1] The cry of victory on the part of the Burgundians was answered by cries of "France! d'Amboise!" These shouts revived the courage of the French who had remained on the rampart, and they renewed the attack. The Sire de Montcler despatched his last reserves against the new comers, but they continued to pour out on level ground and fought valiantly. Their number was increasing every moment, and they succeeded in driving back the reserves to the retrenchment. The Burgundians, cooped up on the platform of the tower, surrendered after having lost half their men. Messire Charles d'Amboise ordered that they should be honourably treated. The tower of the north-west salient was in the power of the enemy, as well as the whole of the curtain stretching from this tower to the north gate.

Day was breaking when the combat ceased, and some hours' repose were needed on both sides. The corner

[1] See Fig. 50.

tower was lost to the besieged; the governor strongly barricaded the adjoining tower opening on to the curtain, and placed a number of small cannon in the upper story of this tower. He had done the same on the broken summit of the western tower of the gate. He wished to hinder the enemy from gaining ground on the curtains, and outflanking—particularly on his right—the retrenchment connected with the old wall surrounding the abbey, and meeting the tower on the north-east corner.[1]

A short time before the end of the struggle, the two bodies destined for the sorties were on their return, the foot soldiers through the abbey postern, and the men-at-arms, not through the east gate, but through that near the castle on the west. The foot soldiers brought in a hundred prisoners; the horse had lost a third of their party. The fortune of these two bodies had been as follows :—The foot soldiers, operating on the left, had come upon the enemy unawares, making their way through the brushwood of the western slope of the plateau as far as the gorge of the enemy's battery, C,[2] had fallen on the guard, spiked the guns, and, taking advantage of the confusion, had taken the attacking column in flank, had entered the battery, A, whose pieces they had also spiked, but, seeing themselves too far advanced, had beat a retreat, descending the slopes straight towards the west. As they were not vigorously pursued, they had entered the lower town, surprised and captured two bodies of guards, set fire to some huts erected by the besiegers, and regained the town. Charles d'Amboise, at first surprised by the audacity of the attack, but quickly perceiving that it could do him no serious damage, had given the strictest orders that nothing should divert his men from the assault, and had contented himself with sending against the troops of the besieged two

[1] See Fig. 48.   [2] See Fig. 56.

or three hundred men to keep them back and compel
them to seek the slopes, without troubling to pursue them.
The men-at-arms had followed the governor's instructions,
had fallen upon the small encampment above the mills,
and, leaving the *coutilliers* there to complete their commission (the latter had re-entered about two o'clock in
the morning by the east gate), they had pursued the road
indicated as far as the base of the plateau, and had arrived without hindrance at the boundary of the French
camp, charging the posts in a direct line at full speed.

This attack had thrown confusion into that part of the
camp which was occupied by the baggage, the carts, and
camp servants. Stacks of forage had caught fire amid
the disorder thus occasioned. But the assailants had soon
observed three or four hundred horsemen close upon them;
they had then made straight for the north, and buried
themselves in the thick woods upon their right; they
next wheeled towards the left, reached the banks of the
stream, whose left bank they followed without interruption, but with the loss of a third of their comrades, who
had strayed, or been captured or killed. They supposed
they had fallen in with a body of the French in the lower
town, and were preparing to pass it at a gallop, but they
turned out to be the Burgundian foot soldiers.

Charles d'Amboise, at the first report of this attack
on the rear of the camp, had been much disquieted, supposing that succour had arrived; but being soon cor-
rectly informed, had sent out men-at-arms to cut off
this body of adventurers, and was only the more eager for
the assault.

Messire Charles d'Amboise was accustomed (in this respect differing from the warriors of the time) to surround
himself with young captains of intelligence and energy,
who kept him constantly informed of all that took place

in the army, during the march and on the field. When the information furnished was found to be exact, and was reported in cool discretion and without exaggeration, Charles d'Amboise would praise these young officers in presence of all his captains, and recompense them liberally. If, on the contrary, the reports were false or tainted with exaggeration, or incomplete, he would inflict severe and public censure on the reporters, and assign them some subaltern and humiliating duty, such as guarding the baggage or superintending the camp servants.

When Charles d'Amboise learned next morning the damage caused on the border of the camp by a few Burgundian men-at-arms, the loss of his men encamped at the mill and in the lower town, and the spiking of six of his pieces of ordnance, he was much annoyed, but could not refrain from saying to his captains: " We have to do with brave men, who defend themselves valiantly. I beg you, gentlemen, to take care that their wounded and prisoners be treated with all the respect due to soldiers who do their duty." Then about the second hour of the day he sent a herald to the retrenchment of the besieged, to ask a parley with the governor. The Sire de Montcler having ascended the terrace, the herald spoke as follows: "Sir Governor! Monseigneur Charles d'Amboise, commanding the army of our lord the king of France, sends me to you to require of you to render up the town and castle of Roche-Pont, which you are withholding contrary to the treaties and defending against their lawful lord. Henceforward the said *cité* is in the power of the army of our lord the king of France, and a longer resistance will only cause the useless loss of a great number of brave men. In consideration of your brave and noble defence, Monseigneur Charles d'Amboise will let you go forth—you and your men—with your lives and property. May God

have you in his keeping and guide you to a wise decision."
"Sir messenger," replied the governor, "Messire Charles
d'Amboise is a captain too well acquainted with war to
think himself master of the town and castle of Roche-Pont
because he has got possession of a tower and a curtain.
He knows what it has cost him to advance even so far;
and there is still a considerable space between this retrenchment and the castle, and the castle is good and
defensible. I acknowledge no other lawful lords of Burgundy, and of this city in particular, than the Duchess
of Burgundy, daughter of the noble and puissant Duke
Charles, and her illustrious husband Maximilian. I am
here to defend their property against all comers, and I
will defend it as long as I have a sword in my hand.
Nevertheless, tell Messire Charles d'Amboise that if he is
willing to exchange prisoners, man for man, I am prepared
to do so. If he prefers to leave things as they are, I give
him my word of honour that his people are being well
treated."

"Well, then," said Charles d'Amboise, when the herald
had conveyed this answer to him, "this *cité* will be
damaged for a long time to come!"

During the 24th of September, the rain did not cease to
fall in torrents. Besiegers and besieged were at a hundred
paces from each other. They were employed in burying
the dead, whose numbers were especially great on the
side of the French, and both were preparing for a fresh
struggle, though the bad weather greatly impeded the
workers. Figure 58 shows the position of the besieged
and the besiegers.[1]

After the losses sustained since the commencement of
the siege, the garrison scarcely reckoned more than two

---

[1] The black lines show the part of the defence still occupied by the besieged, the grey-tinted lines the parts gained by the besiegers.

FIG. 58.

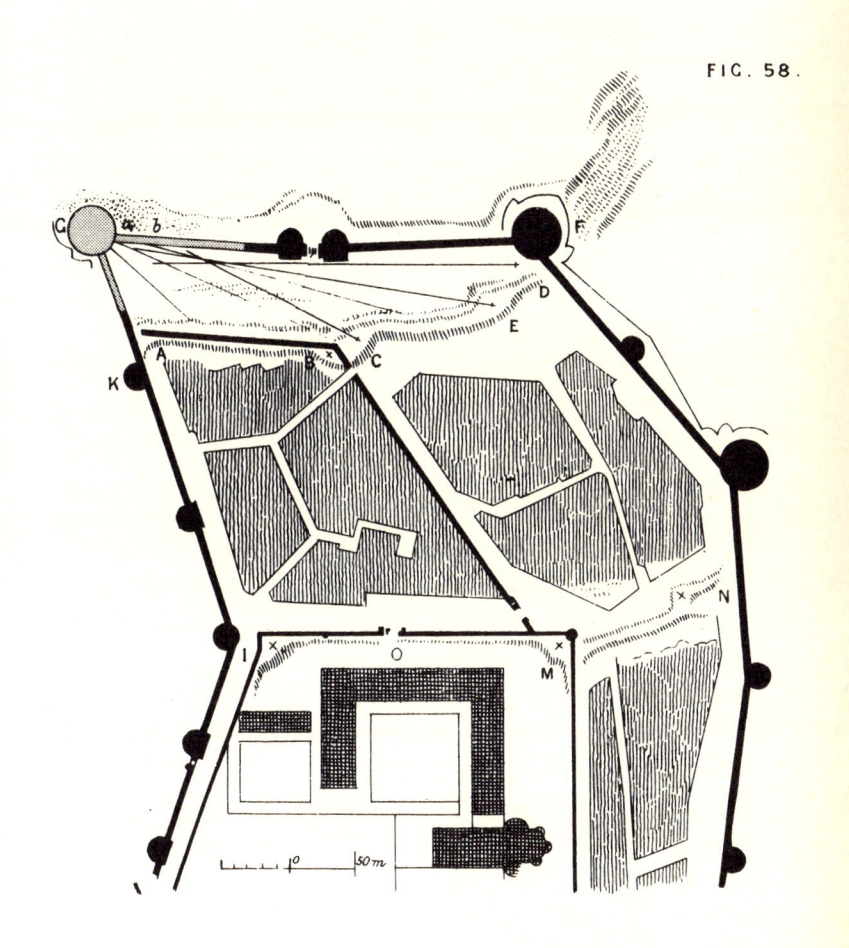

TAKING OF AN ARTILLERY TOWER.

thousand available men, for typhus was already devastating the town; three-fourths of the wounded crowded together in the abbey were attacked by it. The good monks tended them with their utmost care, but they themselves were largely sacrificed to the contagion; and of a community of a hundred and fifty in number scarcely more than fifty survived. The progress of the besieger, however, seemed only to increase the determination of the inhabitants, and the women worked heartily at the defences. They were the first to cry shame on those of the defenders who manifested despondency.

During the night between the 24th and 25th, the Sire de Montcler strengthened the retrenchment. From A to B[1] he took advantage of the ancient enclosure-wall of the abbot's pleasance, then occupied by dwellings. A culverin was mounted on a terrace at B. The retrenchment leading from C to D, which had been made of earth and the *débris* of the houses demolished at this point, was armed with three culverins at C, at E, and D.

The French on their side had cleared the platform of the conquered tower, G, had well gabioned the parapet, and mounted three pieces pointed at the retrenchment, and a spirole directed against the tower, K, which remained in the power of the Burgundians.

The women, children, and old men were employed in strengthening also the second retrenchment, I, M, behind the abbey wall, and the junction, M, N. This second retrenchment was armed with three pieces. Places of egress were reserved at the extremities and through the gate, O, of the abbey.

The rain continued during the 25th of September, which passed without any serious engagement. The combatants were trying one another's strength. The garrison was not

[1] Fig. 58.

numerous enough to allow of their leaving a post at the *tête du pont*. This work was abandoned on the night between the 25th and 26th, and the enemy entered it without striking a blow.

But as they were fired on by the bombard of boulevard I,[1] they did not advance along the ascent, but took shelter behind the cavalier of the left bank. The Sire de Montcler conjectured, however, that the French were preparing a real or feigned attack on this side.

During the night, thirty-six feet of the northern curtain, near the tower, G, fell into the ditch, reaching from *a* to *b*; the miners had been working for two days to accomplish this. On the morning of the 26th of September, the besiegers opened fire against the retrenchment. The dominant position of the tower, G, gave them a great advantage; and though the garrison did their best to reply, the culverins, C and D, were dismounted and the gabions thrown down about noon, when orders were given for the assault. A strong column of infantry advanced through the breach, *a b*, cutlasses in hand, and in fine order. But from the platform of the tower, F, which had remained in the power of the Burgundians, two culverins fired simultaneously on this column. Messire Charles d'Amboise supposed that the pieces in this tower had been silenced, and so they had been. But during the night, the Sire de Montcler had hoisted up three of the small pieces of the lower battery through the vault holes, and had masked them under the rubbish of the parapets. This discharge produced disorder in the column of the assailants. Fortunately for them, the pieces of the outer boulevard, in the power of the French, began to fire in their turn on the platform of the tower, P, and soon silenced the Burgundian spiroles.

[1] See Fig. 48.

The assault was vigorous, well directed and well sustained, while from without the French did not cease firing on the gate and tower F, so that those of the garrison who had remained in the upper works of the gate had to abandon them and escape by the curtain and tower F.

Messire Charles d'Amboise, standing on the breach, *a b*, was continually sending reinforcements to the assailants, and when he saw his people too fatigued he would replace them by fresh troops. The Burgundians had not enough men to do the like, so that about four o'clock they were exhausted, and some were beginning to file off along the ramparts. At length a vigorous effort forced the centre of the retrenchment, and the French pushed forward through the street running along the old wall of the abbey. The Sire de Montcler, however, retreated in good order in three columns, two along the ramparts, and the third by the road in the middle. When he saw his men sheltered behind the second retrenchment, he discharged the *pierrier* placed at M, and the culverin mounted at I, so that the assailants fell back in disorder. Then, followed by some brave men—his last reserve—he fell on the French coming along by the abbey and the western rampart. From the top of this rampart the assailants were also exposed to a shower of darts. Night was advancing: the brave men who had kept close to the governor were urging forward, attempting to recapture the first retrenchment. Many of the Burgundians who had retired behind the second retrenchment, seeing the enemy fall back, began to issue forth in their turn, filled with fresh ardour.

Messire Charles d'Amboise, however, was able to keep his troops at the first retrenchment, and had some small pieces brought up which fired on the groups of Burgundians who were still distinguishable in the torchlight.

The combat lasted thus for two hours more, in the midst of confusion, and the Sire de Montcler was obliged to sound the retreat several times to rally his troops.

In this engagement he had lost nearly five hundred men taken, killed, or wounded. About ten o'clock at night there was silence on both sides; the Sire de Montcler, retreating to the second retrenchment, sent back all his men who had remained on the ramparts beyond this retrenchment, and prepared to defend this last line vigorously—the castle being his only refuge should that be taken. But on reviewing his troops, he observed the absence of a body of five hundred Germans, whom he had posted in the abbey to protect the retreat of the defenders of the first retrenchment.

These Germans, seeing the unfavourable position of affairs, and taking advantage of the general confusion during the last struggle, had gone away through the abbey postern.

The governor had only a thousand men remaining. He endeavoured to persuade his men that the Germans were shut up in the castle by his orders; but few were deceived by this, for it was evident to all that after the taking of the corner tower the Germans scarcely cared to fight for a cause which had no great interest for them, and which they regarded as lost.

The fate of these runaways was, by the way, miserable enough. To support themselves they took to plundering in the outskirts, were surprised by a corps of French gendarmerie employed as scouts round the camp, and put to the sword or hanged as thieves. The few who succeeded in escaping perished under the blows of the peasants in arms against marauders.

It seemed hard to the Sire de Montcler to abandon his second retrenchment without awaiting an attack; so as he had scarcely any need to economise the provisions in the town, he had a double ration distributed to his men, and encouraged them by cheering words, preserving his animation in mien and gesture when among them. He told them that succour would soon arrive, and that if they resisted a few days longer Charles d'Amboise would be obliged to raise the siege.

Having examined the retrenchment, and posted men in the houses behind and in the northern building of the abbey, the Sire de Montcler was preparing to take some repose, when he was informed that along the slopes, above the bridge, the sentinels posted on the boulevards thought they perceived some movement on the part of the enemy. He went immediately towards that quarter, and saw in effect a black mass that appeared to be advancing up the slope like the rising tide, opposite to the boulevard, B.[1]

To summon the garrison of the castle and to draw them up in this boulevard—they were only two hundred in number—required only a few minutes. The escarpment of this boulevard, whose platform was on the level of the castle ditch, rose but slightly above the acclivities (about twelve feet). Before the assailant had placed his ladders, the governor fired on that moving mass, which the darkness of the night did not completely hide from view. The balls from the culverin and the bombards made furrows among them; shouts were heard, and the assailants, separating into two columns, set up their ladders on the two flanks of the boulevard.

Nearly at the same instant the second retrenchment was vigorously assaulted, and to facilitate this night attack, the assailants set fire to the houses between the first and second retrenchment. Thus, having the fire at their back, they could clearly see the defenders, while the latter were

[1] See Fig. 48.

blinded by this mass of flame, whence the French seemed to issue like black shades. The Sire de Montcler was hastening on horseback from one point of attack to another, cheering on his men, and exposing himself to the projectiles ; and both the attacks were well sustained. From the abbey building the arbalisters and bearers of small cannon inflicted very serious loss on the assailants, who, despairing of forcing the retrenchment at this point, were moving towards the junction, M N.

It was evident to the brave governor that the place was lost, and that nothing was left for him to do but to rally the remains of the garrison in the castle, if he could reach it. But he was determined that this retreat should cost the enemy dear. He therefore sent a reserve which he was keeping in the abbey to reinforce the defenders of the boulevard, B.[1] This reserve consisted of a hundred men at most ; but they were brave fellows ; their orders were to defend the boulevard at all cost, and if they were outflanked to return into the castle as soon as possible, to raise the bridge, and not let it down again till they saw him return with the remains of the garrison through the enemy, through whom he would force a passage.

Then he took up his position resolutely at the head of the *débris*, which still defended the retrenchment, and, availing himself of the houses and the abbey walls, he gave way only step by step, obliging the enemy to besiege every house and every enclosure, and taking advantage of the lanes and passages to resume the offensive, and inflict losses on the French. Exasperated by this, the latter set fire to the houses which they could not break open. The abbey resisted for more than two hours after the besieger had taken the retrenchment. The defenders, seeing their retreat cut off, fought with

[1] See Fig. 58.

desperation; for the postern was occupied outside by a large body of men. The church and the principal buildings were in flames.

The Sire de Montcler maintained the struggle in the streets and houses of the town till daybreak, and then debouched with four or five hundred men who remained to him in the open space before the castle. He found it almost entirely occupied by the enemy, whom some brave men were still resisting.

He rallied this greatly diminished body, and entered the castle, whose bridge was immediately raised. The town was taken, but much damaged, as Messire Charles d'Amboise had predicted. He gave the strictest orders to stay the flames and stop pillage, and to save the lives of the unarmed inhabitants. But there were many victims. The wounded and sick shut up in the abbey had perished in the flames; women, old men, and children, were lying on the pavement and in the houses. The 27th and 28th of September were spent by the French in re-establishing order among the troops after the combat of the night, in removing the wounded and burying the dead. Messire Charles d'Amboise, during the two preceding days, had lost a thousand men; he was anxious to end the struggle. During the night of the 28th, therefore, he had twelve pieces of ordnance brought up in front of the castle, provided them with gabionades, and once more sent a herald to summon the garrison to surrender.

The reply was that the garrison would not surrender till it saw itself incapacitated from continuing the struggle.

On the morning of the 29th the twelve pieces began to open fire against the defences of the gate. The besieged could only answer the attack with small pieces mounted on the summit of the towers. But in the evening all these summits were dismantled, the roofs pierced, and the machicolations destroyed.

Moreover, in the course of the 30th of September and 1st of October, four large bombards were mounted in front of the outer tower of the gate. In the evening this tower was falling in ruins into the ditch.

Messire Charles d'Amboise, before commencing the assault, again proposed to the governor to capitulate. The latter then appeared on the ruins, and declared that he would surrender the castle on condition of being allowed to quit it with his troops, their lives and baggage being spared, and with colours flying, and to go wherever they chose.

Charles d'Amboise on his side, then came forward on the breach, and gave his word of honour that these conditions should be granted. The two captains then approached and held out their hands to each other.

The city and castle of Roche-Pont were again subjected to King Louis XI. The Sire de Montcler had but five hundred fighting men left; and even of these there were a full third wounded. Messire Charles d'Amboise gave them a safe-conduct, ordered that they should be supplied with provisions, and entertained the Sire de Montcler and his captains at his table. Two days afterwards they took their departure for Flanders with the foreign troops that were still with them.

CHAPTER XIII.

THE CITÉ OF LA ROCHE-PONT IS FORTIFIED BY ERRARD DE BAR-LE-DUC, ENGINEER TO THE MOST CHRISTIAN KING OF FRANCE AND OF NAVARRE.

IN 1606, Henry IV. had succeeded in subjugating the religious and feudal factions that had imperilled France for more than thirty years. He cherished great designs which his skilful policy, his patriotic soul, his military talents and the advantageous alliances he was able to form, promised to render successful. But Henry IV. left nothing to chance, and would not embark in any enterprise after his accession to the throne, till he had made every preparation to insure its success.

When he saw the moment arriving at which he could effectually intervene in the affairs of Germany—a part of which had its eyes directed to France, and was only waiting for a signal from the Louvre to escape from the incessant rivalries of the princes and from religious contentions —he took measures not only to facilitate a successful intervention abroad, but to strengthen his frontiers and establish depôts and centres for provisioning his troops. Assured of the good-will of the Swiss and tranquil as regarded Italy—thanks to the alliances he had formed in that Peninsula—and wishing to act at once in the east, and on the Pyrenean side, he turned his attention to the defences of Roussillon and of the line which unites Burgundy with Champagne.

Henry IV. had been engaged in partisan warfare; but then he had only his own life at stake. As a sovereign he thought it his duty not to run risks; and before launching into the great enterprises he had in view, and which might change the face of Europe, he wished to put fortune on his side as far as possible. For more than six years, in concert with Sully, he had lost not a day or an hour in preparing for France, which had been a prey to civil war and invasion at the end of the sixteenth century, a future of the noblest order, and which might have secured to it the most honourable destiny, if the hand of an assassin had not in a single day destroyed hopes founded in a wise policy and the most thoughtful foresight.

This prince knew by experience that in war a check is always possible, even when fortune is, or seems to be, entirely on our side, and that the talent of a general consists in his ability to discover new resources after a reverse. Success in arms is secure in proportion to the foresight exercised in preventing a first reverse from becoming a disaster. Henry IV. therefore set about preparing a good line of retreat and supply in the rear of the army, which he was intending to lead in person towards the east. He put in a state of defence the towns and important strategic points from Châlons-sur-Saône, passing through Beaune, Dijon, Langres, along the course of the Haute-Marne, and from Langres to Chaumont, Saint-Dizier, Châlons, Reims, Laon, Péronne, and Amiens. Verdun and Metz had been visited by him, with a view to examining their defences. At Metz he had ordered works of considerable importance. The town of La Roche-Pont was comprised in that portion of this line of defence which lay between Dijon and

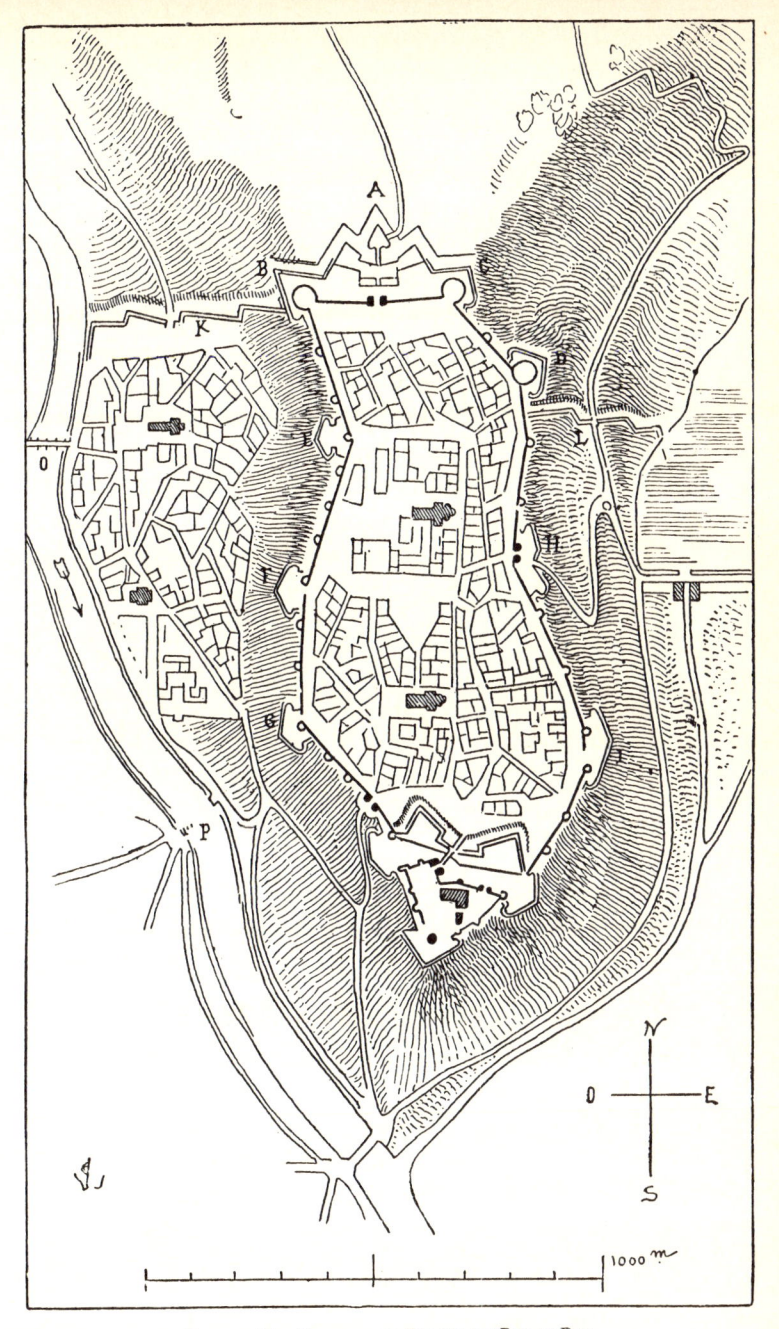

FIG. 59.—THE BASTIONS OF ERRARD DE BAR-LE-DUC.

Langres. The engineer Errard de Bar-le-Duc had been entrusted with these operations, beginning with Châlons-sur-Saône. He had, we may observe, merited the confidence reposed in him by the king, for he had given proofs of considerable ability and ingenuity.

Errard de Bar-le-Duc made use of the ancient walls, considering them suitable for defence at close quarters; but he constructed works outside which would command the country, and force the besieger to commence his operations at a distance of one thousand or one thousand two hundred yards. The system of boulevards was still maintained, but these, instead of presenting only an isolated obstacle, defended each other by crossing their fire, and were, in fact, true bastions.

The three great round towers on the north of the *cité* of La Roche-Pont were then much dilapidated. Errard had them terraced, and then surrounded them with earthworks with walled escarpments. Towards the plateau fronting the north he had a great tenaille constructed with a double ditch and ravelin. Fig. 59 gives the plan of the *cité* after the operations planned by Errard. Besides the works just mentioned, indicated at A, B, C and D, the king's engineer raised the bastions, E, F, G, H, and I, which crossed their fires, and whose orillons masked small pieces designed to flank the old ramparts.

Most of the old towers were lowered and terraced to receive cannon. The ancient castle, of which little more than the donjon and some outbuildings remained, was surrounded by a bastioned enclosure, with a tenaille on the town side.

The lower town, towards the west, though reduced to narrow dimensions, continued nearly in the condition already described. As to the upper town, after the conflagration of the last siege, it had been rebuilt in a very indifferent style. Under Francis I., the abbey had been secularised, and its ancient church was served by a Chapter. The old stone bridge near the outflow of the rivulet still existed, and at O was a second wooden bridge connecting the two shores. The bridge, P, had fallen into ruins and had not been rebuilt.

From the bastion, B, to the river, and from the bastion, D, to the pool, Errard built two fronts, K and L, *à crémaillères*,[1] to command the slopes of the plateau on the

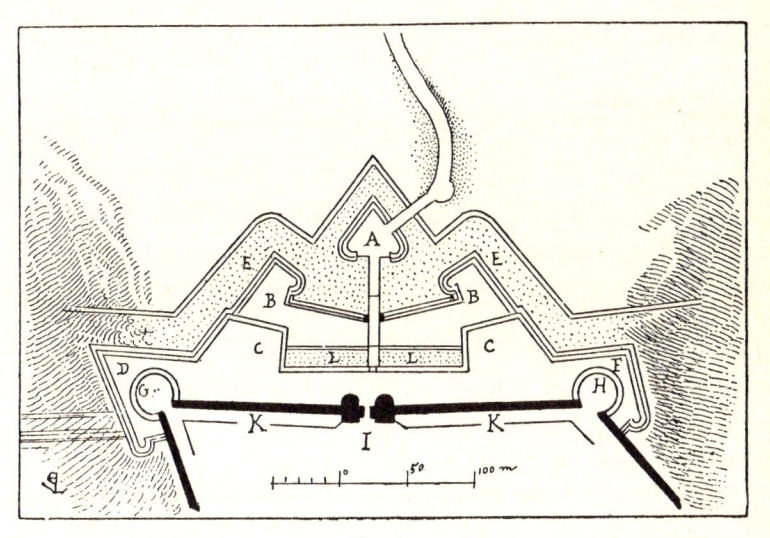

FIG. 60.

right and left, and to hinder an assailant from occupying a position on the east and west flanks of the *cité*.

For the time, these works appeared strong, and the axiom in fortifications, "What offers itself as a defence ought to be defended," was already pretty generally adhered to. Fig. 60 gives the northern work which was destined to

[1] In plan not straight, but broken by a series of returns each in advance of the other.

sweep the plateau, and to render difficult the approach to the cité on this its very accessible side. This work consisted of a ravelin, A, whose height above the level of the plateau was not more than six feet; next of a first tenaille, B, with orillons, eighteen feet above the plateau, and a second tenaille, C, three feet above the level of the tenaille, B. Two bastions, D and F, enveloped the two great towers, G and H, which were terraced. The platforms of the latter

FIG. 61.

rose three feet above the platforms of the bastions. The gate, I, of the fourteenth century, had been preserved and repaired, and the curtains, K, terraced to receive cannon.

The road passed over the right face of the ravelin, and thence at right angles to the centre of the tenailles.

A wide fosse, E, protected the exterior works, and a second fosse, L, the curtain of the second tenaille.

Fig. 61 gives a sketch in perspective of the bastion, F.[1] No use, however, was made of these defences till about thirty years after their construction.

[1] Of the general plan, Fig. 59.

CHAPTER XIV.

THE SIXTH SIEGE.

ABOUT the beginning of July, 1636, France, governed by the Cardinal de Richelieu, saw its northern frontier invaded by the too celebrated Jean de Weert, with an army of Hispano-Belgians, to which the empire had added a numerous body of cavalry, composed of Poles, Hungarians, and Croats. These allied troops advanced into Picardy, and Paris was, for the moment, anticipating a siege; but the enemy were delayed by the siege of Corbie, and, having taken this town, in which they left a garrison, they retired for fear of being taken in rear by the Dutch.

The French army soon came in its turn to besiege and retake Corbie. At the same time, an attack on Burgundy had been concerted by the Imperial troops, while the army of Condé was besieging Dôle, which was holding out for the Spaniards. But the Imperialist army having had to wait long for the necessary reinforcements, did not start at the same time as that of the Hispano-Belgians, and did not cross the frontier till the 22nd of October; which gave time for the French troops employed at the siege of Corbie to pass into Burgundy, to assemble the troops of the province, and to receive the reinforcements sent to the Prince de Condé by the Duke of Weimar and the Cardinal de la Valette. Being unable to raise the siege of Dôle, the Imperialists directed their course to the Saône, which they passed, and sent a body to seize the little *cité* of La Roche-

Pont, the capture of which would give them a centre for attacking Dijon or Langres, and enable them to isolate the Prince de Condé. The town of La Roche-Pont was but scantily furnished with artillery, and had a garrison of only a thousand men, when the Imperialist forces presented themselves before it on the 2nd of November. They numbered six thousand men, and brought with them thirty pieces of ordnance, of which twelve were of large calibre. They were commanded by Galas, and were expecting to take the place in a few days, for the captains knew by their scouts that the garrison was weak, scantily provisioned and unprepared for an attack.

However, Count Rantzau had been sent by the French generals to re-victual Saint-Jean-de-Losne and La Roche-Pont, and to place an experienced captain in the latter. The count arrived before La Roche-Pont two days previous to the Germans; he left a thousand men there, with Rincourt as governor—ordnance munitions and a convoy of provisions; but having only two or three thousand men left him, he thought himself not in a condition to attack the Imperialist army, and therefore marched to Saint-Jean-de-Losne, which he entered on the 2nd of November, in the teeth of the Germans, who were already beginning to invest the town. Immediately on his arrival before La Roche-Pont, Galas summoned the place, offering the garrison the most favourable conditions, and the inhabitants respect for their persons and property. The envoy of the Imperialist general was sent back as he had come, and attack and defence were respectively prepared for.

Rincourt's nature was one of those which are apparently nonchalant and cold, fond of repose, and never appearing discomposed; he was of middle height, with a little embonpoint. His pale face, blonde hair, and dull blue eyes, would be deemed no indication of a soul of firm temper, but rather of one quite destitute of elasticity—an *esprit blasé*, or at least an impassive disposition. Rincourt had however given proof of his ability on many occasions, and Count de Rantzau, who knew him well, esteemed him highly. On leaving him in the place, he had given him these simple instructions—" Hold out here to the last man: for the rest act as you judge best." To Galas's messenger, Rincourt had replied: " My instructions are to defend the place, and I shall defend it."

Rincourt, while making the arrangements necessary for the defence, and enquiring into the stores of provisions, was aware that if he allowed himself to be shut up at once in the town, the enemy would have made a breach in less than a week, and the taking of La Roche-Pont would be at most an affair of fifteen or twenty days. The stock of provisions scarcely admitted of so long a resistance; and at this time of the year it was difficult to add to them, even if the place were not closely invested. The governor resolved, therefore, to take the initiative and to hinder the enemy's approach-works to such an extent, that however favourable the weather might be, the enemy would have difficulty in maintaining his position.

He sent for the mayor and notables of the town, and asked them what they intended to do, and whether the inhabitants would remain at home with their hands folded, while the king's men were fighting to defend the town. They assured him that, on the contrary, the inhabitants were disposed to defend themselves, and that even the women would mount the ramparts if necessary; that all of them knew how the enemy had behaved in Picardy, and thought that the worst course was to trust to their promises, and that if they must die, it was better to die fighting. "If it be so," replied the governor, "and if your acts respond to your words, you may be assured that the Germans will not enter this place; but, you must be doing. Have you any artillerymen among the inhabitants?" "We have some; all our young men are hardy and robust, and many know how to make use of musket and pike." "Well, assemble them to-night, and let all the volunteers, armed or unarmed, be with you to-morrow morning, in the open space before the castle. Whatever you hear this evening, do not let your attention be diverted from this object, and do not be alarmed."

When night arrived (and it comes early on the 2nd of November), Rincourt prepared for the transport of two small pieces of cannon, and ordered two hundred men to mount their horses—for he had some cavalry—accompanied by four hundred foot soldiers; took care that the artillerymen should be at their guns in the works of the tenaille, leaving their captains precise instructions; summoned four hundred men to appear at three o'clock in the morning; and about ten o'clock sallied forth with his six hundred men and two guns through the gate of the outwork.

The night was foggy and perfectly dark. The governor had taken the precaution to envelope the wheels of his two guns with pieces of cloth and canvas, and to have the crowbars, powder spoons, and rammers, carried by the servers, to avoid noise. On issuing from the ravelin, he directed the two cannons obliquely right and left, so as to keep them within musket shot from the centre column; the cavalry was escorting them. He himself, with his three or four hundred foot soldiers, marched straight for the enemy's outposts. About a thousand yards from the outwork he met them, making soup in front of their fires. Falling suddenly on the sentinels and neighbouring posts, he threw himself into the very heart of the enemy dispersed among the orchards, and killing all who resisted, drove them before him.

In conformity with the instructions they had received, the artillerymen then brought their pieces into position, and fired right and left towards the two extremities of the encampment. The Imperialists believed themselves attacked along the whole extent of their front, and took some time to concert their defence.

As soon as Rincourt saw the enemy drawn up in considerable numbers before him, he hastily drew off the right and left of his small band towards the two guns and the cavalry. The Germans then advanced in a compact, but not very orderly body, looking for the assailant, and not knowing whether they should go towards the east or west of the plateau in pursuit of him. Then, after a renewed discharge of the pieces, the two small French corps, cavalry and infantry, rushed upon the flanks of the column, killed or took about a hundred men, and fell back with all speed to the outwork, protected by volleys discharged with as good aim as circumstances allowed from the bastions of the tenaille.

This affray terminated at midnight, without loss. Rincourt sent his men to rest, and at three o'clock in the morning sallied forth once more with the four hundred foot soldiers, summoned for that hour; this time without cannon or cavalry. He went along the western edge of the plateau, and when he saw himself within musket shot of the advanced posts, drawing out his musketeers in a long line, he commanded a general discharge; then moving off obliquely, he executed the same movements a few seconds afterwards, on the eastern side, after which he retired.

The enemy were completely puzzled by these attacks. They had passed the whole of the night on the look-out, and in the morning determined to establish their first lines about a mile from the tenaille, placing advanced posts behind intrenchments hastily thrown up. They then opened the trench about half a mile distant.

Throughout the day the heavy guns mounted on the platforms of the tenaille kept up a fire on these advanced posts, killed some men and overthrew the intrenchments. During the night of the 3rd of November, Rincourt, who had observed that a considerable body of the enemy was advancing up the river, perhaps with the view of passing the night there, and attacking the front K[1] in the rear with cannon, sent out two hundred of his infantry, under efficient command, through the ravelin of the outwork, and made a sortie with three hundred men through the gate of the front, K. He attacked the posts along the river, while the first troop was skirmishing with the advanced posts established along the western slopes of the plateau. When the first troop saw itself too much pressed, it rapidly descended the western slope to rally Rincourt's force, who on his side was retreating after having thrown the enemy into confusion.

The besiegers, however, being on their guard, went in pursuit of the five hundred men from the town with vigour, and in increasing numbers. But this had been foreseen by the governor; and a second body of four hundred men, which during the action issued in its turn from the ravelin, descended the western slopes at full speed, and fell upon the flank of the Imperialists.

On this the five hundred men commanded by Rincourt faced about. There, also, two or three hundred Germans were killed, wounded, or threw themselves into the water. The losses of the French were insignificant.

While these continual alarms in some degree fatigued and disconcerted the besiegers, who did not suppose they had before them a garrison numerous enough to dare

[1] See Fig. 59.

to act on the offensive, they restored confidence to the besieged, and gave them a high idea of the military talents of the governor.

Rincourt continued to preserve his cool aspect and nonchalant demeanour, though he was constantly on the alert, and gave his orders with precision. Seeing the turn things were taking the *dizainiers* of the town assured the governor of their entire devotion, and of the good-will of the volunteers, who deemed themselves capable of guarding the ramparts unaided; he might therefore commence operations outside in full confidence, and "amuse" the enemy. This was exactly what Rincourt wanted.

The Imperialists in the meantime continued to advance with their trench. On the evening of the 5th of November it was fifteen hundred feet from the salient, and in the rear there was a pretty good *place d'armes*, surrounded by an epaulement with cannon at the angles and abatis of trees, at the foot of the bank. Every night the governor found means to disquiet the enemy, often at intervals of two or three hours, so as to keep him incessantly in alarm.

Galas, in the meanwhile, had sent two pieces of ordnance to the right bank of the stream out of sight of the besieged, and on the 7th of November he mounted them on this bank so as to attack the front *à crémaillère*, K,[1] in the rear. The wooden bridge had been burned by the besieged, and the stone bridge barricaded and furnished with a cavalier on the left bank, which swept the right bank. Behind the houses of the western faubourg, Rincourt established a battery armed with three cannons, which had been taken from the arsenal during the night. On the morning of the 8th of November the houses which masked the three pieces having been thrown down,

[1] See Fig. 59.

these guns opened their fire against the besieger's battery, which was soon silenced.

That same day the trench was nine hundred feet from the outwork, and a second *place d'armes* was commenced at this point (Fig. 62). The governor resolved to overthrow the enemy's works. At two o'clock in the morning he first sent out a troop of five hundred men to attack the *place d'armes* on the west, while a second troop of two

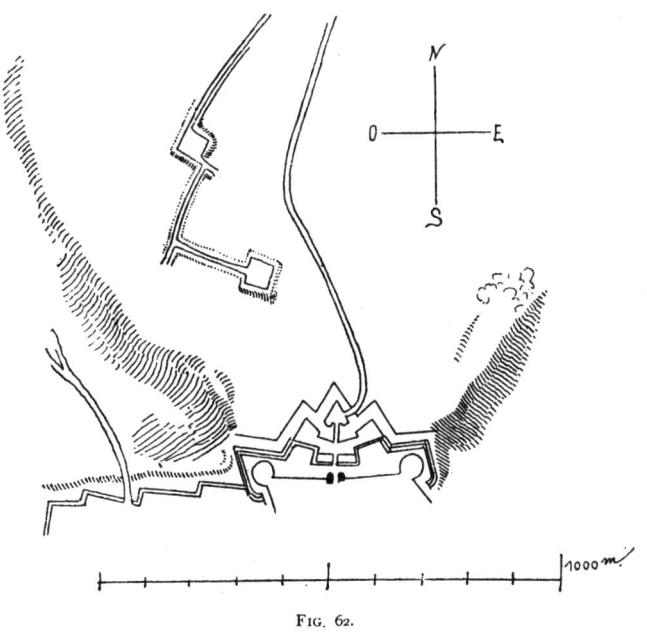

FIG. 62.

hundred men was to attack it on the east, and himself going out with four hundred men to continue the offensive, if the former had a chance of succeeding, or to protect its retreat. His men were armed with pikes, cutlasses, grenades, and pistols.

The besieger had at this point from twelve to fifteen hundred men to protect the workmen. The first troop of the garrison advanced resolutely against the flank, throwing grenades into the trenches, and destroying the gabions and fascines. They were soon attacked by all the Germans posted at this point; but knowing that they were going to be immediately reinforced, they maintained their position in the middle of the *place d'armes*, making use of every obstacle to intrench themselves. This struggle was visible only through some bivouac fires at a considerable distance, and the explosions of the grenades. The townspeople, that they might recognise each other, had put shirts over their buff coats, or their *pourpoints*. The second troop soon arrived from the east, and a part of the besiegers was thus attacked on both sides. The latter retired, and rallying about a hundred paces behind the *place d'armes*, attacked in their turn the people of the town on the two flanks; the struggle recommenced with violence, the French not being willing to abandon the place. They would, however, have been ultimately overwhelmed by numbers, if Rincourt had not come up in the midst of the *mêlée* with his reserve of four hundred men (Fig. 63). He fell upon one of the flanks of the numerous troop of the Germans without uttering a sound. These then fell into confusion, and commenced a speedy retreat. Soon, in spite of the officers, the route was complete, and the fugitives went off and alarmed the neighbouring posts, and even the camp, asserting that they had been surprised by a large body that had come to succour the besieged.

Galas was not certain whether this was a concerted sortie or whether succour had reached the besieged between his lines and the place. Collecting all the troops at his disposal, and ordering two or three hundred men to mount their horses, he betook himself to the abandoned works. Rincourt had not waited for him; but having damaged the trench for the length of a hundred paces,

FIG. 63.—NIGHT SORTIE—THE ATTACK ON ONE OF THE BESIEGERS' PLACE D'ARMES.

scattered the gabions, set fire to heaps of fascines, spiked two guns, which the enemy had abandoned, broken open some casks of munitions, and taken away the tools of the pioneers, retreated with his men. This sortie had cost him about fifty men; he brought back his wounded.

When Galas came up none but the dead of both parties and some wounded remained in the works. In his anger, he broke his cane on the back of the first soldiers he met with, calling them cowards and traitors, and threatening to decimate the whole troop entrusted with the guard of the trench. The mischief could not be repaired in the few hours of night that were left. They were quite bewildered in the midst of these scattered gabions and trenches filled up at some points; and when day appeared the besieged discharged three or four volleys from the tenaille in the midst of this confused host, which then retreated to the first *place d'armes.*

To increase his embarrassment, about ten o'clock in the morning, a message sent from Saint-Jean-de-Losne informed the Imperialist general that this insignificant town was holding out, that the continual sorties of the garrison were fatiguing the troops, that the siege would be longer than was supposed at first, and that, in fact, his presence would be necessary to direct the attack and make head against the Count de Rantzau, who was occupying the town.

The possession of Saint-Jean-de-Losne, which he supposed was already in the hands of his troops, was still more important to the Imperialists than that of La Roche-Pont. For Saint-Jean-de-Losne secured to the Germans the passage of the Saône; but if this town held out they might be cut off by the Prince de Condé, who, on raising the siege of Dôle, or taking that place, would fall upon the rear of the Imperial army.

Galas was therefore much embarrassed. To raise the siege of La Roche-Pont, and to march with all his forces against the Prince de Condé, was perhaps the wisest part to take, but this would have interfered with the plan of the campaign on which the Imperialists founded the most brilliant hopes; it would have been to abandon that conquest of Burgundy which a few days before Germany had regarded as certain; it would have been a manifest check at the very commencement of the campaign.

Galas therefore adopted a middle course, which in war is always the least desirable; he resolved to leave before La Roche-Pont sufficient troops to invest it closely, knowing that the place had not provisions sufficient to last long, and to finish the siege of Saint-Jean-de-Losne. This place fallen, he might resume his original plan.

On the evening of the 9th of November, after having appointed a commander for the troops remaining before La Roche-Pont, and leaving his instructions, he quitted the camp to go and rejoin the army before Saint-Jean-de-Losne.

These instructions were in substance as follows—the establishment of a line of investment around the place and the continuance of the attack on the northern salient, under good protection and taking the time necessary for the works. He had also a plan made out for a battery of bomb mortars. He had sent for four of these engines to bombard the town.[1] Galas's lieutenant was of Italian origin, and was named Forcia: he was an impetuous man, serviceable for a bold stroke, a great talker, a fairly skilful engineer, but wanting in persistency and perseverance, and continually changing his plans. By dint of flattery and the admiration he manifested on all occasions for the

---

[1] Bombs, invented by the Dutch in the beginning of the seventeenth century, were already used in sieges.

military talents of Galas, Forcia had succeeded in persuading him that no one was better fitted than himself to act for the general, to enter into his designs, and put his plans in execution. Forcia, we say, had appeared to appreciate the wisdom of Galas's designs, and had promised to follow his instructions implicitly and to the letter. But where is the flatterer, however astute, who does not leave in the mind of the person flattered—however wanting in judgment—a feeling of mistrust. Accordingly Galas in quitting the camp of La Roche-Pont, had instructed a young lieutenant who acted as his secretary, and whom he left with Forcia, to take note of all that transpired and to keep him informed of the minutest details by frequent messages.

Rincourt allowed his troops the night of the 9th for repose, as half the garrison had been engaged the night before. On the morning of the 10th one of the spies whom he was careful to employ in the country, and even in the camp of the enemy, came to inform him that Galas had departed the evening before with an inconsiderable escort, and that the Imperialist troops were placed under the command of one of his lieutenants. This news set the governor gravely thinking; he knew that Saint-Jean-de-Losne was still holding out, and he gained a glimpse of the real state of affairs. Devoted to the Count de Rantzau, he felt it his duty more than ever to give the enemy so much to do as to render it impossible for him to think of reducing the number of troops assembled around La Roche-Pont, to reinforce those engaged in the siege of Saint-Jean-de-Losne.

The garrison was full of confidence and determination; and the militia of the town asked to share in the sorties. This militia consisted of a body of about twelve hundred men, which Rincourt had divided into companies of one

hundred men each, commanded by ten subalterns and a
captain. He had divided these companies into two battalions of six hundred men each. The first was composed
of the robuster men who had had some experience in
arms; the second was composed of the householders, men
of mature age inexperienced in war. These latter were
especially employed as guards of the ramparts, as a daily
and nightly patrol, and as a police for the town. With
the regular troops, therefore, the governor had at his disposal, even after the losses he had sustained, and after
leaving in the town artillerymen enough to man the guns,
about two thousand two hundred men.

The women of Roche-Pont had also offered their services.
Rincourt formed them into brigades of ten; and their duty
was to bring ammunition, prepare the provisions, repair
military accoutrements, and make fascines and bags.

Even since the enemy's arrival, the governor had been
able to get some cattle, grain, and fodder into the town,
affording a supply for sixteen days longer.

He had good hopes of getting rid of the Germans before
the end of this period. The townspeople, moreover, were
rationed like the garrison, and the inhabitants were obliged
under pain of death to deposit all the provisions they had
in the public store-houses. The two churches of the upper
town had been converted into hospitals for the wounded.

If the spirits of the garrison were kept up and even
raised, such was by no means the case with the Imperialists. Forcia lost no time in announcing to the German
troops that he was appointed commander-in-chief; he
called the captains together and thought it incumbent
upon him to address them in a somewhat long and high-
flown discourse, accompanied by theatrical gestures.

This had but a slight effect on the minds of the officers,
who were for the most part veterans, and who had no

great respect for Forcia. They returned to their quarters, therefore, somewhat depressed, and auguring no good for the prospects of the siege. Following the instructions left him by Galas, Forcia gave orders for the complete investment of the place.

Deducting the losses suffered since the beginning of the siege, and the desertions, Forcia when entrusted with the command had little more than five thousand men. The object to be secured was to maintain at the point of attack a body of troops numerous enough to prevent the sorties of the garrison from not being formidable to them, and to distribute around the *cité* posts sufficiently well connected and defended to cut off all communication between the town and the outside; for it was certain that the inhabitants would be reduced to famine before many days elapsed.

Prudence therefore demanded that a line of contravallation should be established, and provided with artillery, that every point should be efficiently guarded, and that the garrison should be so occupied as to make vigorous sorties impossible. These tactics must infallibly result in the surrender of the town at no distant time. Such were in substance the instructions of Galas. But Forcia had a more ambitious aim; these methods appeared to him tedious and unworthy of him; and he saw himself in imagination master of the place, and sending the news of its capitulation to Galas in a message worthy of ancient Rome.

Still he dared not formally disregard his instructions, but he resolved merely to affect compliance with them, eager to show the army how an engineer of first-rate ability can conduct a siege. He believed that three thousand men would be enough to keep the besieged in awe on the north, to prosecute the approach-works vigorously and to take the place. With two thousand men he made sure of intercepting all communication between the inhabitants and the outside. Accordingly he established a post of two hundred men along the river on the left bank, two hundred yards from the angle of the curtain K;[1] a second post of two hundred men on the right bank, in front of the destroyed wooden bridge O; a third post of one hundred men, opposite the ancient bridge P; a fourth post of three hundred men, two hundred yards from the stone bridge; a fifth post of three hundred men along the rivulet to the south-east of the escarpment of the castle; a sixth post of two hundred men behind the embankment of the mills on the east; and a seventh post of three hundred men above the pool to the north-east—in all sixteen hundred men. Four hundred men were commissioned to connect these principal posts, or to strengthen them at need. The rampart L[1], prevented the besieger from making his way between the pool and the town, the fifth, sixth, and seventh posts communicated with headquarters only by a long détour, and could not be supported by the posts of the right bank unless a bridge were thrown across below the stone bridge. This was a serious disadvantage. Forcia had no idea of taking possession of the stone bridge by a sudden attack, as this passage was commanded by a cavalier and by the bastions of the castle. He preferred throwing a bridge across below to put his posts in communication with each other.

Wishing to keep all his artillery to batter the place and to effect a breach quickly, he did not provide any of these posts with guns, but contented himself with ordering them to erect a strong palisading, and to raise epaulements for shelter. The instructions he gave were wanting in precision, but he often cited Cæsar and

[1] See Fig. 59.

Vegetius and Frontinus, and some of the great captains who had shed a lustre on Italy in the preceding century. While urging vigilance on his captains he merely went with them to reconnoitre the ground, and to determine their posts; but did not trouble himself further to know whether his orders were understood and strictly carried out. The investment was only a concession made to the general-in-chief, and his attention was entirely given to the attack on the north. He could not even avoid observing in presence of his officers that up to that time the works had been feebly conceived and executed; a remark which soon reached the ears of Galas.

Rincourt took advantage of the respite allowed him by the besieger to organize his little garrison more effectually. We have seen that he had six hundred militiamen capable of acting outside the ramparts. He set about equipping these men, who were but imperfectly armed. The castle contained a hundred muskets, which he distributed to those who knew best how to use this weapon, but had not been provided with it. The rest he armed with strong pikes, breach-knives, and partisans. Not counting artillerymen, he had remaining sixteen hundred soldiers—three hundred being horsemen—whom he formed into four bodies of four companies of infantry of eighty men each, commanded by a captain, and three companies of horsemen, one hundred strong.

The town contained thirty-two pieces of ordnance of various calibre. There were sixteen mounted in the north work; two on the cavalier behind the bridge; one in the bastion of the donjon; two in the bastion F[1] and one in each of the seven other bastions; in all twenty-eight. Two were placed in the tenaille of the castle, and two were kept in reserve. The enemy's arrangements

[1] See Fig. 59.

were soon made known to the governor, either through spies or the reconnaissances made by his best officers, or himself personally; he took care not to disturb the carrying out of those arrangements, and contented himself with doubling the guard at the bridge, which was raised to two hundred men.

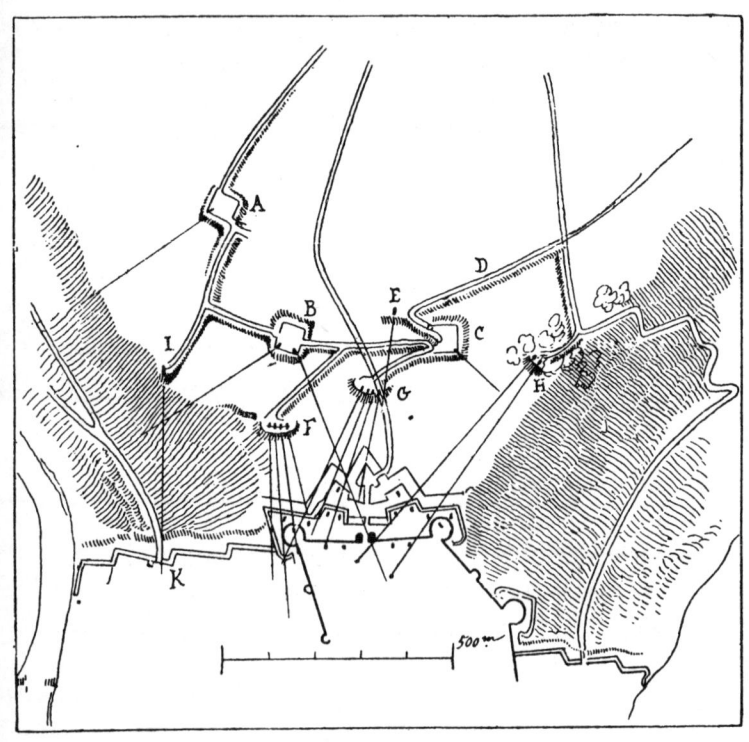

FIG. 64.

During the night of the 11th of November, Forcia had a second breach opened, and marked out the approach-works, as shown in Fig. 64. Besides the two *places d'armes* A and B, already marked out, he planned a third, C, to be reached by a new trench D, next two batteries at G and F, for two pieces each, and a battery for two mortars H. He had the first trench lengthened at I, with a piece at its extremity sweeping the curtain K. Two pieces mounted in the *place d'armes* B commanded the battery F, and the surroundings; a piece mounted at E commanded the battery G; and a piece mounted in the *place d'armes* C swept the outside of the western battery. He thought he should thus provide for every contingency. If the besieged determined to attempt some bold stroke, they could not advance far, and if they succeeded in taking either of the batteries G, F, he could crush them. The two batteries G, F were intended to silence the fire of the north-west salient and of the left half of the tenaille. That done, he could—secure against the right-hand fire —advance as far as the counterscarp, set up a breach battery, and take the place by the north-west salient. Meanwhile, the mortar battery would render the right of the work untenable, crush the defenders of the ancient terraced walls, damage the gates, and prevent the besieged from attempting anything at this point. The plan was not badly conceived; nothing remained but to execute it.

The phlegmatic governor had the gabionades of the work strengthened, and traverses and *paréclats* raised, especially on the platforms of the two great towers. He had shelter places arranged on the platforms of the earthworks. Moreover he kept up a continual fire on the workmen, so that they could scarcely make any advance except during the night. Sometimes at ten o'clock at night, sometimes at midnight, at two o'clock in the morning, or shortly before daybreak, Rincourt would alarm the enemy's camp by sorties of no importance considered with reference to the final result, but which greatly exhausted the besiegers.

These sorties were effected by one or two companies while the others rested. In this way he exercised the militia, and accustomed them to fighting.

By the 15th of November the besieger's works had scarcely made any progress. However the *place d'armes* C was made, as also the parallel which connected it with the *place d'armes* B; and the trenches were commenced which were to lead to the two batteries. The bomb-mortars were mounted, and began to fire towards evening. But they produced more noise than damage to the besieged. Their fire was badly directed, and most of the bombs burst too soon or too late. The besieged became accustomed to them, and kept out of their way when they saw them coming. For a dozen bombs fired the first evening, two men were wounded, and one gun-carriage damaged.

On the morning of the 25th of November the weather, hitherto fine, suddenly changed. About nine a fine snow fell, and was soon after followed by a deluge of rain, accompanied by squalls. During the night of the 15th, the men on guard in the trenches were up to their knees in water; it was impossible to work. The rain continued regular and heavy during the whole of the 16th. Rincourt took advantage of this disagreeable state of the weather. The bridge which had been thrown across the river by the Imperialists, below the stone bridge, consisted of a floor six feet wide, laid partly on trestles, partly on boats collected in the valley and linked together. This was a clumsy contrivance, for the water on beginning to rise lifted the boats proportionately so that it was extremely difficult to maintain the connexion between the floor resting on the boats and that laid on the trestles. Accordingly in spite of the rain the besiegers worked all day on the 16th to prevent the rupture of this bridge. The governor who passed all that day in examining the environs, had perceived from the top of the platform of the cavalier the precarious condition of the besieger's bridge, and at night he had some large trunks of trees thrown over the parapet of the stone bridge, which struck against the boats and trestles and impeded the current, which kept on rising. At midnight twenty of these trunks had accumulated against the boats, and the river continuing to rise, the bridge was carried away. A light appearing for an instant at a certain point of the valley of Abonne apprised Rincourt of the destruction of the bridge. The signal was given by one of the spies.

Secure, therefore, against being cut off on his right by the Imperialists, the governor sent out three hundred militiamen and three companies of soldiers, kept under arms after supper, by the western gate, next to the castle; and another three hundred of the militia, and two companies by the eastern gate. This second troop was commissioned to make for the causeway of the pool, attack the enemy's post established beyond the embankment, outflank it on his right and pursue it hotly along the rivulet. Rincourt commanded the foremost troop of six hundred men. He descended the slope of the bridge, crossed the rivulet by means of planks and trestles which he had ready prepared behind the cavalier, and attacked the post of three hundred men established at two hundred yards below the stone bridge. Finding themselves attacked by a body much more numerous than themselves, they quitted the bivouacs in all haste, and set off along the left bank of the rivulet to join the second post (consisting) of three hundred men established between them and the dam, as the bridge was broken. This was just what Rincourt anticipated. At the same time, in an opposite direction the post at the pool embankment was in flight, pursued by the second troop of the besieged,—depending on getting the support of the post at the rivulet and that of the bridge, since they were outflanked on their right. These two posts—that of the bridge and that of the embankment—retreating as fast as the nature of the ground permitted in an inverse direction, to the post at the rivulet, the latter supposed it was an attack, and fired several arquebusades at the two troops of these outposts. They recognised each other with difficulty, and these eight hundred men thus collected, saw themselves attacked on two sides by Rincourt and the second troop of the besieged. The combat did not last long, in consequence of the confusion into which they were thrown as much as through the numerical inferiority Few resisted, many sought the marshes, and two or three hundred laid down their arms and begged for quarter. Of those who had betaken themselves right and left to the marshes, about a hundred managed to reach the camp in the morning, the others were killed by the peasants.

Forcia, informed in the middle of the night of the attack on his south-eastern posts, got a thousand men under arms. But the weather continued as bad as ever; the captains obeyed with a very ill grace; they had lost all confidence, and it was not until daylight that Galas's lieutenant was able to go down into the valley. His three posts were taken, and he found from two to three hundred men dead or wounded on the banks of the rivulet.

Rincourt had quietly gone up again into the town with his two troops and his prisoners by the castle gate, about three o'clock in the morning. He had not lost more than fifty men, killed, wounded, or strayed. Forcia returned to the camp about ten o'clock in the morning. But from the top of the donjon, at the first glimmering of daylight, the governor had seen the troop of Imperialists defiling in the direction of the posts that had been taken. Without an instant's delay, placing himself at the head of four companies of foot soldiers, fresh and ready for the struggle, and of his three hundred horsemen, and after having fired several volleys on the besieger's works, he courageously sallied forth by the ravelin and rushed impetuously upon the trenches. The enemy, taken by surprise, without a commander, and out of heart, fled, and Rincourt succeeded in spiking the guns of the two foremost *places d'armes*, spiking and throwing down the mortars along the slopes, breaking the gun-carriages, overthrowing the gabionades, and taking a quantity of workmen's tools.

When Forcia returned, it was to learn this fresh disaster. His captains murmured loudly. He called them cowards and ignoramuses, and they retorted sharply, and abuse was lavished on both sides. Happily for Forcia a messenger came from Galas that evening enjoining him to raise the siege of Roche-Pont and to fall back upon the Saône without an hour's delay.

Saint-Jean-de-Losne had held out and had suffered no damage ; the Imperialists, surprised by the inundations, and fearing to be cut off by the French army, determined on returning home.

If that French army had been led by a Rantzau and a Rincourt, not a German would have repassed the frontier ; but the Duke of Weimar and the Cardinal de la Valette, who might have destroyed the invaders, were by no means energetic in the pursuit. The Imperialists, however, lost in this expedition, by which they hoped to gain the most brilliant advantages, all their baggage, a good part of their artillery, and a third of their force.

CHAPTER XV.

THE TOWN OF LA ROCHE-PONT IS FORTIFIED BY M. DE VAUBAN.

BORN at Saint-Leger de Foucheret, in the middle of Burgundy, Vauban, who loved and was well acquainted with this beautiful province, had occasion to visit Roche-Pont several times. The situation of the fortress and its strategical position attracted his notice, and suggested a plan connecting this little town with a line starting with Besançon, passing through Dôle, Auxonne, La Roche-Pont, Langres, Neufchâteau, Toul, Pont-à-Mousson, Metz, Thionville, Longwy, Montmédy, Sédan, Mézières, Rocroy, Avesnes, Maubeuge, Valenciennes, Lille, and ending at Dunquerque. The date was 1680; it was a second line. Would to Heaven it had always been maintained by works accommodated to the means of attack! but if the French know how to take, they are but remiss in keeping what they have taken.

The fortress of La Roche-Pont was exposed to attack only from the northern plateau, and the artillery of Vauban's time could make a serious impression only on that side, as the town was protected on its two sides, east and west, by escarpments and two watercourses. Batteries placed on the hills east and west were either dominated by the artillery of the town or must have been placed at a distance of eighteen hundred yards—*i.e.*, out of range—

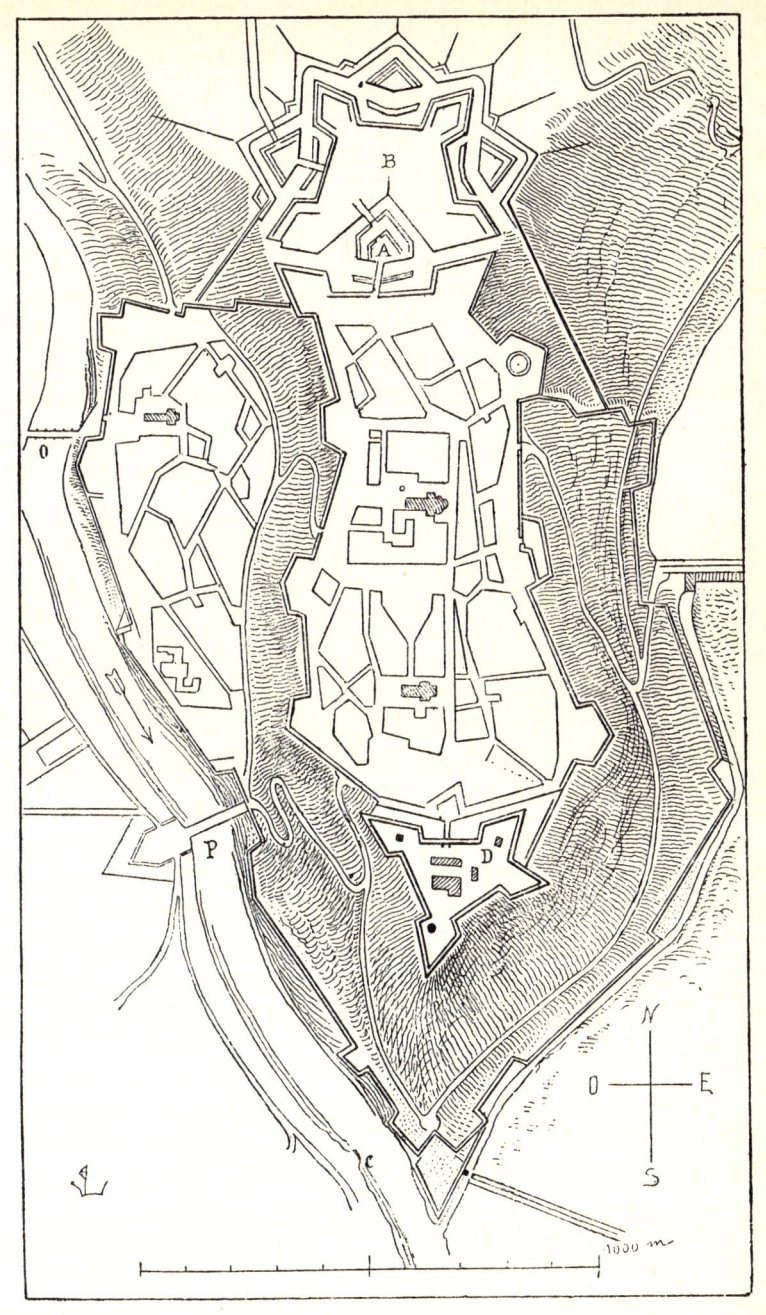

FIG. 65.—VAUBAN'S DEFENCES.

to attain the level of the ramparts. Vauban decided therefore to construct outside the ancient town a large work on the north, which should command the plateau. At the same time—for he was economical of the money of the state—he thought he might avail himself of part of Errard's works, especially the bastions which that engineer had raised on the east and west fronts, and improve the defence of the castle, which would then become a good stronghold. Besides this he planned works, only revetted at the base, along the river, to protect the lower town. On the rivulet side, in like manner, he planned a flanked front for musketry, to secure that side from approach, and to keep some land useful either for the cultivation of vegetables in case of siege, or for pasturage. A weir placed at the mouth of the rivulet, with a flood gate, allowed the inhabitants to inundate the meadows situated on the east of the escarpment.

Fig. 65 presents the general plan of the works laid out by Vauban. At first he had thought of making on the north, before the front fortified by Errard de Bar-le-Duc, a horn-work before a demi-lune; but he could not thus effectually sweep the divergent points of the plateau. He determined, therefore, on the plan given in Fig. 65, making use of a part of the northern revetments of Errard de Bar-le-Duc. In advance of the northern front, in lieu of the narrow and contracted defences of Errard,[1] he made a great demi-lune, A (Fig. 65), with a tenaille behind, and next the bastioned work, B, which swept the whole plateau. As to the rest of the town, making use of the old bastions, he strongly flanked them and disposed the stronghold as shown by the plan, D. The roads of the upper town were widened and improved, and the houses detached from the ramparts. The ancient bridge at C had been

[1] See Fig. 60.

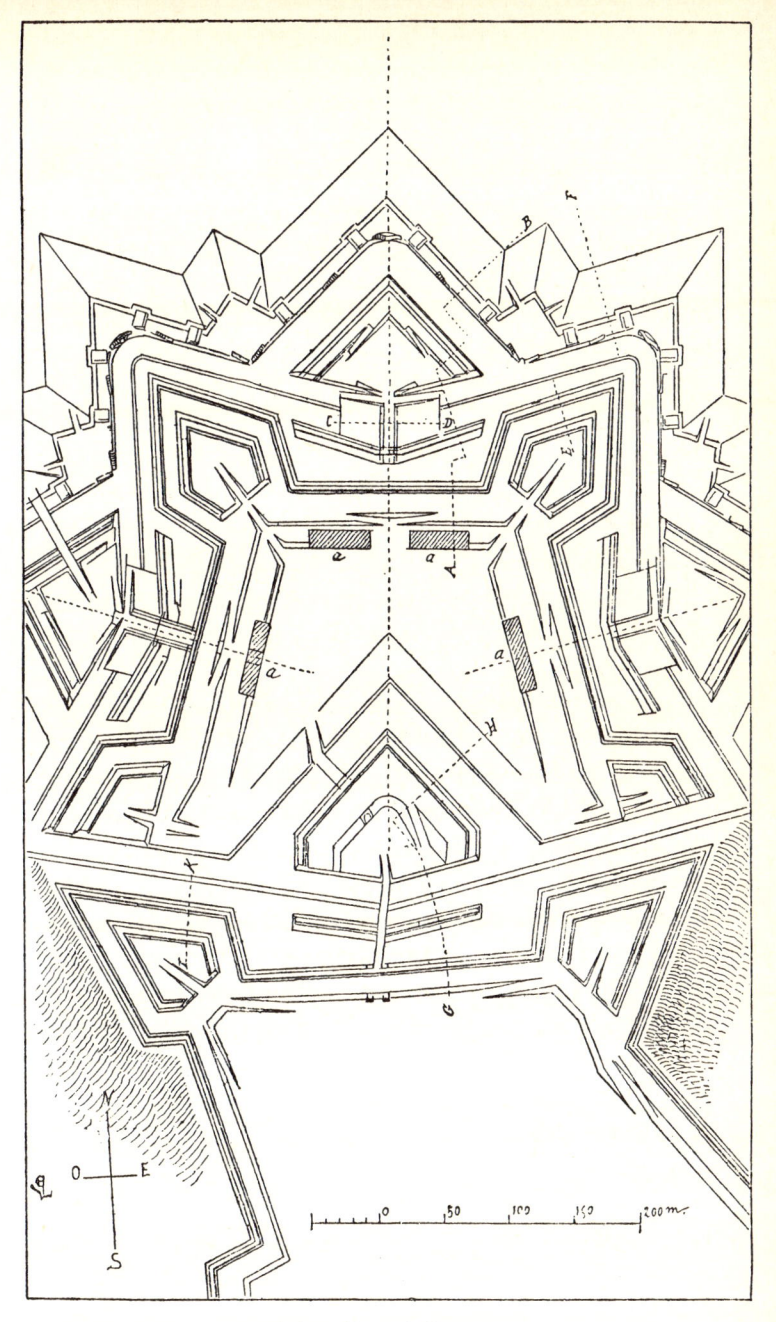

FIG. 66.—Vauban's Outwork.

destroyed by a swelling of the river, and was not rebuilt; but at P, in 1675, a new stone bridge was built, with a *tête du pont* of earthwork. At O a foot-bridge still existed in 1680. The town had again extended along the left bank, and the importance of the *cité* above was diminishing.

Fig. 66 presents on a larger scale the plan of the outwork constructed by Vauban. Before the three fronts of this work, demi-lunes with tenailles behind defended the approaches.

Four barracks were built at *a*. Cavaliers arose on the bastions, and the covered ways, with their *places d'armes*, were furnished with traverses. In the event of this work being taken, the main body of the fortress could still hold out some days.

Fig. 67 gives the sections of these works, which were cased with masonry, presenting a strong defence which only a regular siege could affect.

But it is desirable to point out the reasons that determined the plan of this work, and the method adopted by the illustrious engineer.

Vauban fortified according to the nature of the position, and was not one of those *esprits routiniers* who, when once a certain system has made good its claims, insist on applying it on all occasions.

The fortresses, which, like that of La Roche-Pont, are situated at the extremity of a promontory and present only a narrow front to the besieger, assuredly give certain advantages to the defence, since they have scarcely to fear more than one attack and are accessible only on one side; but this position is not without its drawbacks, especially if, as in the present instance, a fan-shaped plateau spreads outside the fortress; for then the besiegers sweep the defences with converging fires, to which the besieged can oppose only a narrow front unprovided with considerable flankments. On the east side the large bastion, in the middle of which Vauban had left standing the fifteenth-century tower, which thus gave him a good revetted

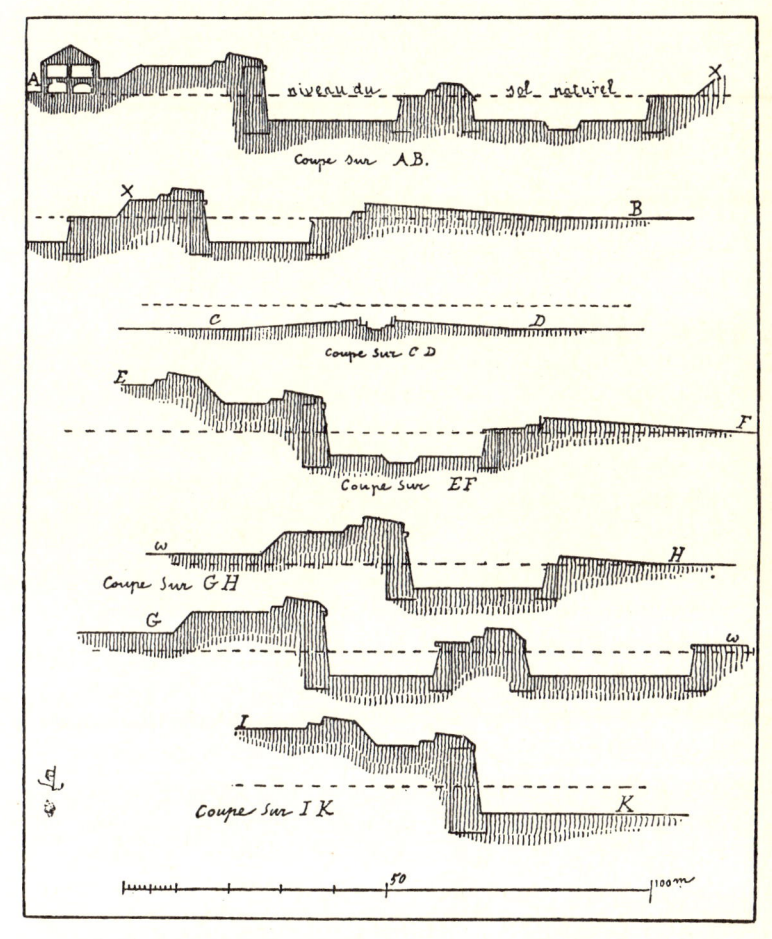

Fig. 67.

cavalier, sufficiently flanked the eastern brow of the outer plateau; but on the western side such a flankment failed entirely, on account of the outward bend caused by the promontory. To obviate these disadvantages Vauban inclined his capital some paces eastwards.[1]

He had thought at first of suppressing the south flanks of the two extreme bastions, but in that case the exteriors of the east and west faces of these bastions would have been too slanting to sweep the crests of the plateau effectively, while the two curtains answered this object. Besides, the enemy could not then, without risk, commence his trenches on the slopes of the plateau and rapidly approach fronts insufficiently flanked. Vauban therefore set out the plan of the great outwork according to the following method (Fig. 68):—To the outside he gave a length of 180 toises, or 1,156 feet. To the western side, *a c*, 1,120 feet; to the eastern side, *b d*, 1,054 feet—that is, he placed the points *c* and *d* according with the edge of the plateau; the two angles *a* and *b* being equal to one another. On the centre of the side *a b* of the polygon he erected the perpendicular, *e f*, having a length equal to one-sixth of *a b*. From this extreme point, *f*, were drawn the lines of defence, *a g*, *b h*, on which the lengths of the faces of the bastion, *a k*, *b i*, were set off equal to two-sevenths of the outer side, *a b* To find the flanks of the bastion, according to the method usually adopted in these defences, points *k* and *i*, he described arcs of a circle, *k l*, taking *i k* as the radius. The point of intersection of this arc with the line *b h* gave the length and the direction of the flank of the bastion; but, not having been able to trace a regular half-hexagon, and the angles *a* and *b* being less obtuse than those of a regular hexagon, by proceeding in this manner, the gorges of the bastion would have been too contracted. Therefore, to determine the flank of the bastion, from the points *i* and *k*, he let fall perpendiculars to the lines of

[1] See Fig. 65.

defence, $a g$, $b h$, and the point h gave the re-entering angle in the curtain, $h g$, parallel to the side $a b$. This

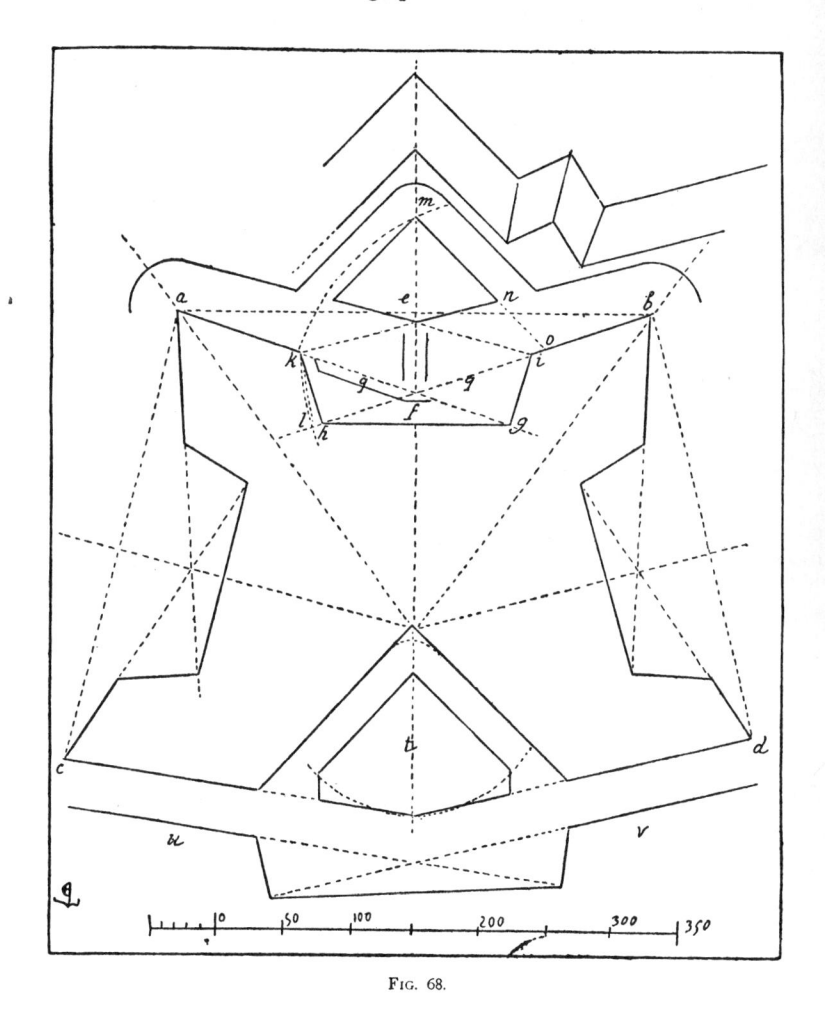

Fig. 68.

exposed the flanks a little too much, but enabled them to sweep the outsides more effectively, and in this particular case that was the principal consideration.

The width of the ditch of the main work was fixed at 112 ft. 7 in., to the rounding of the counterscarp; and this was determined by a tangent to this rounding, drawn from the angle of the epaule of the opposite bastion.

The ditches being dry, Vauban sunk cunettes in the middle, 23 ft. 4 in. wide and 6 ft. 8 in. deep. Double caponnières connected the tenailles with the demi-lunes. The demi-lune was set out as follows:—Taking *g k* as radius, the arc *k m* was drawn. Its meeting with the perpendicular, *e f*, prolonged, gave the point of intersection *m*, the salient of the demi-lune. From *m*, the face *m n* was directed upon a point, *o*, taken on the face of the bastion at 31 ft. 3 in. from the angle of the epaule, *i*. The width of the covered way was fixed at 31 ft. 3 in., and that of the glacis at 124 ft. 4 in. The internal *places d'armes* were 100 ft. across the demi-gorge and 133 ft. 4 in. along the faces. These *places d'armes* were closed by traverses. The ditch of the demi-lune was 89 ft. 7 in. in width. The tenailles, *g*, constructed in the direction of the lines of defence, were 43 ft. 9 in. wide at the base.

Cavaliers were made on the bastions to obtain convenient views over the slopes of the plateau. Their faces and sides, parallel to those of the bastions, had to be placed at a considerable distance from the epaulements, in order that the un-cased external foot of the talus might leave the necessary room for the easy working of the pieces of artillery.[1]

The same method was followed for the sides *a c* and *b d*. The width of the ditch was increased to 100 ft., and the great demi-lune, *t*, was so formed that its faces had a length of 332 ft. and its narrow sides 66 ft. The old bastions restored and enlarged, *u v*, were armed with cavaliers, and the escarp of these bastions was 6 ft. 6½ in.

[1] See Fig. 67, the section on E, F.

higher than that of the bastions of the outwork,[1] which difference, for that matter, was favoured by the conformation of the ground.

All the escarps and counterscarps were cased with strong masonry, with counterforts in the terre-plein; as shown in the sections of Fig. 67 and Fig. 69.

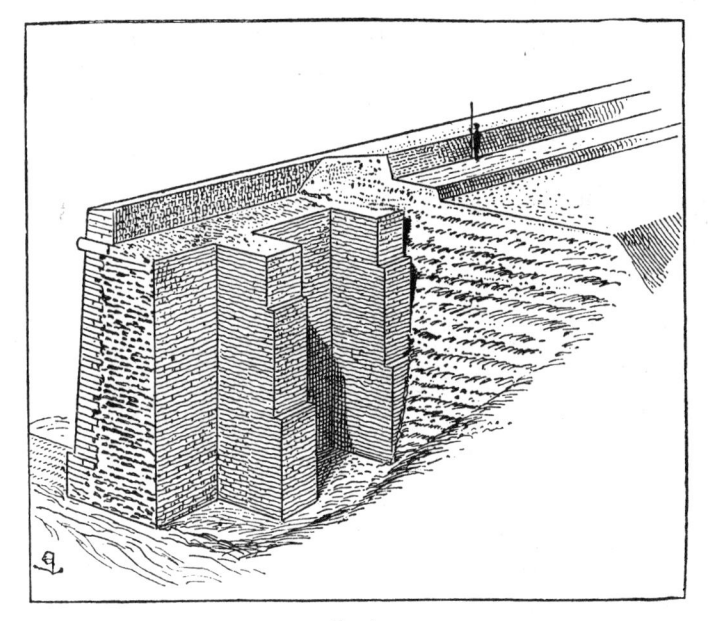

Fig. 69.

The works communicated with each other by posterns. As the fortress of La Roche-Pont was only assailable on one side, the number of cannon necessary for its defence might be, it appeared, in proportion to its extent, inconsiderable. The number amounted to thirty twenty-four pounders, ten twelve- and four-pounders to arm the demi-lunes.

[1] See Fig. 67, the sections on G H and I K.

At the end of the reign of Louis XIV., the efforts of the coalition were directed towards the north-eastern frontiers, and the garrison of La Roche-Pont did not get a view of the enemy. However, during the course of the eighteenth century, this fortress was kept in passable condition.

CHAPTER XVI.

THE SEVENTH SIEGE.

ON the 31st of December, 1813, the grand army of Bohemia, one hundred and eighty thousand men strong, and commanded by Prince Schwartzenberg, crossed the Rhine at Bâle, entered Switzerland, and penetrated into France. Its right bore down on Belfort, Colmar, and Strasburg, its centre marched for Langres, its left for Dijon. The same day the Prussians were crossing the Rhine at Mayence. The invasion of the eastern frontier had to be met by sixty thousand men, at most, echeloned between Epinal and Langres; and this force consisted only of dispirited soldiers and of recruits scarcely knowing how to use their arms. Prince Schwartzenberg's army—which had some reason to fear being attacked on the side of Savoy by the forces commanded by Prince Eugene, and knew that the *débris* of the army of Spain had orders to make for Lyons with all speed—wishing to secure its base of operation, left detachments before Bésançon, Dôle, along the Saône and between Dijon and Langres, with injunctions to occupy the most favourable strategic position. La Roche-Pont was to be taken; and the generalissimo of the Bohemian army imagined that it was not in a condition to hold out eight-and-forty hours, for he knew that it had no garrison, and that the citizens were little disposed to defend themselves.

Among the inhabitants of La Roche-Pont were some royalist families, whose emissaries had assured the commander-in-chief of the Bohemian army that the whole population were impatiently awaiting the arrival of the Allies to declare for the Bourbons. Prince Schwartzenberg was too clear-sighted, and knew too well to what illusions the royalists were ready to yield themselves, to place an unlimited faith in these statements; and he was anxious not to encounter serious obstacles during his first stages, that he might put himself as speedily as possible in communication with his allies on their way from the north-east. He therefore informed the royalists of La Roche-Pont that it was undesirable to provoke a political manifestation on his march; that the best means of assuring the success of the Allies was to remain quiet; that his troops, in conformity with the proclamation issued by the coalition on entering French territory, would respect property; that they were not animated by a spirit of vengeance, and that their glory would consist in concluding peace as quickly as possible, so as to restore to Europe the repose it so much needed.

In the meantime Napoleon, on learning that the German troops had entered France from the south through Basle, had sent pressing orders into the Bourbonnais, Auvergne, and Burgundy, to make a levy of conscripts as soon as possible and send them to Paris. At the same time the depôts of Dauphiny and Provence, as also the conscripts in the eastern departments, were to assemble at Lyons to close to the enemy the approaches from Switzerland and Savoy, and if necessary to operate on his rear.

The prefects of Burgundy, Picardy, and Normandy, and of Touraine and Brittany, were to appeal to the communes to form companies of National Guards *d'élite*, who were to march to Paris, Meaux, Montereau, and Troyes.

These arrangements were hardly made in time to present a serious obstacle to the invaders. The civil authorities and the regular troops began to make a hasty retreat before the armies of the coalition, and were leaving the inhabitants to themselves without arms or guidance. It thus happened that some bodies of troops coming from the south found themselves in an isolated position, and uncertain whether they ought to continue their route or fall back. Such a case happened on the Saône; three battalions of infantry, certain artillerymen called to Vincennes to assemble at the great central depôt which the Emperor was organising there, and some detachments of various arms making their way for Dijon, to push on thence towards Troyes—found themselves on the flank of the left column of the army of Bohemia. They retraced their steps, and made a rather long détour, hoping to get beyond the enemy's right, and resume the route for Troyes through Beaune, Sémur, Montbard, and Châtillon-sur-Seine; but surprised by bad weather and snow, during a night march in the mountains of the Côte-d'Or, they lost their way, and found themselves in the morning at Saint-Seine, which was already occupied by a body of Austrian pioneers. The French were much limited in point of munitions, and had no artillery. They could not force the passage, and were obliged to fall back into the valley of Suzon, hoping still to find the road from Dijon to Langres clear. But at Thil-le-Châtel they came upon another body of the enemy, and had to retire towards the small town of La Roche-Pont, for it was evident that they were cut off. The colonel who commanded this small column was instructed, should it be impossible to reach Langres, to take up a position at Auxonne or at La Roche-Pont, to keep his ground there, and to form a nucleus of defence until the arrival of Augereau's force, which was to march from

Lyons through Mâcon, Châlon, and Gray, to fall on the rear of Prince Schwartzenberg.

Such were the events that had happened at this juncture at La Roche-Pont. Conformably to the last orders transmitted by the prefect, companies of National Guards had been promptly organised. The inhabitants of La Roche-Pont, like their neighbours of Auxonne, Dôle, and Saint-Jean-de-Losne, preserve military habits; and sieges—not without reason, as we have seen—are a tradition among them. There were always companies of archers and arbalisters at La Roche-Pont during the Middle Ages, and at a later date bombardiers and artillerymen. Under the Consulate La Roche-Pont had been a depôt for the army concentrated between Dijon and the Swiss frontier to pass the Saint-Bernard, and munitions had been stored there; some siege pieces had also been placed there, and still remained. At the approach of Prince Schwartzenberg's army the population of La Roche-Pont was in agitation; and even before the prefectoral instructions had arrived, three companies of National Guards, one of which was of artillerymen, had been spontaneously formed. All had old muskets of the time of the Revolution, or good hunting weapons. The lower town, occupied in great part by rich families, of which several were devoted to the royal cause, did not share in these preparations for war. Some indiscreet revelations made the upper town aware of the intrigues of the royalists. The mayor was a man who had been conspicuous for his devotion to the Emperor while the Empire had been in vigour; but who, seeing its fortunes decline, became daily more and more of a royalist.

If he had not actively opposed, he had at least obstructed the formation of a company of National Guards *d'élite*, endeavouring to gain time. The little citadel of La Roche-Pont was occupied by a company of sixty veterans, for the most part invalided, under the orders of an old one-armed captain of engineers, who had served in almost all the campaigns of the Empire. When it was known that the enemy had entered France, Captain Allaud—that was his name—had asked for orders from Dijon, but had not received them. However, he employed his men in restoring and replenishing the arsenal. He enjoyed a certain amount of authority in the upper town. The male population of the *cité*, composed in great part of men who had been soldiers—all the youth had left in the first months of 1813—never called Captain Allaud anything but "the Governor," and had applied to him to form companies, only asking for munitions. Now the arsenal of La Roche-Pont contained a good supply of powder and balls, about twenty old bronze pieces of small calibre, six twenty-four pounders, two howitzers, four small mortars, and about a hundred muskets past service. The six gendarmes remaining till then at La Roche-Pont had been summoned to Dijon at the beginning of January.

Captain Allaud asked for co-operation in repairing the arms, making cartouches and cartridges, repairing the parapets, the traverses, and epaulements, and fabricating gabions and fascines; and the women made bags for earth,—as if it had been possible to sustain a siege with the sixty veterans and the three companies of National Guards, forming a total of two hundred and sixty men. The Prefect of Dijon had transmitted the order for these select companies of National Guards to fall back upon Langres, but the order had not arrived. The royalists shrugged their shoulders on seeing these two hundred and sixty National Guards exercising on the platform of the outwork, and went so far as to joke in the places of public resort about Captain Allaud's *garrison*. He could not put up with raillery, and talked aloud to his men about running their swords through the jokers. High words and even blows were exchanged in the *cafés*. The mayor ventured to interpose his authority; he was insulted and called a traitor, and the captain was informed of the intrigues set on foot by the royalists. At night the captain had the gates of the *cité* shut, and the antagonism between the upper and lower town was increasing in violence. "If the Austrians come," said the captain, "the houses of these royalist traitors will be the first marks for our balls!" Both parties became excited, and the mayor had the impudence to ask the captain on whose authority he was acting. "I am the *commandant de place*," replied the veteran, "since there is no other officer here, and La Roche-Pont is a defensible place. . . To prove it to you I arrest you!" And he had the mayor conducted to the citadel.

Great was the excitement in the town, but the royalists were in a feeble minority, and dared not stir. They cried "Vive le Gouverneur!" in the taverns. The mob attempted to plunder the mayor's house, which was situated on the *cité*, and the captain had great difficulty in putting down the disturbance. "Rascals!" cried he to the fellows who were already breaking in the doors of the house, "I will have you shot like dogs. Sacrebleu! you can break open doors; we shall see whether you have so much pluck when the Germans come! Here," added he, turning to a dozen veterans, who were following him, "clear the place of this *canaille!*" and, setting the example, he dealt blows in abundance with the flat of his sword on the backs of the plunderers.

It was the morning following this riot when the French corps above spoken of presented itself before La Roche-Pont. It was welcomed in the upper town with every demonstration of joy. An army come to their help magnificently accoutred and provided would not have been better received. But this troop, exhausted by fatigue, and having eaten nothing for twenty-four hours, without artillery or munitions, had all the appearance of a band of fugitives. Covered with mud, and scantily clothed, these poor soldiers seemed scarcely able even to defend themselves. But in such times of distress, so much do people cling to any semblance of hope, that the sight of a friendly uniform revives every heart. Seeing themselves so well received, these brave fellows made their entrance into the city in good order, and presented when defiling through the streets, in spite of their exhaustion, a martial appearance which redoubled the enthusiasm of the inhabitants. A colonel, three chiefs of battalions, and some captains, of whom one belonged to the artillery, composed the staff. Two hours after their arrival, these soldiers, most of whom had seen much service, having rested well and brushed themselves up, presented a very different appearance.

The news brought by this small corps proved clearly enough that there was no time to lose, if they wanted to put the town of La Roche-Pont in a condition to defend itself with honour, if not with hope of success. The colonel, of course, took the command; his name was Dubois. He had been in the campaign in Portugal, then in Russia, whence he had returned captain, and having been appointed *chef de bataillon* in the Saxon campaign, he had distinguished himself at Dresden, and had been a colonel from the date of the battle of Leipzig. He was a man of about thirty, but appeared to be much older. He had scarcely seen anything but the disastrous side of French glory. His countenance, therefore, did not bear that impress of confidence which was exhibited by many of his brethren in arms, who had been less tried than himself by the misfortunes of the times. Of the war in Spain he had seen only the miseries, the privations, the failure of order, the utter disintegration. With Ney on the return from Moscow he had learned what the performance of duty is without the prestige of glory. At Dresden, the regiment to which he was attached had lost half its men; and the disaster of Leipzig had followed. With each grade in his promotion was associated a mournful date.

Colonel Dubois had an appearance of coldness that served to hide his natural timidity and profound distrust of his fellow-men. It must be allowed that there were reasons for his distrust of men and things. Entering the service at the age of twenty as a common soldier, though he belonged to an honourable family in Poitou and had spent his earliest years in the bosom of his family, he had seen only the sinister side of warfare, and his first companions in arms did not respond to his ideal of the soldier's character. It was still worse when he went to Spain. His delicate nature had fallen back on itself, and allowed no sign of pity or even sympathy for anyone to be visible. Yet so profoundly does what we call "heart" imprint itself on every action, even when its possessor attempts to conceal its slightest manifestation, that this man, in appearance so cold, and who was not known to have a friend, exercised a moral authority over his soldiers which was very rare at that time.

The soldier—an infallible judge in this matter—is able to discover the weak side of the officer; but he only esteems him and confides entirely in him when he recognizes besides military talents a soul of energetic vigour and a heart that beats in unison with his own. The soldier's glance can penetrate without difficulty a cold and harsh exterior, and soon discovers whether this appearance conceals insufficiency, stupidity, or pride; or whether it is only the countenance of a man accustomed to command—the exterior of a soul really accessible to all human sentiments.

In an action Dubois could see his men fall without the slightest show of emotion, and would not permit a soldier to leave his place to help them; but after the battle he was the first and the most attentive in relieving the wounded, and would take no rest till they were carried to the ambulances.

Of the three battalions (they were not complete) which he commanded, two belonged to his own regiment; the third was composed of fragments drawn from all sides. Nevertheless, after two or three days' march, all these men, as well as the companies of various arms which he was to lead to Troyes, knew Colonel Dubois better perhaps than he knew himself. These brave men, after some hours' rest were well satisfied to submit to circumstances and remain under the orders of their Colonel de *Bois*, as they used to call him—and thought it a fine joke to defend themselves in this *nest* of La Roche-Pont, cut off from all help.

Though in concert with Captain Allaud he made the most needful preparations for defence—were it only to save his own honour—Colonel Dubois wished to ascertain whether it was possible to reach Langres and Troyes without compromising his troops. He therefore instructed a young orderly officer of energy and intelligence, by whom he was accompanied—giving him two attendants and two guides from the town and known to the captain, all mounted—to reconnoitre the route and return as quickly as possible.

We have seen that before the colonel's arrival the defenders numbered three hundred and twenty men, of whom sixty were veterans. Among these men about fifty were capable of serving the guns, having been artillerymen. The troop brought by the colonel consisted of three battalions, in all one thousand four hundred and fifty men, twenty-five artillerymen, and thirty dismounted horsemen; total, one thousand eight hundred and twenty-five men, including officers.

Provisions were the first question. The colonel, having learned the arrest of the mayor, summoned him into his presence, and soon heard the confession of the municipal magistrate. He gave him to understand that the proofs of his royalist intrigues were sufficient to justify his being shot there and then, and that the only means of avoiding this unpleasant necessity was to set about provisioning the city without a moment's delay. He added that he only commanded the vanguard of a *corps d'armée*, marching from Lyons in the rear of the enemy, while the Emperor was to take them in front: it was important therefore for the town of La Roche-Pont to be in a position to resist for some days, and if it were obliged to surrender for want of provisions, the Emperor's Government would lay blame on the mayor, as having an understanding with the enemy, and then it was all over with him.

The poor mayor, more dead than alive, promised everything, and swore by all the saints that he was devoted to the Emperor, and that in four-and-twenty hours the fortress should be supplied with all the provisions that could be found in the neighbourhood. " I don't know what there may be in the neighbourhood," replied the colonel; "you probably *do ;* but I have to tell you that by four o'clock to-morrow afternoon—it is now a quarter-past six —there must be on this spot, first, rations of meal, meat, and wine for a garrison of two thousand men for twenty-five days at least; secondly, the inhabitants of the town must also be provisioned for thirty days; and that if this is not done, I shall be unfortunately obliged to send you back to your place of confinement, where you will await the decision of the Emperor's Government; I am going to give you twenty men to accompany you and help you. Planton! ask the major to come here!" "But, colonel," said the mayor, "you must be aware that at this time of the year I shall have great difficulty—" "You prefer then to return to prison immediately?" interrupted the colonel. "Major!" said he when this officer was introduced, "Monsieur le maire de la Roche-Pont engages to provision the town within twenty-four hours. Here is a list of what is required. You will accompany him, and have twenty pressed men with you—thirty if you want them. You must begin at once. I wish you good luck, Monsieur le maire." Addressing himself to the major, while the mayor was retiring, pale and covered with perspiration, in spite of the cold: "Do not suffer this man to go out of your sight, he is a Royalist; keep him at work, and bring him back here with the provisions." "I understand, colonel." It was many years since the upper and lower town of La Roche-Pont had been so animated. The upper town resounded with the noise of arms, of the excavators going to the works, of guns being taken from the arsenal and mounted in the batteries, and of the repairing of the carriages. In another part the carpenters were at work making platforms. As in former times, women mingled with the workmen and brought bundles of willows cut from the side of the pool to make gabions. Behind every window some were to be seen sewing bags for earth. Wheelwrights were repairing wheels; and all engaged were singing and laughing as if they were preparing for a fête. The meal and forage carts were coming in, while pigs, cows, and sheep were rendering the streets almost impassable.

The lower town presented a different aspect: the *cafés* were full, and all were talking at once and very loud. The mayor, followed by the major, who kept close to his elbow, and by his staff of assistants, was making his visits to the shops and houses.

The whole of the population was at the windows or at the door-sills. Carts were got ready, and the twenty pressed men filled them in no time; if horses could not be found to draw them, the workmen pushed at the wheels. Some large houses, however, remained closely shut.

They had to go through the valley and visit the farmers and millers of the neighbourhood. Many inhabitants of the upper town went down in search of hams, meal, and grains. The grocers' shops and the pork shops were emptied one after the other; provisions were rising in price, so that the last ham was sold, at three o'clock in the afternoon, for sixty francs.

At four o'clock the mayor, followed like his shadow by the major, presented himself before the colonel and gave him the list of all the provisions he had been able to bring into the upper town. The colonel bade him sit down, and examined the account carefully, asking many questions and appealing to the major's testimony respecting the correctness of the statements. The twenty-five days' rations for the two thousand men were found complete, thanks to a good stock of un-ground corn which made up for what was wanting in meal.

The colonel expressed himself satisfied, especially as they had found in the castle some few hundred-weight of biscuit in good condition. "Thank you, Monsieur le maire," said he; "you must be fatigued, and may return home; but as I am not unaware of the ill-feeling of some bad sort of people towards you, you shall have a man on guard posted at your door; and I must beg you not to quit your house except to go to your office, which fortunately is situated in the upper town, which will enable you, when we are invested, to fulfil your functions with the zeal you have just manifested.

"I will also beg you to make arrangements without delay for an ambulance with fifty beds duly furnished—suppose we say to-night—and to send me the surgeons of the town, if there are any at La Roche-Pont, this very evening.... Major! accompany Monsieur le maire while he attends to this business, so that no harm may befal him...."

That same day, at eight o'clock in the evening, the reconnaissance returned and reported what they had seen.

The enemy was at Gray near Champlitte, and was occupying the roads between Gray and Thil-le-Châtel. His force had been seen at Bèze, about eighteen miles from La Roche-Pont. Communication between Dijon and Langres was cut off: and although the enemy had not occupied that town, he was forming a curtain between it and the north to mask his ulterior movements.

The circumstantial details given by his orderly officer confirmed the colonel in the idea that the army of Bohemia was paying but little attention to what was taking place in his rear, but was pushing on towards the capital by the basin of the Seine. "Ah!" said the colonel, when he had heard every particular from the young officer, "if we only had twenty thousand of those men who were lost in Russia, we could make these German and Russian gentlemen pay dearly for their temerity, and few of them would see the other side of the Rhine again."

Colonel Dubois therefore determined to follow the second part of his instructions. He sent a reliable man, selected by Captain Allaud, to Auxonne to inform the governor of the place—if the town was not already occupied—that he was holding La Roche-Pont, that he was in a condition to defend himself there for some time, and that he should wish all isolated detachments and any provisions or munitions that had no particular destination to be sent to him.

Up to the 15th of January the town of La Roche-Pont had not seen a single enemy. The centre column of Prince Schwartzenberg's army was marching in the direction of Gray along the heights of the Seine and Marne basins, and avoiding the Lower Saône. This delay had allowed additional munitions to be brought into the town, and the garrison increased by some recruits who, not being able to join their regiments, were wandering about without orders. Four pieces of field artillery, whose carriages were out of repair, had also been got into the town. The colonel had put himself in communication with Lyons; and Marshal Augereau, still hoping to commence offensive operations, had confirmed the previous orders that had been given— that is to say, to hold La Roche-Pont, and to gain all possible information respecting the enemy's movements in the north.

Towards the end of January the great army of Bohemia had some grounds for apprehending an attack on its rear; and Prince Schwartzenberg knew that from Macon along the ascent of the Saône, and as far as the countries intersected by hills which form a part of Upper Burgundy, a nucleus of resistance was being formed which might at any moment take the offensive and embarrass him greatly. After the battle of Brienne (29th of January), as the result of which the Prussians were thrown back by Napoleon on La Rothière, the sovereigns assembled in Prince Schwartzenberg's neighbourhood deliberated as to whether they should stop short at Langres or risk advancing alone against the troops commanded by the Emperor.

This indecision with regard to ulterior operations led to a more effective concentration and the occupation of a circle of wider radius around Langres.

Orders were then given to a body of four thousand of the allied Bavarians and Austrians to invest La Roche-Pont, and to guard the route from Lyons to Langres.

It was not till the 1st of February that the front of this corps showed itself before La Roche-Pont.

Colonel Dubois had not been wasting time: the garrison was provisioned for more than six weeks, and munitions were not wanting. This superior officer had put everything in order; and his troops, motley in appearance, certainly, but well rested and full of confidence, amounted at that time to more than nineteen hundred men, of whom twelve hundred were experienced soldiers who might be relied upon. The works on the north were well armed and the defences in good condition, duly furnished with palisades, traverses, and appliances for shelter.

On the evening of the 2nd of February, some of the enemy's horse were caracoling at a distance of about two hundred yards from the works; this bravado cost them about a dozen men.

The enemy, however, did not seem desirous of undertaking a regular siege, but took up a position about a mile from the northern salient; he sent detachments to occupy the faubourg on the left bank, and raised an encampment on the eastern hills.

The colonel had blown up the stone-bridge and destroyed the foot-bridges.

On the morning of the 4th of February an envoy appeared on the glacis and handed on to the governor of the place a summons from General Werther, demanding the surrender of La Roche-Pont to the troops of the allied princes. The garrison would be allowed to retire southwards with arms, baggage, and field artillery.

The colonel replied that the place was sufficiently strong and well provided; it would not capitulate till the moment when the breaches were no longer tenable; and he judged that the defence could not be prolonged to any purpose.

The following night Colonel Dubois sent out a hundred men to try the strength of the enemy's outposts and reconnoitre their positions.

By the end of the two following days—the 5th and 6th —the investment was almost complete, and the communication with the surrounding country interrupted. On the evening of the 9th there came another summons from the enemy's general, declaring that if the place were not surrendered within twenty-four hours the bombardment would commence. The colonel replied as before.

In fact, on the 10th of February a mortar battery opened fire, first on the northern salient, about eight o'clock in the evening. The bombs produced no effect, and in ten hours' bombardment only eight men had been struck, the roof of one of the barracks broken in, and two gun-carriages damaged.

The pieces of large calibre mounted on the cavaliers of the bastions of the work did not begin to fire on the mortar battery until daybreak, and silenced it about noon. The enemy appeared then to limit his efforts to the investment; and it was not till the 17th of February, probably in consequence of news received from the north, that he appeared to decide on a regular siege. Perhaps until this moment he had not the needful appliances.

On the night of the 17th, the first parallel was commenced about six hundred yards from the salient of the re-entering *place d'armes* (Fig. 70), as also the communications between this parallel and the depôts. About two o'clock in the morning the governor sent out a hundred and fifty men, who charged the advanced posts protecting the workmen on the western side of the plateau, and forced their passage through to the trench; put the sappers to rout, took some of their tools, and then, seeing themselves taken in flank, rushed up the slopes of the plateau, and re-entered by the postern of the lower town, protected by the fires of the demi-bastion.

On the 18th of February those who worked by day finished what their comrades, told off for night work, had commenced; and the engineers fixed in the parallel the prolongations of the works of the place, which they were intending to ricochet, with a view to planting the first batteries. By the method in which the besieger was proceeding, Colonel Dubois and Captain Allaud had no difficulty in perceiving that they had to do with a methodical enemy, who would conduct his attack according to the rules of the art, and would employ the acknowledged methods of approach against the main work of La Roche-Pont. The commander of the Bavarian engineers, in fact, had drawn out the plan of siege as exhibited in Fig. 70.

On the night of the 18th of February he commenced the ricochet batteries of the first parallel, and the boyaux of communication that were to lead to the second parallel; the works were continued by day. He was intending to direct the siege in the method we are going to describe.

On the third night the batteries of the first parallel were completed so as to fire in concert at daybreak.

The fourth night, supposing the artillery of the besieged to be silenced, they would commence the second parallel, and the fifth night the counter-batteries parallel and perpendicular to the faces to be cannonaded.

The sixth night would be occupied with the continuation of the counter-batteries and the commencement, by sap, of the zigzags about as far as one hundred and sixty yards from the crest of the salient angles of the covered way.

During the seventh night the construction of the counter-batteries would be finished, and they would dig the demi-parallels.

On the eighth night they would continue to advance by sap in zigzag, and arm the demi-parallel with howitzers and mortars, to commence their fire at daybreak at the same time as the counter-batteries.

On the ninth night the sap-fronts would reach the glacis fifty or sixty yards from the salient angles of the covered way, and the zigzags would enter the third parallel, which they would continue by day.

On the tenth night the works would be completed, the third parallel should be finished, and batteries of stone mortars planted there.

On the eleventh night they were to drive two saps a length of twenty-six or thirty yards, right and left of the capital (Fig. 71). They would dig the circular trenches, and then advance straight on the capital by double sap to within range of hand-grenades; twenty-six to thirty yards from the salient of the *places d'armes*. Protected by the fire of the third parallel, this work would be continued by day.

The twelfth night would be employed in tracing the trench cavalier by means of two saps; these works were to be terminated by day.

The thirteenth night, starting from the extremities of the trench cavaliers near the capitals, by double sap, they would crown the salient angles of the covered way. At daybreak these crownings would be finished, and the construction of the counter-batteries commenced. They would get down by means of two saps (Fig. 71) to the *place d'armes*, to establish a lodgment parallel to the rounding of the ditches.

If necessary, they would drive right and left of the crowning two saps which would meet each other in the middle of this crowning. A fourth parallel would, if necessary, be established, on which they would then place the stone mortars of the third parallel. If this fourth parallel was not needed, they would advance from the third parallel by means of a double sap directly upon the salient of the re-entering *place d'armes*.

The fourteenth night the crowning was to be extended along the branches of the covered way as far as the first traverse. The construction of the counter-batteries, and that of the fourth parallel, would be continued. If this fourth parallel were not required, the saps would reach to the salient of the re-entering *place d'armes*, which they would crown. At daybreak the breach batteries would be commenced.

On the fifteenth night these works would be completed; then, if they had been obliged to dig a fourth parallel, they would diverge from that in two saps which would unite to form a strong traverse, under shelter of which these saps would reach as far as the salient of the re-entering *place d'armes*, which they would crown by extending that crowning right and left. They would then have to commence the descent of the ditch.

During the sixteenth night the breach batteries would be terminated, and would begin firing. They would work at the descent of the ditch. If possible, they would get down into the *place d'armes* to install themselves and plant a battery of stone mortars there.

The seventeenth night would be occupied in finishing the descent to the ditch, and they would commence the epaulement of the passage.

During the eighteenth night they would begin to make a breach, and advance the passage of the ditch of the breach, which should be effected in the morning.

During the nineteenth night they would reconnoitre the breach, and the sappers would render it practicable. They would terminate the epaulements of the passage of the ditch, that the assault might be made next day.

Thus, according to the plan of the siege, in nineteen times twenty-four hours the place would be in the power of the enemy.

The lines were fixed upon, and General Werther did not doubt of success, as he did not imagine that La Roche-Pont could be succoured, and was aware of the weakness of the garrison and the inefficient character of its artillery.

Nevertheless, these theoretic calculations were somewhat disconcerted by the energy of the defence.

Colonel Dubois had not men enough to act efficiently at a distance; he did his utmost to economise his strength, and contented himself with impeding the works at the commencement with his artillery. This consisted, as we have seen, of—

Guns of various calibre	20
Twenty-four pounders	6
Howitzers	2
Mortars	4
Field-pieces	4
Total of ordnance	36

A dozen stone mortars and rampart rifles formed the rest of the artillery. The arsenal contained also a certain supply of hand-grenades and fireworks.

At length, on the 20th of February, the batteries of the first parallel, to the number of ten, opened their fire. Each of them was armed with three guns; the first on the right (of the besieger), à ricochet, raked the covered way in front of the right face of the left bastion (of the besieged). The second swept the right face of the left demi-lune; the third, the left face of the middle demi-lune; the fourth, à ricochet, raked the covered way in front of the left face of the left bastion; the fifth swept the salient of the demi-lune; the sixth swept the right face of that demi-lune; the seventh, à ricochet, raked the covered way in front of the left face of the right bastion; the eighth, à ricochet, raked the left face of the demi-lune in the centre; the ninth swept the left face of the right demi-lune; and the tenth, à ricochet, raked the covered way before the left face of the right bastion. Four mortars were mounted between the batteries 4 and 5, 6 and 7. Captain Allaud did not doubt that the principal attack would be directed to the left bastion; he had the gorge of this bastion therefore retrenched during the night. The six twenty-four pounders were placed in battery on the cavaliers of the bastions of the main defence, and well sheltered by traverses and blindages. These six pieces concentrated their fire on the fourth and fifth batteries of the besieger, and succeeded in silencing their fire about noon. Then they fired on battery No. 3, and before night silenced its three guns also. The guns in battery on the cavaliers of the bastions of the work were sufficiently well sheltered not to be in danger from the enemy's projectiles, to which they responded only feebly. But on the night of the 20th February the plans of the besieger had to be modified. At midnight the colonel ordered five hundred men to arm, put horses to his four field-pieces, whose wheels had been covered with rags and wool, and going out by the left demi-lune, he had two pieces placed on the right and two on the left of the road, two hundred yards in front of the glacis, and, on the road itself, the two howitzers, a hundred yards behind.

Then he advanced resolutely towards the communicating boyau, between the third and fourth of the enemy's batteries, whose fire had been silenced. The posts offered but a slight resistance; the sappers fled, abandoning the trench, and were pursued to the batteries at the point of the bayonet.

The reinforcements then arrived, and the colonel drew back his men quietly, by echelons, to the guns. These then opened a simultaneous fire on the enemy with grape; and the five hundred men advanced once more, and brought back some prisoners, but seeing themselves again attacked by a superior force, fell back. This time the Germans did not go beyond their trenches, but contented themselves with a few volleys of grape at random. This skirmish did not last more than half an hour. At one o'clock A.M. Captain Allaud placed two hundred workmen at a distance of two hundred and fifty yards in front of the face of the left demi-lune No. 1, crossed by the road, to commence a trench at this point (Fig. 72). These workmen were protected by a post of one hundred men, and the two howitzers left on the road. This work consisted of two redans, with massive traverse-shelters (see A). It was sufficiently advanced at daybreak to be able to shelter the workmen. When the enemy, who had begun his work again at the trench boyaux, B and C, in order to commence the second parallel, perceived at early dawn the new work executed by the besieged, he hastened to bring the fire of battery No. 1 upon it, for batteries 2, 3, and 4 had not yet been remounted. But from the cavaliers of the bastions No. I. and V., six guns in two hours silenced this battery, No. 1, in spite of the besieger's batteries, 5 and 6. The day thus passed in cannonading, and the Germans could not continue their boyau of communication, B, which was raked by one of the howitzers which the besieged had

FIG. 70.

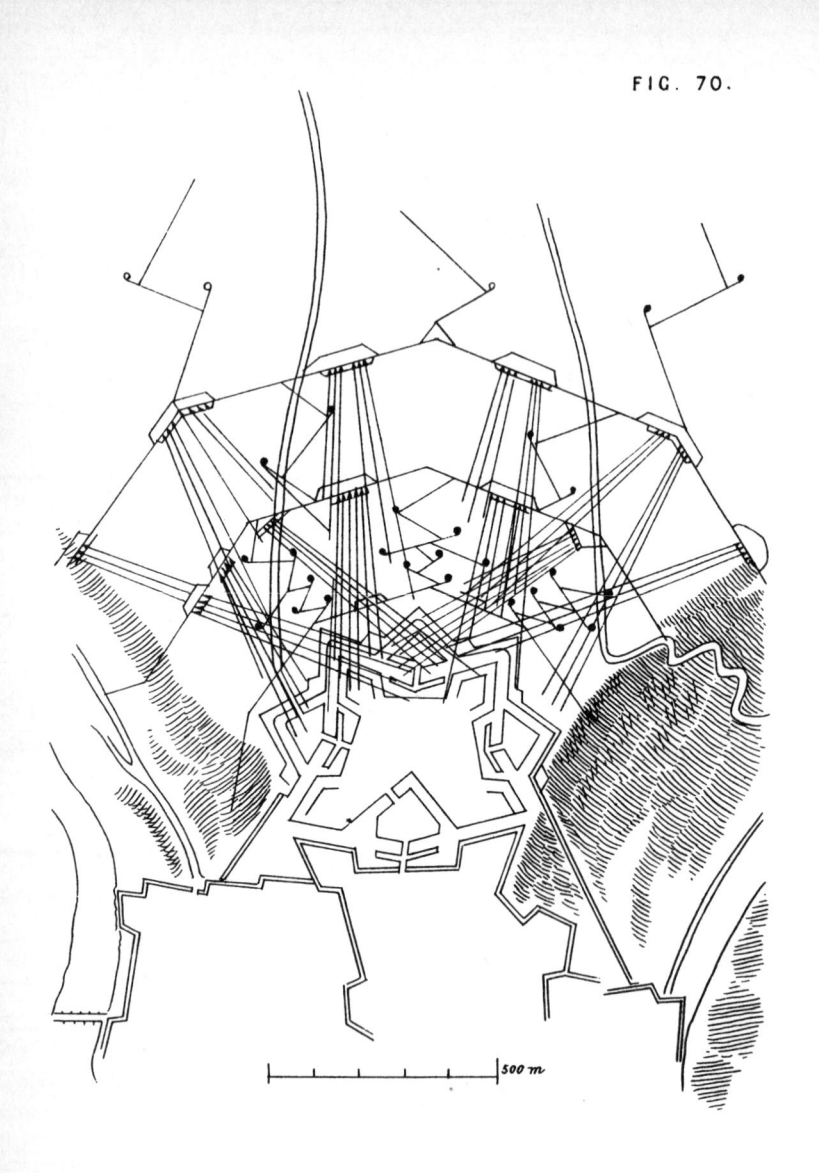

500 m

THE THEORETICAL ATTACK ON VAUBAN'S WORK.

FIG 71.

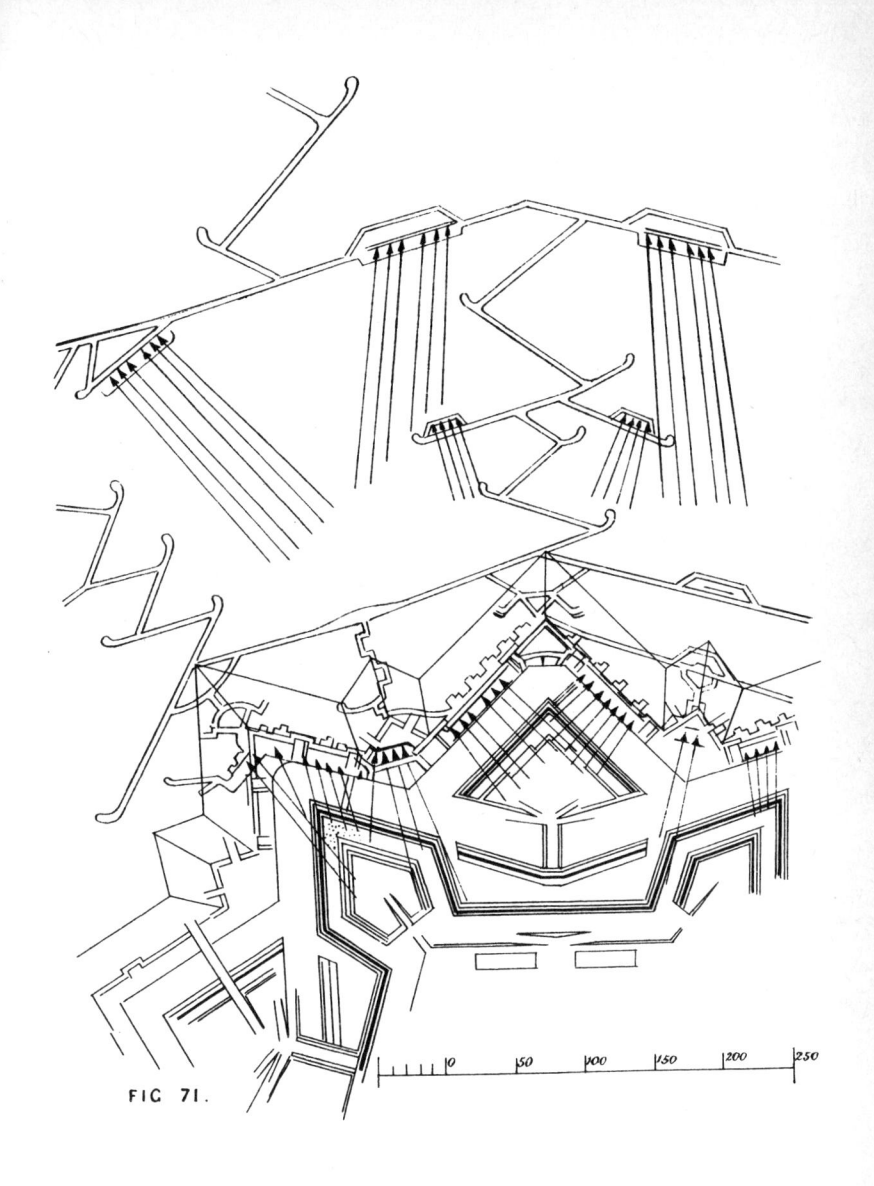

THE THIRD PARALLEL AND CROWNING OF THE COVERED-WAY.

placed behind the great traverse of the salient of the redan on the left. They had to modify the direction of the trench, and follow the dotted line, *a b*.

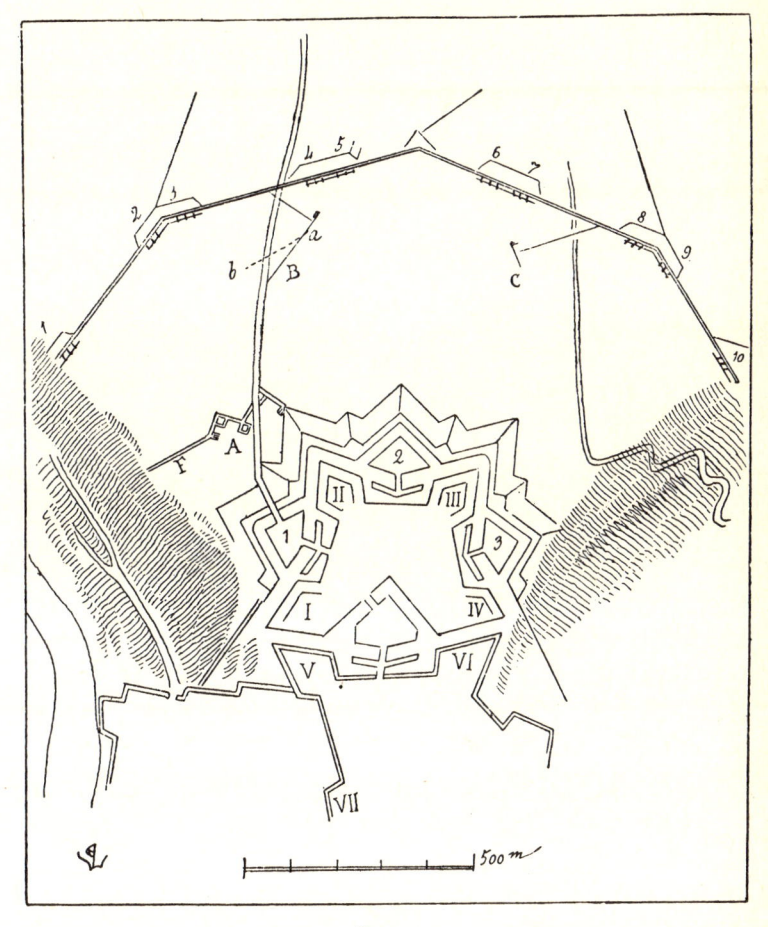

Fig. 72.

During the night of the 21st of February, Captain Allaud completed his redans, enlarged the traverses, and set up blindages for seven guns; and in the morning the work presented on the inner side the appearance (Fig. 73). The gun on the left, A, directed its fire on battery No. 1 ; the two guns on the left return, B C, on battery No. 4 ; the

Fig. 73.

pieces D E, of the right return, on battery No. 1 ; and the two pieces F G, of the right face, on battery No. 6.[1] But

[1] See for the numbers of the enemy's batteries, Fig. 72.

this did not hinder the bastions V., VI., I., II., and III. from firing on these batteries.

That same night, however, the besieger had been able to start his second parallel; but he was evidently embarrassed on his right, and was modifying his plan on this side. He seemed to be giving up an attempt on the place by the salient of bastion No. 2, and was working actively on his left.

During the 22nd of February, the besiegers could not restore battery No. 1, because the besieged kept up a constant discharge on this point. They succeeded only at nightfall in remounting their guns in batteries 2 and 3; and having determined the range before night, discharged the balls of two guns on the salients of the redans. About midnight Colonel Dubois sent out five hundred men, who, traversing the western ridge of the plateau, attacked battery No. 1. A few moments afterwards, a second troop of four hundred men attacked the two batteries, 2 and 3; and the besieger having been dislodged from battery No. 1, the first troop of the besieged came and formed in line of musketry between battery No. 2 and the salient of the redan on the right; while fusiliers posted at the trench, A,[1] and one of the howitzers, swept the ground as far as battery No. 1, in order to hinder the enemy from taking the sortie in the rear.

This operation was completely successful; not only were the works of battery No. 1 damaged, and the three guns with which it was armed (the carriages belonging to these guns, as stated above, were already broken), but around batteries 2 and 3 there was a very sharp struggle, which resulted in the Germans being repulsed, the guns rendered useless, the munitions scattered, and the gabions and earth-bags thrown down. A body of a hundred men had also

[1] See Fig. 72.

been posted by the colonel on the slopes of the plateau to hinder the enemy from making his way along that escarpment to attack the work A.

Under favour of this sortie, two hundred workmen had been placed by Captain Allaud along the western ridge of the plateau, to raise a new work, B C D (Fig. 74), which consisted of three new redans presenting three batteries each for two guns, traced *en crémaillère*, and separated by strong traverses. By the morning of the 23rd of February the first battery, B, was sufficiently strong to resist projectiles.

Moreover, this battery could not be immediately attacked by battery No. 1, which was abandoned, and whose guns were useless. Forty-eight hours at least were required to enable the besieger to restore batteries 2 and 3. Batteries 4 and 5 must change their embrasures to direct their fire on this battery B, and only batteries 6 and 7 could sweep the redans A and B. Now these batteries, 6 and 7, received the fire of the two guns of the right face of the right-hand redan, of the two guns of the right face of the bastion II., of the two guns of the left face of the bastion III., and of a gun of the right face of the demi-lune 2. Every moment it was necessary to repair the gabionades, and replace the earth-bags; and since the beginning of the day the enemy had had ten artillerymen killed, and as many more wounded, in these two batteries.

The German engineer, who had so methodically traced the successive operations of the siege, was evidently embarrassed by the strategy of the besieged. It was in his opinion barbarous, absolutely contrary to rules, and showed an ignorance of, and contempt for the art of fortification, which must end in disaster.

During the night of the 23rd of February the Germans were finishing their second parallel, except in the north-west side. They gave the eastern branch of this parallel an inclination towards the south,[1] and commenced the

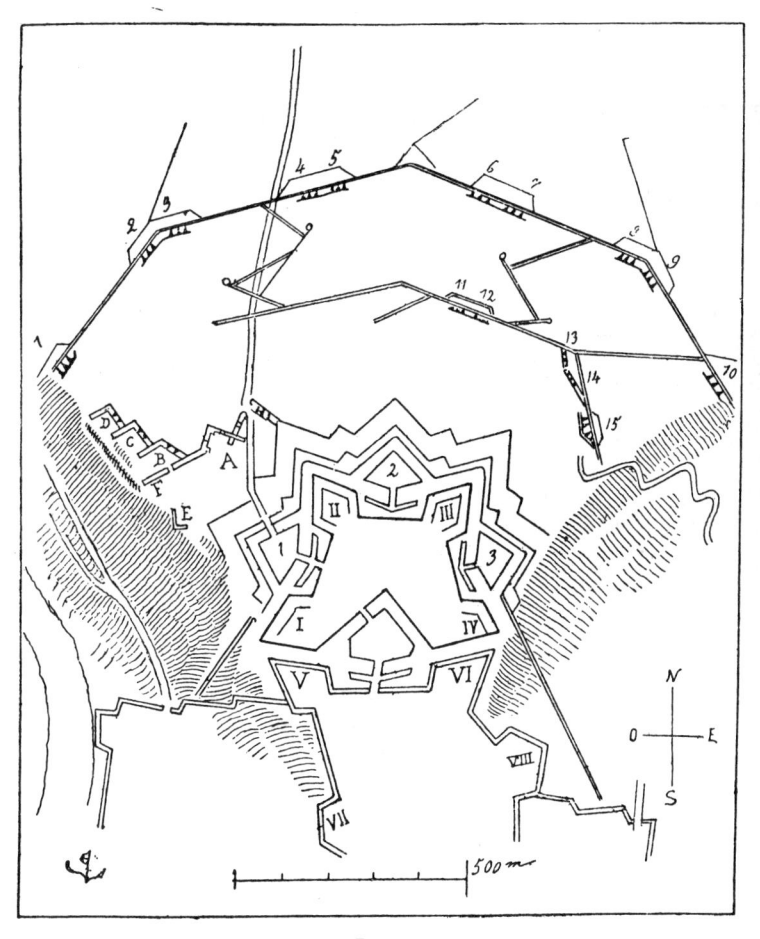

FIG. 74.

batteries 11, 12, 13, 14, and 15. Battery 13, of two guns, was to rake the work A.

[1] See Fig. 74.

But that same night Captain Allaud terminated the second battery, C, started the third, D, had an intrenchment made on the ridge of the plateau, and raised an epaulement, E, to sweep the slopes, with a good parados.

If the besieged succeeded in finishing and arming these works, the batteries 11 and 12 of the besieger would be taken obliquely, the boyaux of communication would be for the most part raked, and the siege would have to be recommenced. The German general was in a very bad humour, and blamed the commander of the engineers, who, with his plan on the table, endeavoured to show that his siege had been duly arranged, according to all the rules of the art; that the ignorant temerity of these Frenchmen could not be foreseen, and that if the Germans acted with vigour, they would be made bitterly to repent of thus advancing wedge-like on the flank of the attack; that such a thing had never been seen, and that if they concentrated three batteries on this salient in the air, they would soon crush it.

On the morning of the 24th of February two twenty-four pounders, placed in battery on the left face of bastion VIII., opened fire on batteries 13, 14, and 15 of the besieger, which they raked, and damaged greatly before they were completely finished. This time the German general proceeded from ill-humour to passion and even menaces; so that the unfortunate officer of the engineers, repairing to these batteries after a violent scene to raise traverses and rectify the line, which he asserted had not been executed conformably to his instructions, had his head broken by a splinter from a gun-carriage.

The direction of the engineering was then given to a young officer, who, after a conference with General Werther, modified the plan of the attack. During the 24th of the month there was scarcely any firing on either side, the besieger firing only at long intervals. The French garrison, which was anxious to economise its munitions, scarcely replied, but worked with ardour at perfecting its advanced works on the west.

A sortie effected during the night of the 24th, to ascertain whether the enemy was re-taking possession of batteries 1, 2, and 3, only encountered advanced posts, which retired after a feeble resistance. These three batteries were in the condition to which they had been reduced by the preceding sortie.

Captain Allaud employed the whole of the night in strengthening the batteries B, C, D. They were armed with six guns, which on the morning of the 25th swept the boyaux of communication and a whole branch of the second parallel.

The Germans scarcely replied, and seemed to be abandoning their works.

They were probably going to try another attack. The colonel was somewhat disquieted at Captain Allaud's novel strategy, which, in face of a bold assailant, presented grave perils. The calmness of the enemy made him fear some unexpected design; perhaps a strenuous attack on that salient which, if it were taken, would furnish the besiegers with an excellent position for rapidly establishing breach batteries against demi-lune No. 1, and bastion II. This salient therefore must be defended at any cost, since they had been led to establish it in order to disconcert the systematic attack of the Germans. Moreover, if they lost it, they would probably lose at the same time most of the guns that armed it; and the defence had only a restricted number.

Thirteen guns armed the advanced work. The two howitzers were placed in battery, one at the extremity of the salient D, pointed at battery No. 1, the other in the right re-entering *place d'armes* of the demi-lune No. 1. Two guns were also placed on the right face of the demi-lune; two guns on the front, between the bastions I. and II., and two guns on the right and left faces of this bastion, to sweep the advanced works if they were taken. In all, nineteen guns and two howitzers. Besides, the ridge of the plateau was well defended by a good trench-shelter with traverses, that the work might not be able to be taken by assault in rear by the escarpment. One of the twenty-four pounders was placed in battery in the bastion V. of the main work, in the direction of its capital, to sweep this slope.

On the 25th of February only a few cannon-shots were exchanged. The mortar batteries of the besieger concentrated their fire on the western redan, without doing much damage; but during the night of the 25th the fire of the bombs was so incessant that it became difficult to labour at these works. It continued during the 26th, but the besieged dismounted three of these mortars with the guns left on the bastions II. and III. The besieged on his side placed the two mortars in battery on the front between these two bastions, and sent projectiles into the batteries 11 and 12.

During the 26th of the month (the weather being clear) the enemy was seen to be erecting three batteries on the north-west, evidently directed against the batteries A, B, C, D, to crush them. They could not reply to their fire; the colonel therefore decided that they should bring back into the town temporarily the six guns of the batteries B, C, D. The bombs continued to fall into the works during the whole night of the 26th; and on the morning of the 27th the fire of the three batteries of the enemy, erected six hundred and fifty yards behind the abandoned battery No. 1, was opened against the redans B, C, D; it lasted the whole night of the 27th, damaged the blindages very severely, and threw down the traverses. On the morning of the 28th the *crémaillère* ceased to be tenable, but the work A had not been seriously injured. The howitzer placed at D had been brought back behind the great traverse F surmounted with a banquette.

About nine o'clock the enemy resumed possession of the battery No. 1, installed four field-pieces there in spite of the fire of the bastions I. and II., and threw an assaulting column against the damaged works D, C, B. This was what the colonel anticipated. The column encountered the fire of the three guns left in the redans A, the howitzer, and a front of fusiliers posted on the great traverse F. Bending to the right and defiling below the crest of the plateau, this column was able to seize the work B, C, D, without excessive loss; and, sheltered behind the ruins of the earthworks, it was able to keep its ground there while the field-pieces of the battery No. 1 cleared off the defenders of the great traverse F. The colonel, however, had brought in again the guns left in work A, and gave orders to his men to fall back. But at this juncture, from the demi-lune No. 1, the bastions I. and II. and the curtain between these bastions, twenty-two guns and some stone mortars poured a tremendously heavy fire into the abandoned work, inflicting very serious loss on the besieger, who was endeavouring to hold his ground there. This cannonade lasted till noon. The colonel, supposing the enemy to be giving way, sallied forth at the head of eight hundred men and fell on the posts which the Germans had begun to fortify. He had his attack sustained by the two howitzers. The work was retaken, but not without the loss of about a hundred men. The great point was to keep it. About two o'clock two field-pieces conveyed behind the ruined epaulements of batteries 2 and 3, and the four of battery No. 1, once more overwhelmed the salient with small bombs, balls, and grape. The bastions I., II., and III. replied immediately, and dismounted some of the enemy's pieces, which were ill-protected by the battered-down epaulements. The colonel made his men lie down behind the traverses ·C, B, F, and awaited a second assault; which was in fact attempted about four o'clock, as the enemy believed the outwork was once more abandoned. The assaulting columns passed the first epaulement; but as soon as they found themselves in the last redan, D, they were received by a discharge of muskets almost at arm's length, from behind the traverse C (Fig. 75), followed by a bayonet charge; this time two hundred Germans remained on the field, and the remains of the assaulting column fell back in disorder to the batteries, which recommenced firing and went on till nightfall.

The besieged remained masters of the place, but under the converging fire of the enemy they could not maintain this wedge-shaped and badly flanked position. There was no advantage in keeping it, sufficient to compensate for the loss they would suffer in resisting fresh attacks. However, the colonel was unwilling to abandon the redans without cost to the enemy. The evening was employed in charging three powder-mines under the salients A and B, and raising earthworks to protect themselves as well as they could. All this night of the 28th of February the bombs fell thick on the outwork: the men were still tolerably protected on the *débris* of the blindages. On the morning of the 1st of March the German artillery recommenced firing on the redans more briskly than the day before, from the three batteries behind and from battery No. 6.

The colonel withdrew his men into the town, and left only one platoon, well sheltered, with orders to fire the

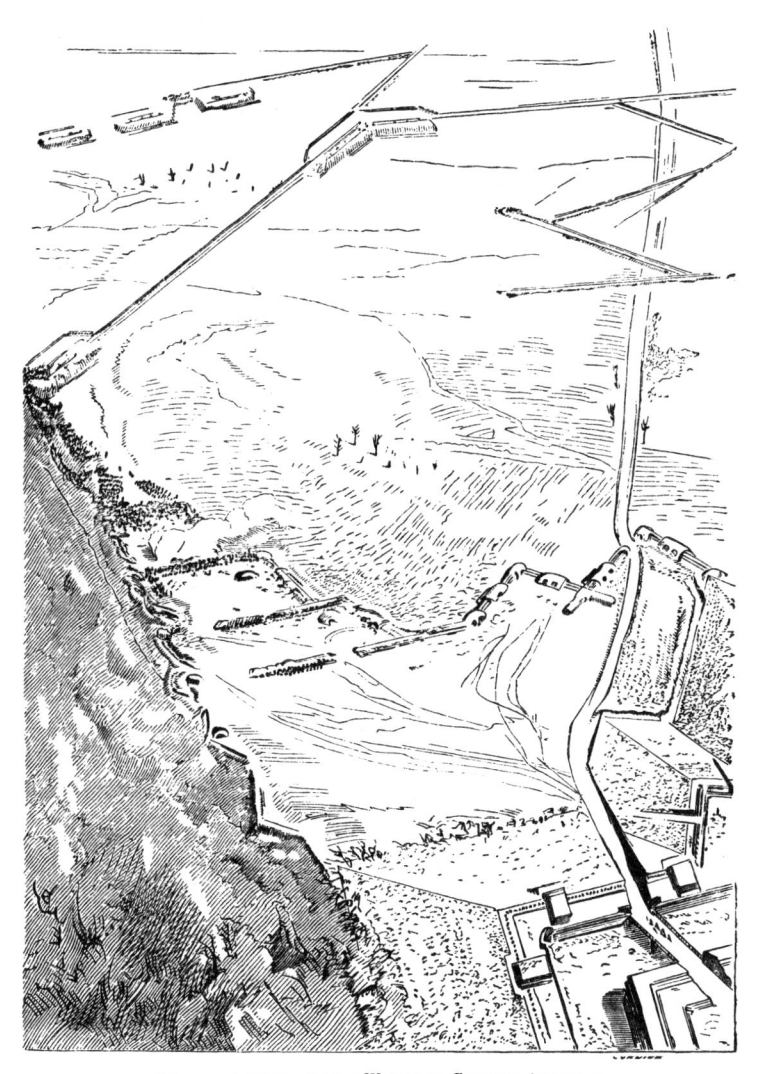

FIG. 75.—ATTACK ON THE WORKS OF COUNTER-APPROACH.

mines only when the enemy thought himself covered by the epaulement of the redan A, and was endeavouring to take up his position there.

The 1st of March passed by without a new assault being attempted by the besiegers. "They will try it to-night," thought Colonel Dubois. He went back about seven o'clock in the evening into the salient, to make certain that the train was well laid; and to encourage his men, he reinforced them with twenty fusiliers, enjoining upon them, when they saw their enemy, to make such a pretence of defending themselves as should be sufficient to draw him on; but to fall back promptly after setting fire to the train.

The bombardment was recommenced about eight o'clock, but at ten ceased for a time; and the colonel, who had ascended the cavalier of bastion II., thought the enemy was about to make a fresh attempt. In fact, notwithstanding the darkness of the night, he saw black masses spreading successively through the works D, C, and B[1]. On arriving at the traverse F, they were received by a volley of musketry, to which they responded by a well-sustained fire. A mass of the enemy might be seen moving along the traverse F, and halting outside the redans A. At this moment three successive explosions were heard which made the ground tremble, succeeded by loud cries. The order was given: from the demi-lune No. I. and bastions I. and II., all the pieces fired together on the outwork for half an hour; after which two hundred men of the garrison sallied forth and rushed on the enemy. The outwork contained only dead and wounded. Captain Allaud then went out in his turn with two hundred volunteer workmen, to fill up the trenches and destroy obstacles as far as possible. About midnight the bombs fell once more on the corner of the defence, and orders were given

[1] See Fig. 74.

to retire within the fortress, so as to avoid unnecessary loss.

The siege had lasted twelve days, and the second parallel, which ought to have been terminated on the sixth day, was not finished. The garrison reckoned about a hundred and fifty men killed and wounded; but they had inflicted more serious losses on the besiegers.

General Werther found the affair a very tedious one, and was much annoyed. Some royalists, who had mansions in the faubourg on the other side of the river Abonne, were on very friendly terms with the troops of the coalition, and manifested their impatience and anger against "this handful of *brigands*" who were holding the upper town and prolonging a useless struggle. The German general was very anxious to come to terms with the garrison: four hundred of his men were already *hors de combat*, and he thought this a great expenditure in taking this "nest," which was supposed to be without a garrison or munitions. The news he had lately received from the north was more encouraging, but he was urged to finish the business.

One of the most zealous of the royalists, who were constantly in the German camp, proposed therefore to pay a visit to the governor, to inform him that Napoleon's armies were retreating at every point, that the capture of Paris was imminent, that the Boubrons would soon return amid the acclamations of the whole of France, and to urge the uselessness of a longer defence.

General Werther readily acceded to the proposal, and on the 2nd of March, Baron de X *** presented himself at the outpost with a German envoy. The colonel received the German officer and the baron in a room in one of the ruined barracks. The German envoy first asked for an exchange of prisoners. This was readily granted by the colonel. Then the Baron de X * * * began in his turn to explain the object of his visit.

Scarcely had he begun when the colonel stopped him: "I do not know, and do not desire to know, sir, whether you come here to speak for yourself alone or as the representative of a certain number of your countrymen; but I will answer you briefly and clearly. I am here on the authority of superior orders to defend the place against the enemies of the country. The political inducements which you urge have not the slightest weight with me. I utterly ignore them. I shall not surrender the place unless compelled by force or ordered to do so by the Emperor's Government. Permit me to add, sir, that the part you are performing to-day is not an honourable one. What do you think of it, *Monsieur le capitaine?*" added he, turning to the German officer. The latter merely bowed slightly. "The prisoners shall be exchanged this very day, if you desire it, man for man," said the colonel, rising. "As to you, sir, if you had not come here protected by a flag of truce, I should have you tried, and probably shot before the garrison, ere sunset." And dismissing his two visitors, the governor enjoined on the officer commissioned to accompany them back to the outposts not to allow them to have any communication with anyone.

The besieger from this day forwards was but slow in carrying on his approach works; he contented himself with terminating the second parallel and setting up three batteries of six pieces each, which opened fire on the 6th of March upon the faces right and left of bastions II. and III., and on the left face of demi-lune No. 2, with the evident intention of making a breach at four hundred yards' distance. Three mortar batteries covered the works with bombs. The Germans were evidently intending to keep the garrison occupied, and put it out of heart; waiting the chance of political events to put the place in their hands. Of the four thousand men under General Werther's command, and who had been reduced to three thousand four hundred by the losses sustained, it was necessary to send one thousand to Troyes; only two thousand five hundred men therefore remained before La Roche-Pont. Besides, the general had received orders to run no risks, but limit himself to a surveillance of the passages from the Saône to the Marne, and blockading the garrison of La Roche-Pont, keeping it sufficiently employed to prevent its taking the offensive, but without losing men in the capture of so insignificant a place. On the other hand, the royalists of the lower town were constantly predicting the end of hostilities and the return of the Bourbons.

On the 12th of March news was received at headquarters that Napoleon had received a check before Laon, that Marmont's force had been routed, and that the allied troops were in full march on Paris. The royalists thought that the moment had come for another application to General Werther to induce him to complete the capture. They were anxious to be the first in Burgundy to declare for the Bourbons, and the cautious deliberation of the general of the allied troops exasperated them. He, too, would have liked to get possession of the place before the anticipated cessation of hostilities. He therefore sent another envoy to Colonel Dubois, to give him the latest news of the armies of the coalition, to inform him that the Allies were just about to enter Paris, which was now without defence, and to summon him to surrender in order to avoid a useless effusion of blood; and to say that if he refused to capitulate he must expect rigorous measures, which he, General Werther, would rather avoid, and of which the governor alone would have to bear the responsibility. Colonel Dubois' answer was exactly the same as before.

He said he could not capitulate, as his defences remained entire.

During the night of the 12th of March, two mortar batteries were planted on the hill slopes of the right bank, and opened fire in the evening on the faubourg of the left bank. The *flèche* which served as a *tête du pont* was broken down by the shells. The German general thought he should thus induce the townspeople to insist on the governor's promptly capitulating. Some of the houses in this faubourg caught fire, and the inhabitants took refuge in the upper town. The garrison could not respond to the fire of the mortar batteries, as they had no more guns of large calibre. The six twenty-four pounders were employed to oppose the enemy's batteries on the north, and they could not disarm the bastions on this side. To complete their distress typhus broke out among the wounded in the *cité*.

Provisions, too, were becoming scarce, and the garrison was placed on half rations.

On the plateau the cannonade on both sides was continuing, and the escarpments of the two bastions II. and III. were much damaged. As the enemy found nothing more to destroy or burn in the lower town on the right bank, he began his approaches on the 15th of March, and established a demi-parallel with two fresh batteries during the night (of the 15th and following day), of four guns each. This was, however, not accomplished without difficulty, for these batteries were only three hundred yards from the faces of bastions II. and III., whose cavaliers still preserved three guns of large calibre. But on the 18th and 19th of March twenty-six guns were brought to bear against the works, and succeeded in throwing down the parapets and dismounting the guns of the besieged.

During the night of the 19th of March, the colonel

endeavoured to mount the cannon that still remained to him; but these pieces of small calibre could effect nothing against the enemy's works. However, the breaches made in the salients of demi-lune No. 2 and of bastion II, were not practicable; and the colonel, wishing to reserve the little artillery he had left, for the moment of assault, retrenched the gorge of bastion II, withdrew its cannon within the fortification and waited the issue. Not to keep his soldiers idle he occupied them at night in trifling sorties which fatigued the besieger. He kept the covered ways in good repair as far as the enemy's fire allowed, and prepared camouflets and *chicanes* for the moment when the assailant should try to ascend the counterscarp.

On the 25th of March the third parallel was finished. The place was thenceforth only defended by musketry, and a few stone mortars, and grenades, which small sallying parties threw into the trenches at night.

The approaches to crown the covered way and set up breach batteries were advancing but slowly, thanks to the activity of the garrison, whose courage seemed redoubled in seeing the enemy approaching and which defended its glacis foot by foot.

On the 1st of April came the news of the capitulation of Paris, the abdication of the Emperor, and the order to suspend hostilities. The garrison was allowed to retire to Nevers, through Auxonne, Beaune, Autun and Château-Chinon.

On the 5th of April Colonel Dubois quitted La Roche-Pont at the head of seven hundred soldiers of all arms, who were all the able-bodied men left him.

CHAPTER XVII.

CONCLUSION.

NOTWITHSTANDING its bastioned enclosure and great outwork which was still existing in 1870, exactly as Vauban had planned it, the town of La Roche-Pont could not have held out forty-eight hours before the German artillery. A few batteries to the north, on the plateau, and on the west and east on the sides of the hills placed at nearly two miles distant would have overwhelmed the place with projectiles without a possibility of replying; for in September 1870 the small arsenal of La Roche-Pont contained only six cast iron guns, and four bronze pieces with smooth bore, two thousand pounds of powder and two or three hundred solid balls.

It was not attacked, though bodies of the enemy showed themselves not far from its walls.

Its garrison consisted then of a guard of the engineers and a brigade of gendarmes.

The inhabitants of La Roche-Pont are, however, patriotic, and mention with pride the numerous sieges they have experienced.

They had organized their national guard as early as August, including an artillery corps. It is true they had not been able to supply these National Guards with more than a hundred flint guns which were lying in the citadel, and about thirty muzzle-loading guns. These brave people were not less determined to defend themselves, and began to cast bullets and make cartridges. They had not the pain of seeing the Germans there.

In 1871, a French captain of engineers, having been in General Bourbaki's army, had entered Switzerland with the *débris* of the corps.

Captain Jean had received a bullet in his breast, not far from the frontier, and had been taken up by some peasants in the environs of Pontarlier, and saved by some Swiss custom house officers who had conveyed him to Lausanne, where he had received the most careful attention. We might give a touching account of that sad period of our disasters; and indeed we must write it if it is to be on record at all, for the Swiss are not the people to make a parade of the zealous kindness they displayed on this occasion in saving our harassed, famished, and frozen soldiers. Peasants and townspeople set out amid the snows of the Jura, to guide and to give shelter to our disbanded and wandering regiments. Some sacrificed their lives in this service of humanity, and emulated each other in offering an asylum and giving assistance to our exhausted soldiers. The behaviour of these excellent people has excited universal admiration.

Captain Jean was living at Lausanne when Monsieur N. .... an officer on half pay happened to be there. His medical attendants thought that the climate would contribute to the cure of the wounded man, who had obtained a congé in the hope of regaining health under the clement skies of this part of the lake of Geneva. His sister had come to join him and was doing all for his cure that the tenderest affection could suggest. His strength was however not returning and alarming symptoms continued.

Captain Jean was from La Roche-Pont; he was on intimate terms with Monsieur N..... and the conversation often turned on the recent war and the resources which through ignorance or inability had not been employed; and they frequently spoke of this beautiful province of Burgundy, placed on the flank of the invasion, and which was so well adapted to mask and protect an offensive movement, if they had had an army of reserve with its right supported by Besançon and its left by Dijon, and abundantly supplied from the basins of the Rhône and the Saône.

The Captain used to employ his leisure in studying the defence of his dear little town whose history he knew so well and which he deemed a strategic position of some importance.

Monsieur N.... spent nearly a month in the company of this amiable and well-informed man, whose feelings were deeply affected by our disasters; but whose active mind sought in these misfortunes themselves a means of instruction, and an opportunity for developing the resources and advantages peculiar to France. This was an inexhaustible subject of conversation for the two friends, and they would continue talking till the sister interposed her authority as nurse to enjoin silence and rest.

In December 1871, Monsieur N.... received the following letter at Paris, accompanied by a bundle of papers.

"LAUSANNE, *December* 10*th*, 1871.

"SIR,

"My dearly loved brother died in my arms the day before yesterday, his death being the result of his wound and also perhaps of grief for our late disasters,—deeply affected as he was by the indelible recollection of the sufferings he had witnessed.

"He retained his consciousness to the last, and I am fulfilling one of his most urgent requests in sending you these papers. It is the only souvenir he can bequeath to you—

as he said to me the day before his death—of the hours you so kindly devoted to a poor invalid.

" My brother often spoke to me of you ; you were able to appreciate his excellencies and noble character, and will receive his bequest, I doubt not, as a mark of the profound esteem he had for you.

"As for myself I cannot quit a neighbourhood where I have lived with my brother, and where we have met with so much sympathy."

Extracts from Captain Jean's papers.

Attack implies a shock or onset ; defence is a resistance to this onset. Whether a piece of ordnance discharges a ball against a plate of iron, or a casing of masonry, or an earthwork ; or an assaulting column climbs a breach, the problem is substantially the same ; in either case we have to oppose to the impulsive force a resistance that will neutralise its effect.

When there were no projectile weapons, or their range was inconsiderable, only a normal resistance had to be opposed to the shock—a man to a man—or if the effect was to be rendered certain, two men to one. But when projectile arms acquired a longer range, the *position* of the attack and defence became a question of importance. Thus were evolved for combatants in open ground the elements of tactics, and for fortification, arrangements of a more and more complicated character.

It is evident, for example, that when it came to a close engagement—a hand-to-hand struggle with an adversary ; if the latter found himself placed behind a circular enclosure, the obstacle that protected him would give him a considerable advantage—an advantage that could only be compensated for by renewing the attack.

To make this very simple principle intelligible at a glance, suppose (Fig. 76) a circular enclosure containing forty defenders separated from each other about a yard

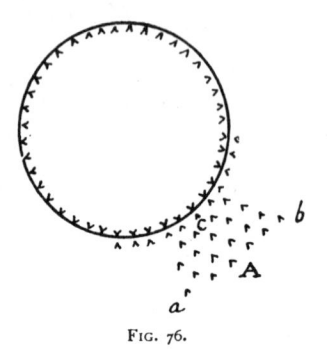

FIG. 76.

apart; a hand-to-hand struggle can only be carried on with a number equal to that of the defenders—or nearly so—and these under cover. It is no use for the assailants to assemble as at A, they can only present a front equal to that of the defence, and if this is energetic, the triangle a, b, c, will be effective only at c.

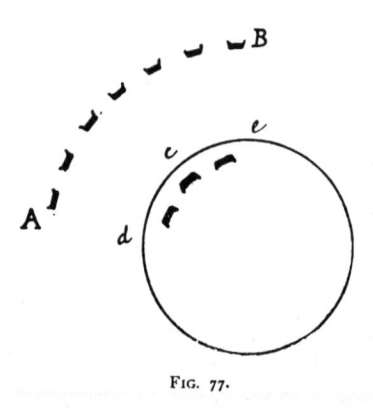

FIG. 77.

But let us suppose the attacking body to possess projectile arms (Fig. 77), and instead of encountering the circular enclosure, the assailants to set up their engines between A and B within fair range. They will overwhelm the segment d, c, e, of the circle with projectiles, while the defenders will be able to oppose only an inferior number of engines to the convergent fire.

To compensate in part for this inferiority the defending party adds appendages to the enclosure (Fig. 78 A), which allow an almost equal front of defence to be opposed to

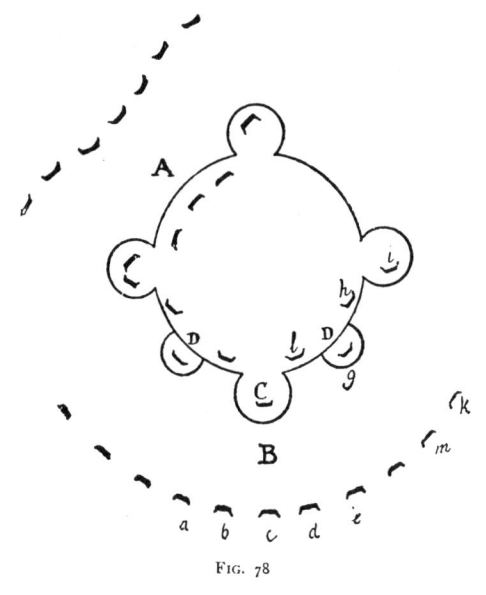

Fig. 78

the attacking front, as regards the number of projectile weapons, and very superior in point of elevation and protection. But the attacking force will thus naturally arrange its engines as seen at B. Thus the projectiles sent from a, b, c, d, e, converge upon the salient C. The defence adds the new appendages D D, and if the engines are well protected, it can make the projectiles g, h, i, converge on the engine K and crush it, secondly the projectiles l, g, h, on engine m and destroy it, and so on.

Besides, these appendages have the further advantage of giving side views over the circumvallation itself and masking its foot.

This principle regulates and will always regulate attack and defence; distances alone modify its applications.

The more eccentric the defence is, the more distant must be the attack, and the wider the perimeter it must occupy; but it should be observed, that the more widely the defence is extended, the more open its flanks are to attack; these flanks therefore must also be capable of being defended, for every obstacle that offers only its own resisting force, without being protected by the action of a neighbouring obstacle, is soon destroyed.

Whether fortifications or plans of battle are in question, the same principle comes into play. "Every part should defend its neighbour and be defended by it." It is clear that the solution of the problem becomes more and more difficult in proportion to the enlargement of the range of projectile weapons, and the extent of fronts of fortification or lines of battle.

Vauban, and most of the engineers who were his rivals and successors, had resolved the problem in view of the range of the artillery of the period.

Suppose a hexagon (Fig. 79), fortified according to Vauban's first method, it is evident that all the parts of the circumference of one thousand, and even one thousand eight hundred yards, are commanded by the curtains, the faces of the bastions and the demi-lunes. If the fortress stands in a level country, the enemy cannot occupy any point in that circumference without being exposed to its fire.

To raise his first parallel and first batteries, he would have to begin his works at the limit of the range of the rampart guns; and, as we saw in Fig. 70, he must erect these batteries sufficiently near the place to enable their fire to tell upon the defences—*i.e.*, at eight or nine hundred yards. At this distance the curtains could be swept, the faces and flanks raked, and the parapets thrown down. As the projectiles reached either point blank, or under an

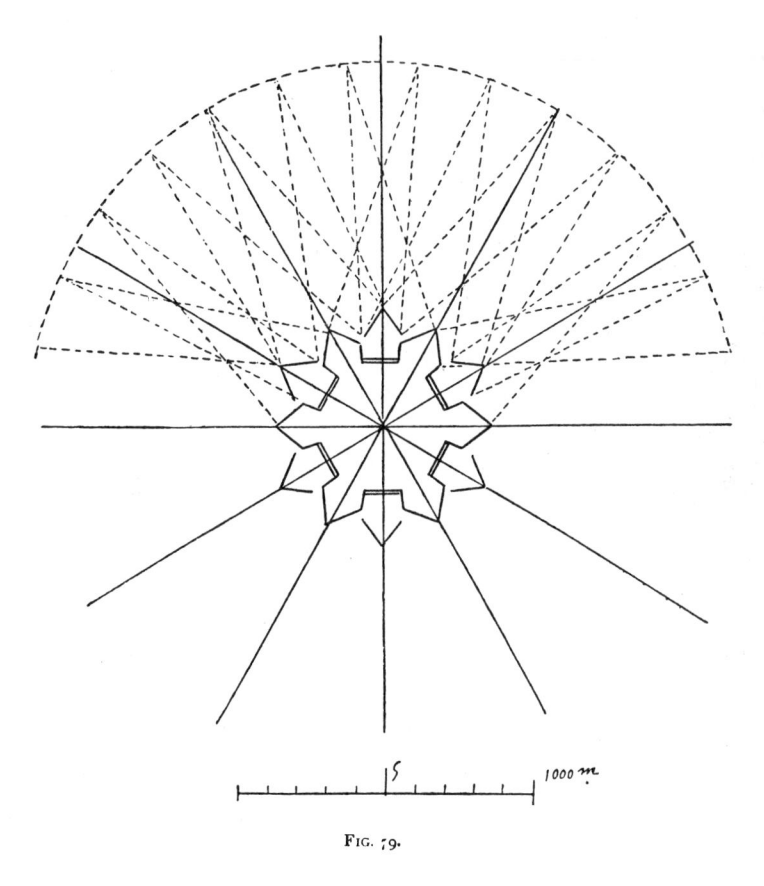

FIG. 79.

angle of about 10° when the ball rebounded, the besieged could protect himself against it for a very considerable time, and keep his own artillery intact.

But as the range of siege pieces in the present day extends to eight or nine thousand yards, the conditions both for the besieged and the besieger are very different. Hence (Fig. 80) the enemy raises his batteries on two or three fronts of the circumference, taking advantage of the rise in the ground, a wall, or a wood to protect his works, and when all is ready, he unmasks these batteries, and

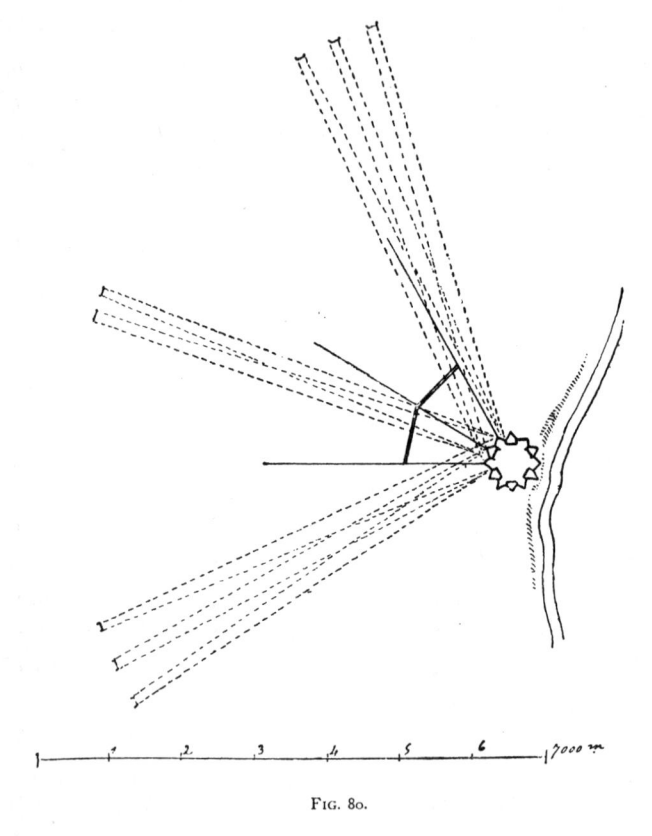

FIG. 80.

covers a segment of the fortress with a quantity of explosive projectiles, which, reaching it at an angle of 25° to 30° burst, no matter where—*dans le tas*, to use a common expression—the distance not allowing an aim at flanks or faces in particular—the besieger being in fact unable to distinguish them. Supposing the besieged able to maintain his artillery and reply, exposed as he is to the deluge of iron on his face and flanks, he has to aim at eccentric points which may vary, to whose position he has no clue but the smoke of the guns, and at an enemy, who, taking advantage of an indefinite amount of space to make his arrangements and shelter his men, is completely free. But to maintain his artillery and preserve his men and munitions, the besieged has only a space relatively limited to move in; he is soon encumbered with *débris* of all kinds, every movement is difficult for him, and he has not even room to repair damages. He tires himself out to no great purpose. If the attack has maintained its fire at a long range for several days, it has introduced such confusion into a great part of the defences, that in two or three nights afterwards the first parallel may be commenced at about one thousand yards, it may be well armed and protected by batteries *en retraite* and trench-shelters, so as to discourage sorties and allow of an advance to crown the covered ways. In what state are the works of the besieged by this time? The flanks of the bastions are as much damaged as their faces, the demi-lunes are untenable, and the ditches partly filled up; disorder and confusion prevail on all sides. No breach is practicable, certainly; but all the works are seriously injured on three or four fronts, and at one thousand yards distance, a breach may be made, and that a wide one. The garrison may sustain the assault to the last, and sell the possession of the *débris* of its work dearly; but in this case the final result is not doubtful.

In proportion to the length of the trajectory, therefore, the defence must remove its defensive arrangement from the centre of the place.

If each front of Vauban's defence was about four

hundred yards in length, it ought to be from thirteen to fourteen hundred yards now (Fig. 81). That is to say, the side of the hexagon which was four hundred yards—*i.e.*, from one salient of a bastion to another—should be fourteen hundred yards. Let A be the main body of

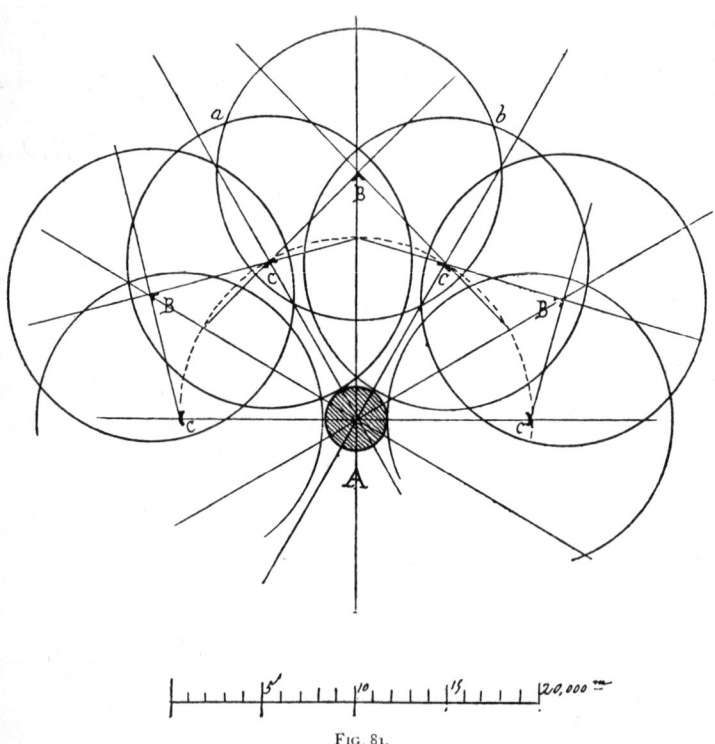

Fig. 81.

the fortress—on a plain suppose; forts will be erected at B and C, the zone of action of each of these works being eight thousand yards, they will protect each other and cross their fires without the possibility of their projectiles falling into the fortress if any of them should be in the power of the enemy.

Fig. 82 presents the block plan of each of those forts B and C, to whose interior arrangements we shall return. But by this excessive lengthening of the *capitals*, the forts B (Fig. 81), may be swept along the whole extent of the arc of a circle *a b* (more than the third of the circumference); they occupy the points of a triangle, and if one of them were taken the enemy would be able to batter two of the forts C. It is therefore necessary, with an extended radius,

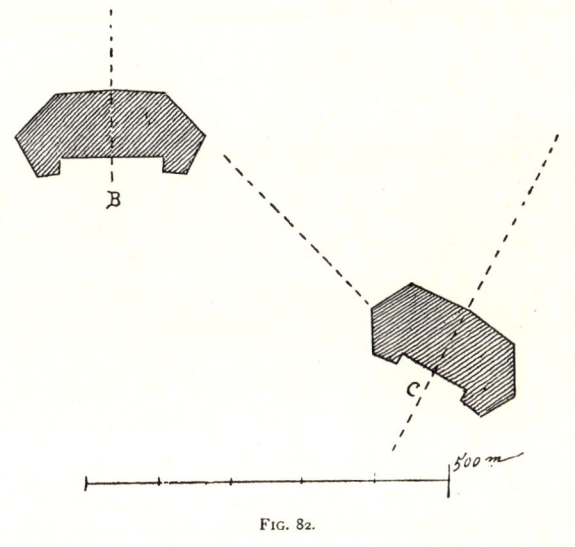

FIG. 82.

to multiply the defences, and to enable them to protect each other in a more effective manner. This is the method indicated in Fig. 83.

Here we have a dodecagon. The forts of the outer zone are seven thousand yards apart, and the works, A, flank each other; a second zone of forts B commands the latter, if required, and the zone of action of these second works extends beyond the outer line of forts. Railways are required to connect the forts of each zone, and to put them in communication with the body of the place.

This extension of the fields of defence may, according to the nature of the ground, be divided into two zones with a central nucleus.

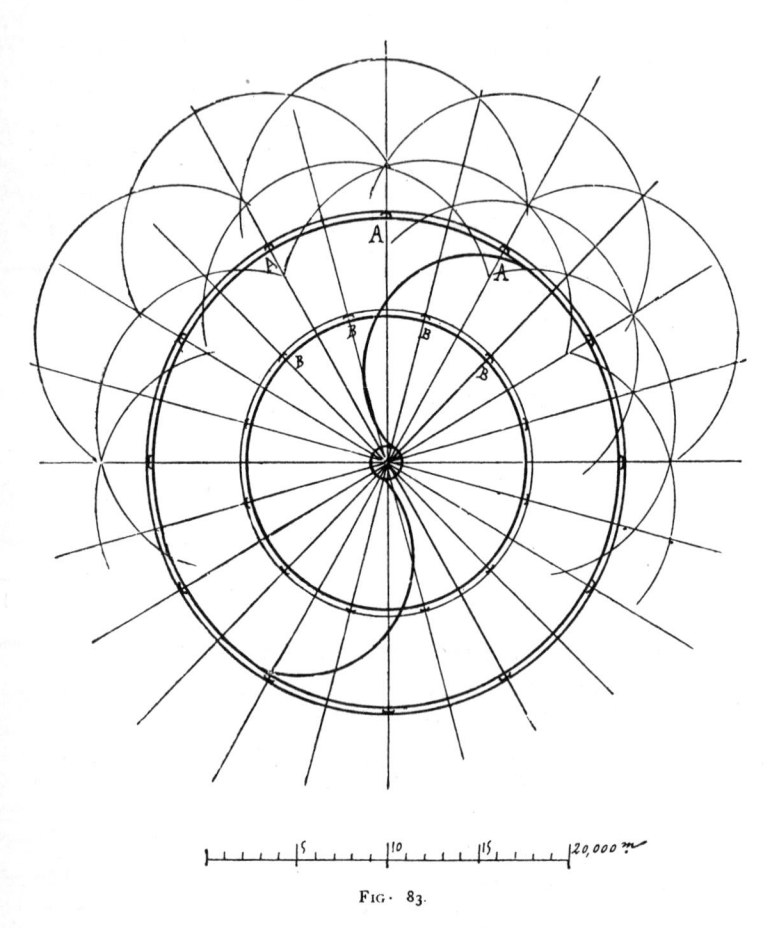

Fig. 83.

The interior zone would consist of permanent works, forming an *enceinte de préservation;* a line of forts at intervals sufficiently strengthened, in case of war, by field works.

The exterior zone would be fixed by occupying strategic

points well chosen and considered beforehand, forming small camps protected by temporary works, and affording security to a numerous army, whose manœuvres the enemy could not espy.

The expenditure entailed by such a system of defence is unquestionably enormous. But as respects this question there is to all appearance an unwillingness to realize exactly the new state of things produced by artillery of long range.

The expenditure involved in the successive systems of defence from ancient times downwards has been a continually increasing one. The wall built round Paris by Philippe-Augustus, would not cost, the running yard, as much as that of Charles V.; the latter, again, must have been less expensive than the bastioned fronts of Louis XIII., and these again would be far from necessitating the outlay (*i.e.* estimated by the running yard, and reckoning detached forts) occasioned by the fortification of Paris under Louis Philippe. Similarly the mounting of four or five trebuchets, and the movable towers required for attacking a fortified place before fire artillery was employed, cost less than the manufacture of the artillery used at the siege of Turin in 1535. The latter again would be far less costly than the French and English artillery at the siege of Sebastopol. Whereas at the time when smooth-bore guns were used a place might be attacked with about sixty pieces, five times the quantity are needed now; since it is necessary to operate over a much more extensive area.

War is therefore a game which tends to become more and more costly, and especially siege warfare. Are we then to conclude that nations will become disgusted with warfare on account of the frightful expense it involves? This is not probable.

At the present day, as in times past, that which costs most is defeat. With forty millions well laid out in France, before the war of 1870, and from forty to eighty millions spent in the war itself, we probably should not have had to pay the four hundred millions which this war cost us, and we should not have lost two provinces which are certainly worth still more than that sum.

Parsimony in military preparations, in times of serious change, such as ours, is ruinous.

The principles to be followed may be summed up as follows: Commit yourself to no superfluous outlay, but spend all that is necessary. Besides, is it after all certain that a good system of territorial defence is so costly as some allege?

Is it a question of building something like a Chinese Wall on our eastern frontier? Is it likely that if a few strong positions rendered impregnable without unnecessary works enabled us to keep an army of observation two hundred thousand strong, secure from any surprise in the elevated valleys bounded by the ranges of hills which stretch from the Jura along Belfort, Remiremont, Epinal, Langres and Dijon, and border the right bank of the Saône as far as Lyons, the Germans would be in a hurry to make their way a second time to Paris? If they experienced the slightest check on such a route, if they were obliged even to halt, what would become of them?

The essential consideration therefore is a good choice of positions; shelter from the approach of an invasion on the flanks, and the avoidance of enormous expenditure in the attempt to defend all points. Let us suppose that Metz had been rendered impregnable, or at least so provided with defences that it could have held out for six months; and certainly the thing was possible. In the first place we should not have lost that town, and secondly the war, notwithstanding our deficiencies in soldiers and in artillery, might have taken quite another turn. Greater sacrifices on the part of the enemy, more prudence, and a still greater loss of men, would have been required to constrain us to a peace accepted before the cannon's mouth.

War is made now-a-days with armies a million strong; this is all very well while the invading force meets no very serious obstacle, either in front of it or on its flanks; when the combinations which such a vast display of forces necessitates are not disturbed at any point, and when the strategic operations upon the ground succeed each other with perfect precision, as one might trace them on a map in our studies. But these enormous agglomerations of men could give rise in a single day to appalling perils, after a grave check on one of their flanks. Such masses can be advanced, fed, and manœuvred only by means of a very complicated, and therefore delicate and easily deranged machinery. The Germans asserted that by the possession of Alsace and a part of Lorraine we had a hold upon Germany. Now their country is almost dovetailed into France. The future will show whether that will greatly benefit them.

In 1870 and 1871 we saw what could be accomplished by the little fortress of Belfort; which was perhaps the only one among our strong places possessing guns of long range, and a garrison well commanded and determined to defend itself.

It persisted in maintaining the offensive over a circle of from twelve to sixteen miles, thanks to a few rifled cannon with which the ramparts were furnished, and which protected sorties through a radius of three to four miles. For a month it hindered the planting of siege batteries; and, in spite of a bombardment of seventy-three days, the town had only four of its houses burned. This defence is instructive, and shows that the old defensive system has had its day.

During the siege the batteries of the besieged hardly suffered at all, and had recourse to indirect firing—that is, they fired over the barracks from the gorge of the castle without seeing the mark, but regulating by observation. This indirect firing, which took no account of the plan of the crests of the defence, and which thus enabled a powerful fire to be directed to any point, without regarding the faces, produced a great effect on the batteries of the enemy, who, on his side, could not see these guns, and did not know how to regulate his fire.

The question, therefore, remains undecided; and, though a long range enables the attack to envelope each work more decidedly with its fires, each battery of the besieger may be subjected to the fire of a greater number of guns by the defence. At Paris, the forts which are by no means planned in view of the present long range, enabled a weak and inexperienced garrison, whose *morale* was none of the firmest, to execute sorties with success to a distance of two miles and a half.[1]

With good troops, then, we might have raised in one night, works which would have enabled us to resume the offensive, and to push further on, to break the line of contravallation, and seriously to embarrass the besieger. It is not therefore proved that long ranges give a greater advantage to the attack than to the defence, while, on the other hand, the long range of rifled cannon may be affirmed to be favourable to the defence; but it would be so only on the condition of the works being planned in view of the new action of artillery, and not according to old traditions, however glorious. The destructive power

---

[1] The battle of Champigny had extended our lines to four thousand six hundred and twenty yards from the Fort de la Faisanderie.

of explosive projectiles puts obstacles in the way of the besieger's approaches; and, in fact, during the late war we never saw employed that old mode of approach with a view to attacking by breach and crossing the ditch.

The Germans were not so stupid as to employ these classical methods. They took up their position on favourable and often commanding points, at three thousand eight hundred to four thousand two hundred yards around our fortresses, which adhered to the old defensive system adapted to ranges of two thousand two hundred yards at most; and covered with shells our works and the towns they were supposed to protect, without risk to a single sapper. We thought that odious and unreasonable; like those nobles of the fifteenth century, who thought it an abominable shame that their feudal nests should be breached with bombards, and declared that the trade of war was thereby damaged. But suppose we should some day condescend to practical consideration, when these old flanked fronts fall into disesteem, and the new generation of military engineers determine to admit that we have to do with artillery of long range, and to take advantage of the fact, a certain degree of superiority might be doubtless given to defence over attack.

How ought these isolated forts, which are destined to replace the salients of our old fortresses, to be planned? They should afford ample space for a large number of fires—even indirect fires—in case of need; consequently extended faces and short flankings—that is, as shallow as possible, and perfectly open gorges. They should efficiently protect the works of counter-approach, and consider defence at close quarters as a question of only secondary importance; for very seldom would there be occasion for it, if indeed the case ever presented itself, which is doubtful.

Referring to the general defensive system shown in Fig. 83, and required the plan of one of the forts, A, the result will be Fig. 84, giving the work at the lower level at

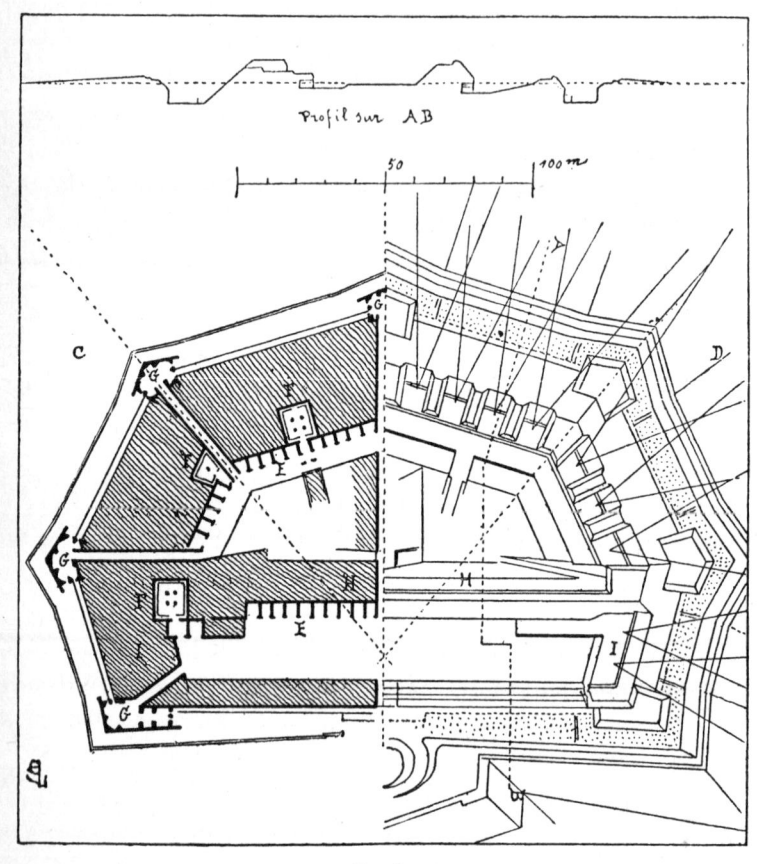

Fig. 84.

C, and at the level of the batteries at D. The counterscarp should be cased up to at least sixteen or seventeen feet above the bottom of the ditch.

The escarp should be made with tipped earth. The masonry works should all be covered and secured from being enfiladed; they form casemates inside E. Beneath the terracings, powder magazines, F, and the passages communicating with the *oiseaux* or lower *orillons*, G, protected by the counterscarp and the covered way, and which are used only if the enemy attempts to pass the ditch. The faces and flanks on the outside are planned on angles sufficiently obtuse to cross their fires. The two faces in the plan (Fig. 84) may be armed with eight guns and the flanks with six guns. This work is separated from that of the gorge by a traverse that efficiently protects this gorge, which possesses its flanks, armed with four guns and its orillons.

From the work of the gorge is a communication into the fort by a covered caponnière, forming traverse in the direction of the *capital* or centre line. The gorge is defended by a curtain for the riflemen, and, at need, for small pieces of artillery. At need also, on the terre-plein of the work of the gorge may be mounted guns of long range, affording an indirect fire in the circumference of a semi-circle, over the great traverse H, if the parapets of the faces are damaged by the fire of the enemy.

Fausse-braies consisting of palings are fixed in the ditch at ten feet from the base of the escarp, to hinder the fallen *débris* of the escarp from filling up the ditch, and to enable its passage to be defended. The well-covered internal masonry works prevent the accumulation of earth on the interior platforms, and afford casemates, which enable the garrison to take rest in perfect security; at any rate along the two faces and the great traverse. Blindages can be set up on the traverses of the batteries, and can be easily repaired every night, as well as the escarp of tipped earth.

It would be difficult to say how many projectiles it would require to render such a work untenable; since we have seen in the siege of Paris, that a marine battery erected on tipped earth on the military road between the forts of Rosny and de Noisy, armed with three guns, had been a mark for the German shells during twenty-four days, without any of its guns having been dismounted, or its escarp suffering more than could be made good each night.

Permanent works should, however, only be established with the utmost circumspection:—1. Because they require a very considerable outlay. 2. Because they are necessarily familiar to, and for a long while studied by the enemy, who takes his measures accordingly.

The important point is to possess an accurate acquaintance with the ground to be defended, and only to establish permanent works in second line, and on points incontestably favourable for defence, supposing an artillery of even a still longer range than the present.

Every centre to be defended should therefore possess works sufficient to prevent a surprise; and in addition at a distance of six to eight thousand yards, a line of forts, crossing their fires if possible, or at any rate connected by strong batteries; and lastly, at a distance of about four thousand yards, positions previously examined and known, suitable for placing very simple works of field fortification, but which at a given moment may offer a resistance sufficient to permit movements on a grand scale —and delay the formation of an enemy's batteries.

In applying these principles to the defence of the town of La Roche-Pont, whose strategical position is one of major importance, since it connects Besançon with Dijon, and forms a salient on the flanks of an army which manœuvres from Epinal and from Vesoul upon Langres and Chaumont, it would be necessary to construct around this place, whose old fortifications are no longer of any value (Fig. 85) eight forts, A, on the brows of the plateaus which

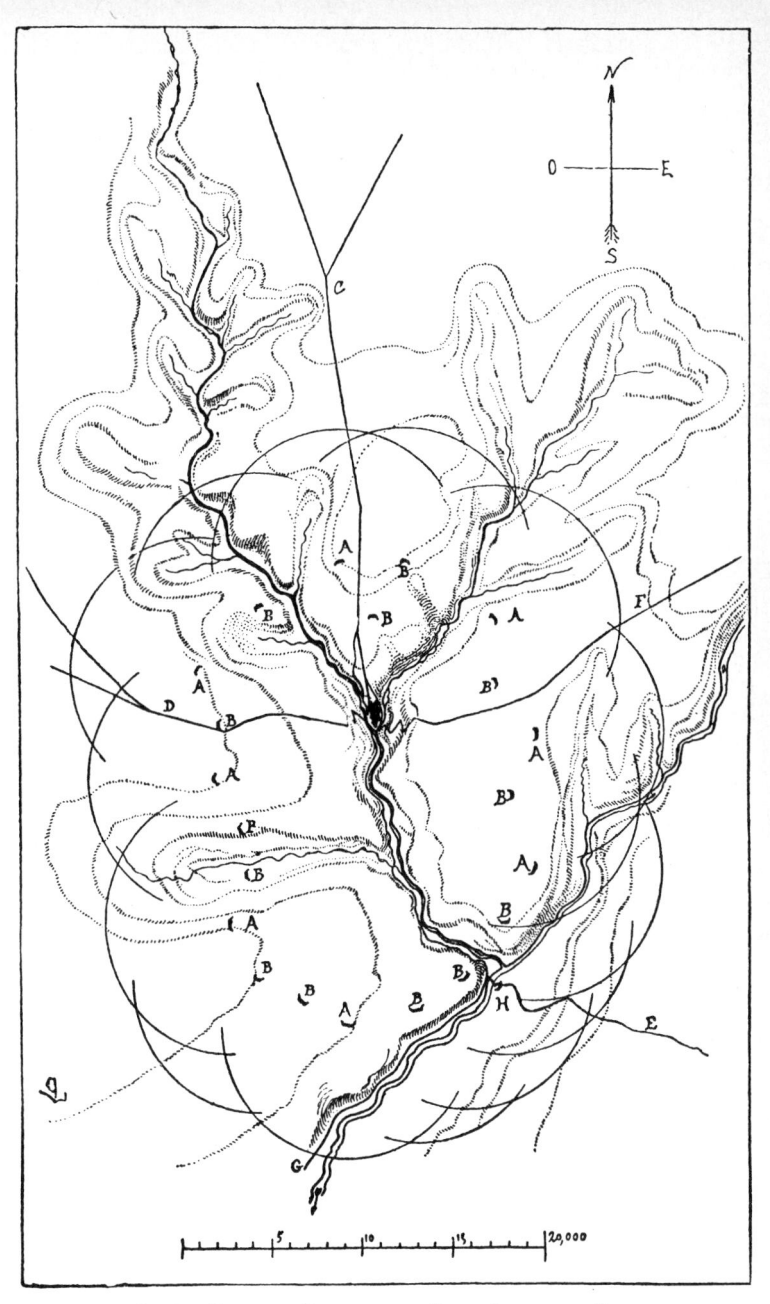

FIG. 85.—DEFENSIVE SYSTEM OF THE GREAT INTRENCHED CAMP.

surround the town, and thirteen batteries or redoubts, B, a little behind or to command the meeting of the river Abonne with the Saône and enfilade the valleys. Thus the group of roads which from the point C lead to Langres and Champlitte, from D to Dijon and Beaune, from E to Besançon and Dôle, from F to Gray and from G to Saint-Jean-de-Losne, would be occupied. A *tête du pont* H, protected by batteries which would dominate the Saône, would enable an army to manœuvre on both banks.

This passive defence would occupy a perimeter of forty miles, and the zone of action of the permanent works, a perimeter of sixty miles.

The purely passive defence would require, for the eight forts, four thousand eight hundred men; for the thirteen batteries two thousand men; for the guard of the intermediary trenches and the service of the *enceinte de préservation*, not including the forts and batteries, eighteen thousand men; reserve in the fortress, two thousand five hundred men; total, twenty-seven thousand three hundred men, whilst the effective investment would require an army of one hundred thousand men. But if this great intrenched camp contained an army of a hundred and fifty thousand men in addition to the troops necessary for the passive defence, this army could besides, on a very extended perimeter or on some advantageous points, occupy within the zone of action of the forts, an *enceinte de combat* defended by field works, which would enable it to assume the offensive at the opportune moment.

The armament of the forts would consist of a hundred and sixty guns of large calibre, and that of the batteries of forty-five guns of long range. With the reserve park this would give a total of two hundred and thirty pieces of ordnance.

Harnessed guns would be also necessary to support the trenches of the passive defence.

Each fort would cost about £48,900. The eight together	£391,200
Each battery or redoubt would cost about £6,000. The thirteen together	78,000
Total	£469,200

To make head against an invasion at all points at once has always been a difficult problem to solve; and it is still more so if we confine ourselves to the defensive, for the enemy starts from a base of operation with a view to concentrating himself upon a point unknown to the defenders. The latter has therefore only a line to oppose to the apex of a triangle of action. He must limit himself to preserving the heart of the country and certain districts that are already naturally protected, and which allow him to operate on the flanks of the invading forces; regions behind which lie extensive tracts of country from which supplies may be drawn.

Let us suppose that on the zone of defence of which La Roche-Pont forms the centre, an army of a hundred and fifty thousand men were assembled, which was able to reach Belfort through Besançon or by the road from Vesoul to Langres through Gray or Châtillon-sur-Seine through Dijon, these towns of Besançon, Vesoul, Langres, and Dijon being themselves in a condition to arrest the enemy's advance: the latter in attempting to make his way to Paris would be obliged either to watch this zone with an army of three hundred thousand men, or to move, and that with extreme caution, along the Lunéville and Nancy routes.

If a defensive zone of the same importance is disposed on the north, a point becomes very dangerous, especially if the capital is provided with an *enceinte de préservation*, and an *enceinte de combat* allowing an army to manœuvre.

Three hundred thousand men therefore would be required to watch the defensive zone of Burgundy and the same number that of the north, and four hundred thousand men to invest Paris; total, one million, without reckoning the troops required for keeping open the communication between the three armies and guarding the base of operations.

It follows that the slightest check might entail a serious disaster.

As the army of Metz under the ramparts of the town was not able to manœuvre, the two hundred thousand men employed in blockading it were rendered inactive for two months.

If the French army had been able to move within a perimeter of 60 miles, with a good supply of provisions, it would have reduced three hundred thousand men to inaction; since the Germans, who leave nothing to chance, reckon—and not unreasonably—that on the field it is desirable to be at least two to one. It would seem then that the art of war now-a-days—as far as resistance to an invader is concerned — consists not in endeavouring to defend any extensive lines which may be taken or outflanked, but in establishing a small number of centres of defence, sufficiently remote from each other and connected by a system of railways in the rear; which are capable of holding out long, and which compel the enemy either to divide in order to watch them or to take them, or to expose his flanks to an attack if he leaves them alone, or to see himself cut off from his base of operations if he advances *en masse* against one of them without covering himself against the others. . . . .

But we must confess to a limited confidence in fortifications on this immense scale. It is certain that they are ruinous : it is not certain that they are effective in proportion to the enormous expense they occasion.

The men-at-arms of the fifteenth century cased themselves and their horses in iron to resist cross-bow bolts, lance-thrusts, and strokes of axe or sword. Fire artillery, which at first aimed at nothing more than substituting powder for the mechanism of engines worked by counterpoise or ropes, and like these discharged only stone balls, becomes improved and uses iron balls and leaden bullets ; and instead of being ponderous and fixed as formerly, moves on wheels and is rendered easily manageable, and at the beginning of the sixteenth century places pistols and arquebusses in the hands of foot-soldiers and horsemen. What plan do the men-at-arms adopt ? They thicken the plates of their armour and line them so thoroughly that they are no longer fit for a charge. This method lasts about fifty years, until it is perceived that the best way to enable cavalry to face artillery, so as not to be crushed by it, is to allow it to move rapidly.

Cannon are made whose balls pierce through and through the wooden planks of a vessel. Immediately these planks are cased with iron. To-day's balls are resisted by the vessel's sides. The plates of iron are doubled . . . . and forthwith the penetrating force of the projectiles is increased ; but those of the next day pierce them. Steel is made to take the place of iron : but after thousands upon thousands have been spent the projectile has always the best of it. But it happens in a naval engagement that an Admiral steams at full speed right athwart an enemy's ship and sinks it ! In fact it is by rapidity of movement and facility in manœuvring that victories at sea are ensured much more than by increased protective plating.

And in the art of fortification we are exactly at the

same point as were the men-at-arms of the end of the fifteenth century, who heaped plates on plates to protect themselves from artillery. It is time the art of fortification should be modified.

It will be objected that a vessel or a horseman can move about, but that a fortress is immovable, and that consequently passive force cannot here be replaced by active force or agility. This is a mistake. Though a fortress cannot be moved, the defensive system of a district can and ought to be studied, in view of various contingencies. In future warfare the plan of temporary fortification ought to play a principal part and may be made to do so. In other terms, an army ought to be able to fortify itself everywhere, and take advantage of every position. It is temporary fortification therefore which it is desirable to render easy, prompt, and efficacious, in order to defeat the combinations studied beforehand by the enemy, to reduce him in certain cases to the defensive, when he was hoping to attack, and to embarrass his movements on the great scale by unforeseen resistance at a point which he expected to pass with ease, and oblige him incessantly to modify his plans by rapidly executed arrangements for defence.

Vauban's fortresses have had their day; who can conjecture what may be accomplished in a future war by the system of defence of which an example has just been presented?

Still the most reliable fortress for a country is a good and well-commanded army, and a well-educated, brave, and intelligent population, resolved to make every sacrifice rather than undergo the humiliation of a foreign occupation.

Captain Jean's papers contained many other critical remarks which cannot be recorded here. These documents sufficiently indicate that, whatever may have been said about the matter, there were among our officers some who worked, and many who had anticipated the dangers to which we were exposed by a blind confidence in our valour and an utter ignorance of the progress made by our enemies. Indeed among these papers of Captain Jean's, numerous notes, dated 1866, 1867, 1868, show the inefficiency of the defensive system then recognised in France, and the necessity of providing our strong places with works adapted to the recent progress in artillery.

Will the town of La Roche-Pont witness the realisation of Captain Jean's projects, or is its military history closed for ever? The future will show.

In the meantime it is engaged in cultivating its vineyards, and its suburbs are invading once more the slopes of the plateau on the south and the west. The lower part of its donjon of the 12th century is still visible above the escarpment of the little citadel, and antiquaries can discover Roman basements at some points in its wall. When cellars are excavated, Gallo-Roman coins are sometimes found with broken pieces of red and black pottery, charred wood, and even flint hatchets.

These evidences of the antiquity of the cité are deposited in a small museum which also contains sculptures taken from the abbey and the castle.

If you go to La Roche-Pont, ascend the ruins of the donjon. From this elevated point the view on a clear spring morning is very fine; towards the south it extends as far as the Saône, showing the little river Abonne, winding along the vale through meadows and orchards. On the north spreads the plateau covered with clumps of trees, and bounded only by the blue outlines of the hills of the Haute-Marne. At your feet the town with its ramparts looks like a vessel moored at the extremity of a promontory. We are reminded then of all the events which this little nook of ground has witnessed, of the ruins that have been accumulated by human passion, and the blood that has been so lavishly shed. We fancy we hear the shouts with which these walls have so often echoed.

Nature however remains the same; the meadows continue to be enamelled with flowers, and clothe with a mantle of beauty the ruins that have been heaped up by the fury of men. A feeling of deep sadness comes over us, and we say to ourselves: "What use is it all?" "What use!" replies at once a voice in the depth of our our soul. "What is the use of independence? What good is the love of our country? What use is the memory of self-sacrifice?" Do not blaspheme, Egoistic Philosophy; be silent before centuries of struggle—before that layer upon layer of the bones of the dead, and those heaps of successive ruins which have formed our country's soil. Though often ravaged, this hill has never been abandoned by its inhabitants; the more affronts it has had to sustain, the more its children have become attached to its side, the more they hold to the soil that has been impregnated with the blood of their ancestors, and the more hatred they feel towards those who would attempt to detach them from this ancestral tomb. This is patriotism; and it is the only human passion that can be dignified with the title of holy. War makes nations, and war raises them again when they sink down under the influence of material interests. War is struggle, and we find struggle everywhere in nature; it secures greatness and duration to the best educated, the most capable, the noblest, the most worthy to survive. And in the present day more than ever, success in war is the result of intelligence and of that which develops intelligence—Work.

Whenever what is called fraternity between nations shall

become a reality, the reign of senile barbarism and of shameful decay will not be far distant.

Before this rock on which so many generations have fought to defend their independence, to resist aggression and to keep the rapacious foreigner at a distance, it is not an expression of regret that is called for—it is rather of homage to the dead which hearts full of gratitude cannot withhold. They do not ask for tears but for imitation.

EXPLANATION

OF SOME OF THE TECHNICAL TERMS USED IN THIS BOOK.

AGGER (Latin), terrace, or platform, which the Romans raised before the fronts attacked, for the purpose of setting up their projectile machines, securing a commanding position, and masking the troops assembled for an assault.

BAILEY, forecourt; court of the outer works, or yard. The stables and the lodgings for the garrison were usually disposed in the bailey of the strong castles of the Middle Ages (see p 169).

BALISTA (Latin, *onager*), an engine for propelling stones, worked by means of strongly-twisted cords.

BARBICAN, exterior defence protecting an entrance, and allowing a large assemblage of men to prepare for sorties, or to protect a retreat. Barbicans were either of masonry or earth, or constructed of a simple palisade. They were always of a circular form (see p. 169).

BASTION, an earthwork, cased externally with masonry, salient beyond the main body of the fortress, and possessing two faces, two flanks, and a gorge, so as to sweep the ground without, to cross the fires, and to flank the curtains. The gorge of bastions is open, closed, or retrenched. Bastions are said to be full when their *terre-plein* is level with the curtains; empty, when their *terre-plein* is beneath that level; armed with a cavalier, when upon their *terre-plein* is raised a battery of earth which commands the country without over the parapets (see p. 278, 310).

C C

BOULEVARD, an earthwork—in use at the time when fire artillery had attained a certain degree of importance—for placing cannon outside ancient defences still preserved. Boulevards were of all forms—square, circular, and triangular (see p. 229).

BRAIE, an exterior defence of trifling height, protecting the foot of the ramparts, and hindering the enemy's approach.

BRETÈCHE, timber construction intended to strengthen and to flank a front or a salient (see p. 184).

CAT, timber gallery, low and long, covered with a longitudinal very pointed and strongly ironed roof. Placed on wheels, these galleries were advanced to the foot of the walls, after the ditch was filled up, and enabled the miners to begin working into the masonry under cover. The name *rat* was given to these galleries in some provinces.

CATAPULT, engine for shooting large darts by means of a powerful bow.

CAVALIER, earthwork raised in the middle of a bastion, or upon any point of the defence, to command the exterior. In the sixteenth century the besieging armies erected cavaliers around defences to mount cannon upon them. Our siege batteries are the modern analogues of these works (see p. 237, 312).

CHEMISE, exterior inclosure of a donjon; the chemise of the donjon consists of a wall which leaves a space of some yards between it and the donjon. A postern with a drawbridge gives a communication between one of the rooms of the donjon and the rampart walk of the chemise (see p. 201).

CLAVICULA (Latin), exterior defence, raised outside the gates of a camp, and which obliged those who endeavoured to enter to present their flank to the defenders of the ramparts (see p. 92).

COVERED WAY, road formed on the counterscarp and protected by the relief of the glacis (see p. 307).

COUNTERSCARP, is the casing of the ditch which is opposite to the defence.

DEMI-LUNE, low work, disposed before a curtain between two bastions, separated from the main body of the fortress by a ditch, and possessing two faces and two short flanks (see p. 306).

DONJON OR KEEP, chief retreat of the defenders of a strong castle. The donjon was always separated from the defences of the castle, and put in direct communication with the exterior (see p. 169).

ESCARP is that part of a revetment of fortifications which fronts the exterior, from the bottom of the ditch to the parapet or crenelation.

FAUSSE-BRAIE, palisade or trench, with parapet, defending the bottom of the ditch, low enough to be masked by the relief of the counterscarp.

GLACIS, sloping ground which extends from the counterscarp of the ditch towards the country, and masks the covered ways as well as the escarp.

HOARDING, wooden gallery which in time of war was put outside crenelations to enable the defenders to see the foot of the ramparts and towers, and to throw stones and materials of all kinds upon assailants attempting to approach.

LIST, interval left between the exterior defences and those of the body of the place (see p. 180).

MACHICOULIS—The wooden hoarding being easily set on fire, it was replaced in France, about the end of the thirteenth century, by stone corbels carrying a crenelation of masonry, and leaving intervals between them for throwing materials upon the assailants who approached the foot of the walls. In Syria, the Christians had adopted the machicoulis as early as the beginning of the thirteenth century.

MANGONEL, engine for propelling large stones from a kind of sling attached to the longer arm of a movable beam heavily weighted at its other extremity.

MERLON, solid space in the parapet between two embrasures. During the Middle Ages the merlons were usually perforated in the middle by a loop-hole. In time of war the battlements were masked by mantelets of wood, which could be raised at discretion by means of an axle turning in two iron collars let into the upper angles of the merlons.

MOVABLE TOWER, timber tower which was mounted on rollers and was advanced to the walls for the purpose of assault. The movable towers were made to command the battlements, and the upper story was furnished with a bridge which fell upon the crest of the ramparts of the towers (see p. 218).

OISEAU, in the fifteenth and sixteenth centuries, a small masonry work which, disposed at the salient angles in the ditch, swept the latter and was intended to bar the passage. The *oiseaux* were masked by the counterscarp. In modern polygonal fortifications this plan has been re-adopted (see p. 373).

OPPIDUM (Latin), a citadel or fortified strategical position, among the Gallic populations. Many Roman camps were formed at the epoch of the conquest of Gaul, on the Gallic *oppida*, which were only a kind of intrenched camps formed upon elevated plateaux. Several of our French towns occupy the sites of ancient *oppida*—Langres, Laon, Béziers, Carcassone, Uzerche, Sainte-Reine (Alesia), Le Puy-en-Velay, Semur-en-Auxois, Avalon, Puy d'Issolu, &c.

ORILLON, projecting part of faces of bastions, intended to mask the flanks and to shield the guns which arm these flanks (see p. 280).

PARADOS, mound of earth disposed behind the guns in battery, to shelter them as well as the servers from reverse firing.

PARALLEL, trench parallel to the sides of the polygon of a fortress, supplying a covered communication for planting and serving the siege batteries. Formerly these parallels were required for approaching and planting the breach batteries. These parallels communicated with each other by trench boyaux traced in zig-zags, so as not to be raked by the fires of the place (see p. 330).

PARECLAT, epaulment of earth, or formed with gabions raised on the ramparts, or in the middle of bastions, to shelter the defenders from the splinters of bombs and shells.

PLACE D'ARMES, space defended by an epaulment, intended to enclose a body of men and to protect it from projectiles (see pp. 288, 307).

POSTERN, secondary gate, small gate, generally masked (see p. 170).

RAMPART, epaulment raised with the earth taken from the ditch sunk on the outer side ; also a wall crowned with a parapet and rampart walk. It signifies a permanent defence.

RAVELIN, name originally given to demi-lunes. A work consisting of two faces, open at the gorge, low, and intended to sweep the exterior between two bastions (see p. 279).

REDAN, work presenting a salient angle and a re-entering angle (see p. 305).

RETRENCHMENT, a work made to augment the defensive strength of a place within the permanent fortifications, so as to present a fresh obstacle should the latter fall into the power of the enemy ; the retrenchment consists of an epaulment of earth raised with the material from the ditch sunk on the outside.

STIMULUS (Latin), barbed iron crook, which, fixed on a short stake stuck in the ground or in the bottom of conical holes, protected the approaches of a defence (see p. 80).

TENAILLE, work consisting of a curtain having at each extremity two demi-bastions (see pp. 278, 306).

TRAVERSE, a mound of earth disposed across covered ways, *terre-pleins*, bastions, and curtains, to shield the guns and the defenders against enfilade, oblique, or ricochet fire (see p. 335).

TREBUCHET, engine for propelling large stones, very similar to the mangonel, but whose counterpoise was suspended from the beam instead of being fixed to it.

TRENCH, road sunk in the ground, the earth being thrown up on one side only, or on both sides, for enabling the approach of places under cover.

TRENCH-SHELTER, temporary defence, consisting of an exterior epaulment made with the earth taken from a trench, in a way to shield the soldiers upon a front, around a camp or a post, and enable them to fire under cover. The trench-shelter is destined to play an important part since fire-arms have acquired a long range and a rapid discharge. The Romans, in their day, made use of trench-shelters in the field.

VINEA (Latin), a wooden mantlet, also a timber gallery, set up perpendicularly to the *agger*, and which affords approach to the platform under cover. The wooden towers intended to attack the ramparts of the besieged were rolled forward on these wooden galleries (see p. 83).

THE END.